BESSIE, MIKE AND ME

Ireland and Scotland in six weeks . . . by motorhome

Jackie Williamson

Print ISBN 978-1-8380752-6-2

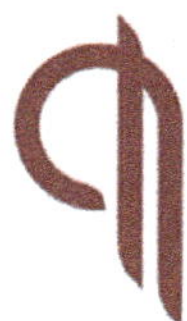

Published in 2020 by
Llyfrau Cambria Books, Wales, United Kingdom.
Cambria Books is a division of
Cambria Publishing.
Discover our other books at: www.cambriabooks.co.uk

For Mike: driver, planner, navigator . . . and hero, for putting up with my awful map-reading!

Acknowledgements

Huge thanks to:

My husband Mike, for his brilliant map reading, superb organisational skills and for making the journey possible in the first place.

My best friend, Lesley Hall-Wood, for her inimitable wild-life drawings. They bring the story to life in a way my words never could.

Everyone at Nameless Writers of Pembrokeshire, for their interest, support, constructive criticism and good ideas: Pam Treneer, Carolyn Denman, Rob Barnes and David Western.

Special thanks to Pam and Lesley for the extra feedback, endless cups of coffee, phone chats and long lunches in which we've stirred the cauldron and plotted our way through our pages.

Archie Douglas: my 'Scotland editor'.

Wayne Musgrave for his photograph of Llangynog.

Tim Murray: classic car enthusiast extraordinaire.

Sam Sheddon at The Scotsman newspaper for allowing me to reproduce extracts from an article about The Glen Coe Massacre, and Holly Lennon for writing it in the first place.

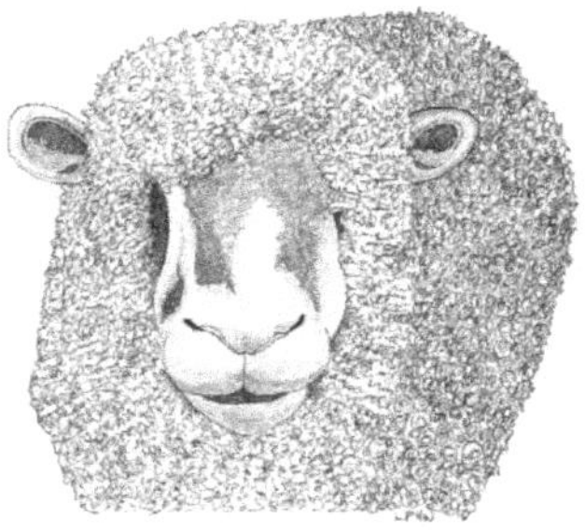

Contents

The Beginning

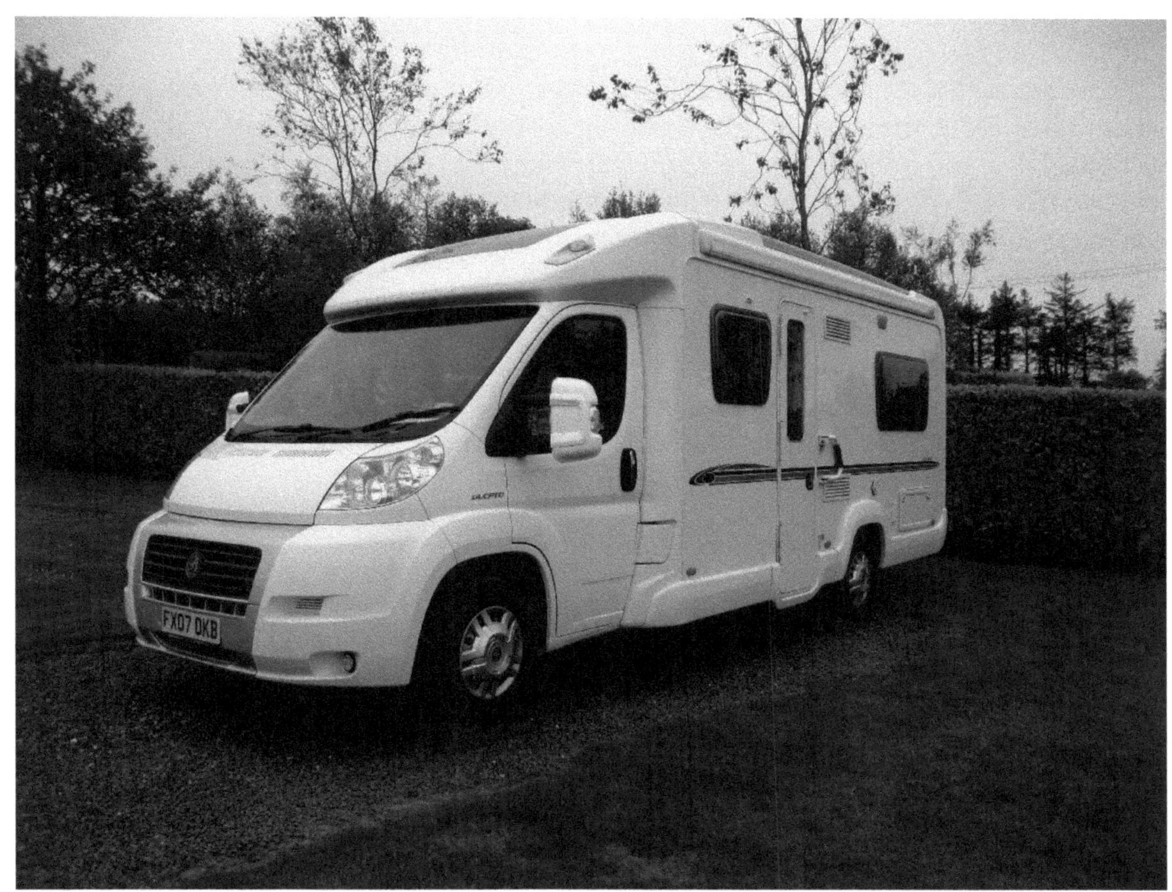

Bessie

The summer of 2007 saw the publication of my book, *Cevamp, Mike and Me: tales of romance and adventure in the Irish Sea*. Published as a paperback, the first edition soon sold out, later appearing as an e-book on Amazon Kindle. It continues to sell and I am pleased to say there have been numerous requests for a sequel.

Cevamp was a small wooden yacht in which I and my police officer husband Mike spent all our free time and holidays, sailing around the Irish sea, from north Wales to Scotland, Ireland and the Isle of Man. Our many adventures and near-disasters are chronicled with as much honesty and humour in the book as I could muster: as any sailing couple will tell you, life on board can sometimes put a strain on the good nature of even the strongest relationship!

After four years *Cevamp* was usurped by an easy-going catamaran in which we were accompanied by our crew of two beagles. But after a few years of horrible summers and dog-overboard incidents, we made up our minds to have a break from sailing, whereupon we took up scuba diving – a slightly odd pastime for people living, as we did then, in land-locked Oxfordshire.

Taking early retirement in 2003, we moved to Pembrokeshire from where, after a few years, we again felt the call of the sea. The next yacht was April Rose an 18-year-old Westerly Tempest that Mike, in a deeply romantic gesture, renamed *Jacqueline*. We kept her for about eight years, sailing in and around our old Irish Sea haunts together and, memorably, Mike sailing solo around the island of Ireland.

Plenty of material there, you might think, for a sequel. And here it is: *Bessie, Mike and Me*. But the *Bessie* of the title is not a yacht. She's a motorhome. We sold *Jacqueline* in 2016, *Bessie* took her place the same year and we continued our adventures on dry land.

This book is the account, originally in blog format, of a six-week trip in the early summer of 2017, when we toured Ireland and Scotland. I hope it will be useful to other motorhomers planning a similar tour, especially when it comes to the difficulties of driving a large vehicle along roads that were originally designed for horses and carts! I haven't included route maps – it's easy enough to plan your own journey from the pages of any decent road atlas and this book was never intended as a prescriptive itinerary. It's more of a personal account of the sort of holiday we love, in quiet countryside and coastal locations mainly away from the hubbub of major tourist attractions. If that's what you like too, then our story could be just what you're looking for as an aid in planning your trip.

Bon voyage!

Jackie Williamson

PART ONE: Bessie Goes to Ireland

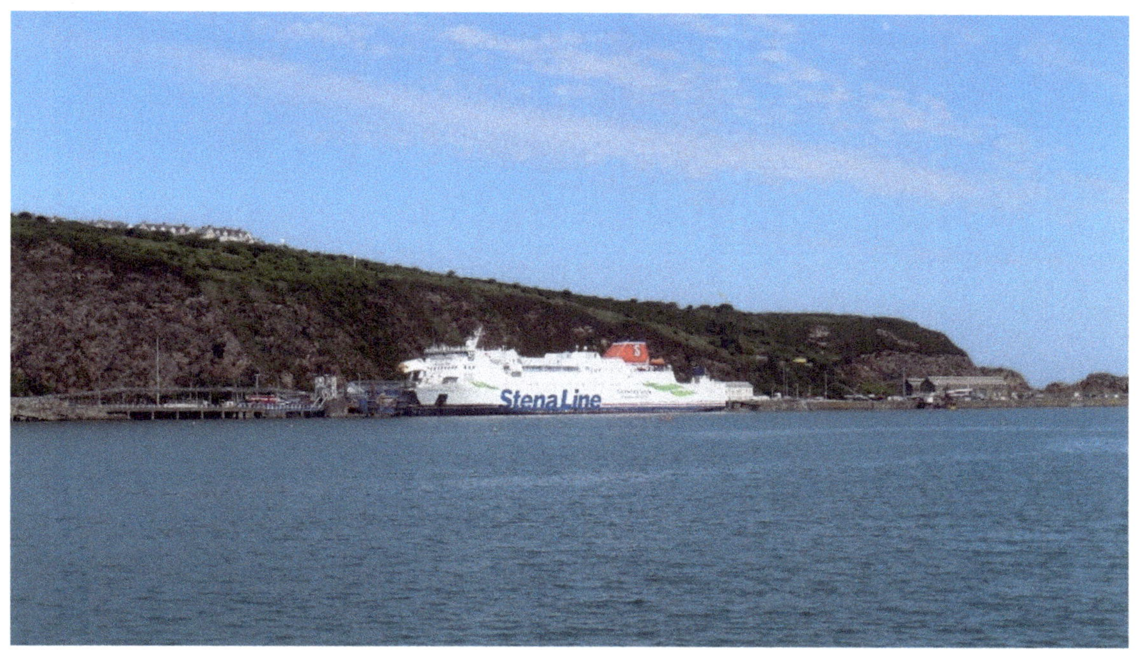

Fishguard Bay

County Wexford – Rosslare

County Waterford – Waterford

County Tipperary – Tipperary

Wednesday, 10th May

The first post – bear with me. This one is long. In future they will be shorter. I promise.

***

Well here we are in the Emerald Isle. After lots of frantic preparation, most of which was to do with making sure my 92-year-old mother had everything she needed and would be properly cared for in my absence, it was a relief to make the 10-minute drive from home to the ferry port at Fishguard.

We got there late on Monday night, in good time to catch the 2.30am sailing. *Stena Europe* rolled in about half an hour later, quickly disgorged her cargo of cars, lorries and motor bikes, and we were soon on board. We've made the ferry crossing a few times but as we clanged and clattered our way up the ramp I felt that familiar flicker of anxiety. What if the ramp doors weren't shut properly? What if there was a storm and one of the big lorries rolled over? What if we sink? All that weight . . . how on earth does the ferry stay afloat?

Despite my fears, it was a calm and peaceful crossing and the ferry was more than half empty. While we were in the queue waiting to board, we'd counted about 16 cars, half a dozen big lorries and six motorhomes and caravans. Mike and I sat in the quiet seats at the front of the ship and once we'd polished off our midnight feast we settled down to read and doze until we docked at Rosslare around 6am on Tuesday morning.

In retrospect, we wouldn't do the overnight crossing again. It did save quite a lot of money but we were exhausted from lack of sleep. We were both already tired from sorting out things at home, packing the van with food, clothing (the usual packing nightmare) and all the other bits and pieces we thought we would need for our six-week tour of Ireland and Scotland. A lot of this had to be done at the last minute because we didn't know until Friday afternoon that we were free to go – there was a possibility we would have to delay it so I could have further treatment on my clavicle, fractured, along with a couple of ribs, when I crashed off my bike in the Brecon Beacons back in March. After two months of will-we-won't-we operate, the orthopaedic consultant recommended waiting until we got home before sending me for further tests, scans and x-rays.

Once off the ferry and clear of Rosslare we found a lay-by where we could pull-over and get a couple of hours of much needed rest. This was one of the few lay-bys we found in Ireland that wasn't closed off with height restriction barriers to exclude vehicles the size of Bessie, a practice that we guessed was intended to ward off undesirable travellers.

Slightly more rested after our nap, although still a bit woozy, we trundled on to Waterford where, again, it was almost impossible to park. The riverside car park has height restrictions and the roadside spaces were all taken. After driving around for what was beginning to look like a fruitless task, we spotted a big Tesco store with a two-hour limit and dived in there. We walked back into town and down to the quayside, where we met up with our good friends Dave and Faye. They had left Milford Haven on the previous Sunday afternoon in their Vancouver sailing yacht *Green Jacket* and sailed the 100 plus nautical miles through the night, across the Irish Sea and up the River Suir to Waterford. Over excellent coffee in The Fat Angel, a warm, welcoming and historic café in Cathedral Square, we caught up on each other's' travel news before parting with a vague plan to keep each other posted as to our whereabouts so we could get together again later in the trip.

The Fat Angel is in a corner of old Waterford known as the Viking Triangle, so called because of the city's 1000-year-old Viking Walls. Faye and I spent a few minutes in the square outside the café pondering on the futility of war while we studied a memorial to 'the boy soldier'. John Conlon was believed to have been only 14 years old and the youngest recorded Allied soldier to be killed in World War 1 when he died in the Battle of Ypres, although there is some dispute over this. The sculpture is also a memorial to the 1,100 Waterford troops who died on the Western Front, as well as the men, women and children of the city who died in other armed conflicts, including the Irish War of Independence.

From Waterford we drove another 50 miles or so to the Glen of Aherlow Caravan Park. The site is peaceful and well managed and the Galty Mountains are awesome. Everywhere is so green and the trees here are spectacular, with all their fresh young leaves and blossom on the hawthorn. I don't think my pictures do it justice but these, photographed from our pitch, give you an idea.

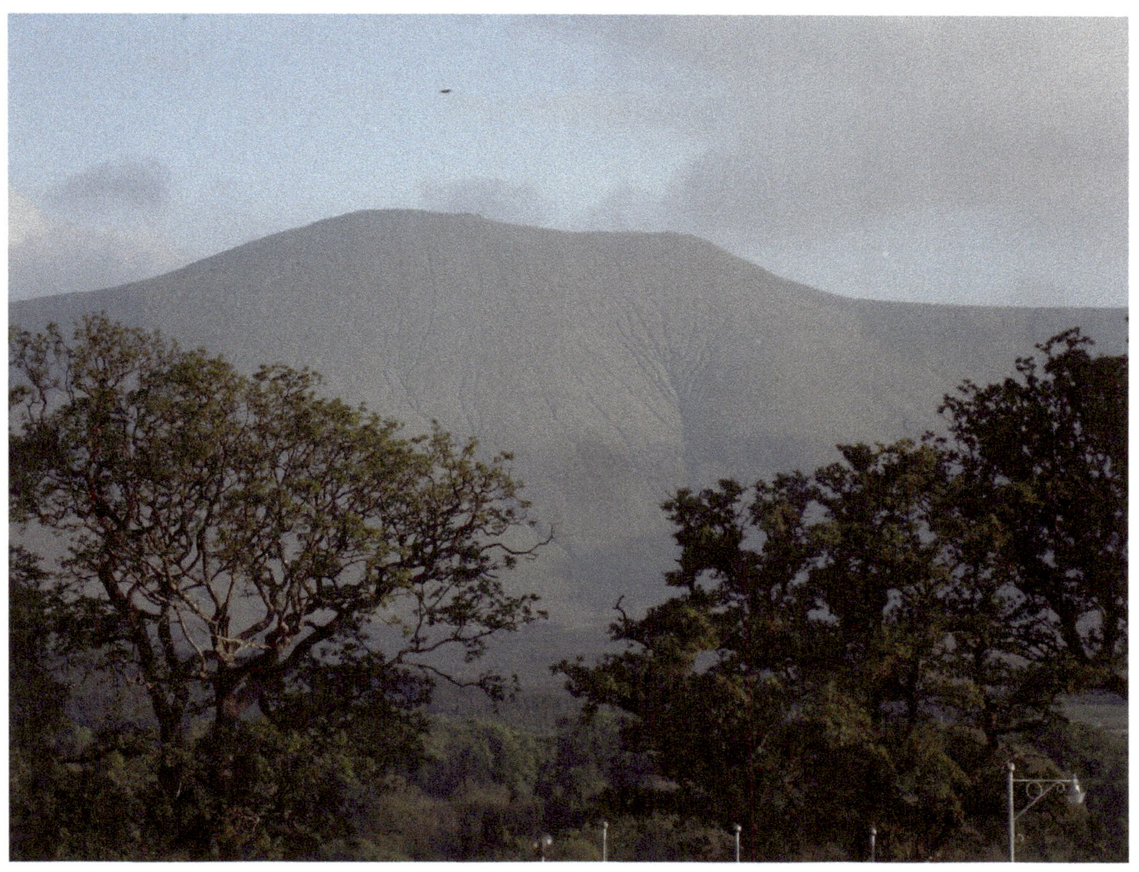

Galty Mountains

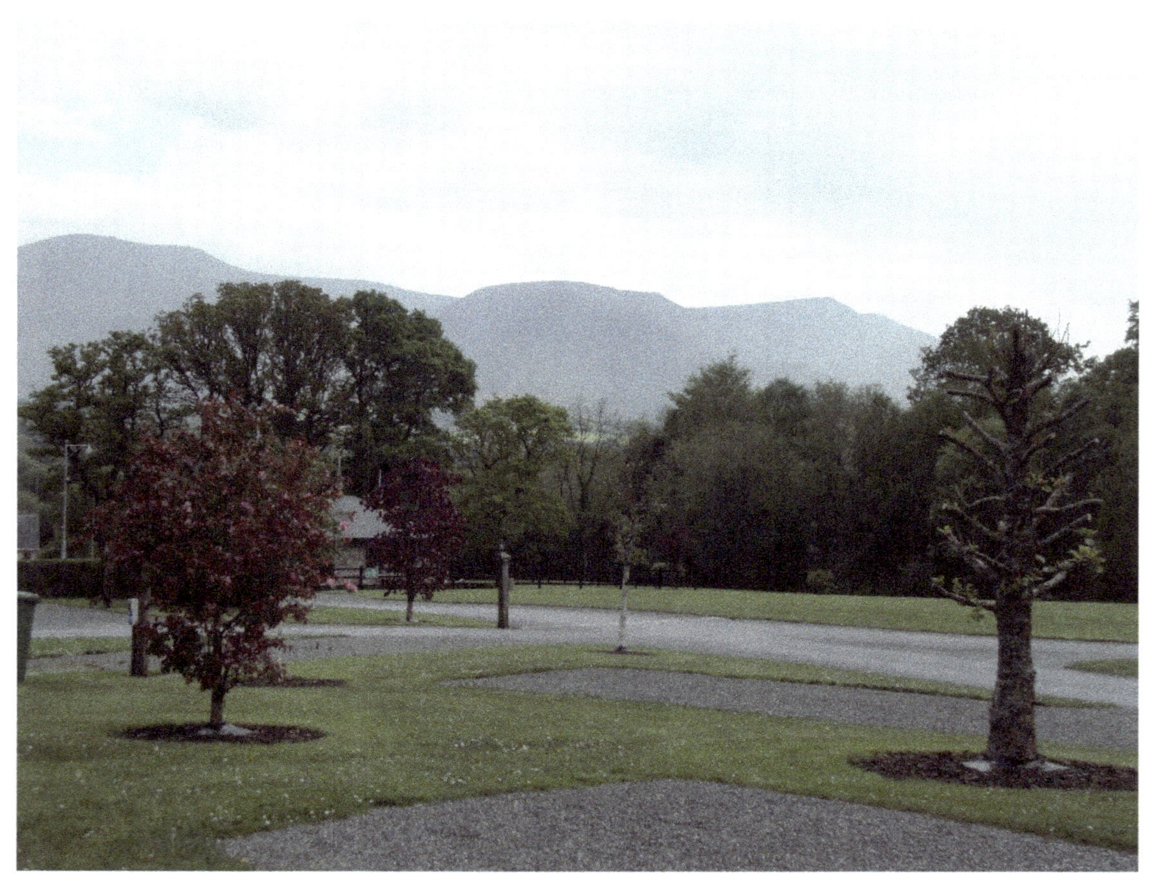

Glen of Aherlow Caravan Park

We were in bed by nine o'clock, slept like logs and didn't properly wake up and get ourselves moving until ten this morning (Wednesday). We had a quick breakfast and then Mike got the bikes down from the rack on the back of the van ready for us to go exploring. Another warm and sunny day – ideal weather for cycling in shorts.

We started with a short circular ride through the Glen of Aherlow to restore my confidence after my accident and then we set off for Tipperary. It was a long way (sorry – very bad joke). There was a pretty steep climb of about a mile and we were grateful for the electric power assistance on our bikes, although Mike was slightly concerned the battery on his was running a bit low. Mine was better, but not much.

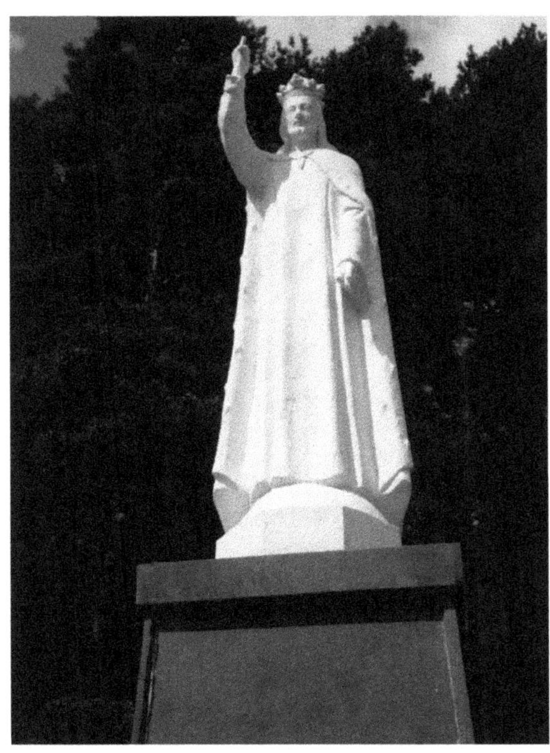

Christ the King

Unlike dynamos, the batteries on e-bikes have to be charged from a mains electricity supply – however much muscle-power you put into your cycling the batteries will eventually run down. And of course, the more you ask of your battery, the quicker it will die on you. Our bikes have a range of around 150 miles, possibly more, depending on how much assistance you need from them, and we never do that much in a day. But even short distances add up and, before you know it, you're running low. And in a motorhome you don't always have access to electricity, so you can't charge them up every night.

But to get back to our little excursion, we pedalled almost to the top of the hill where a big lay-by is dominated by the gleaming white statue of Christ the King, with miles of countryside spreading below.

We stopped for a break there and chatted with a group of motor-cyclists-of-a-certain-age from Wexford. One of them was a keen road-cyclist too and he tightened up my handlebars – they'd become a bit wobbly after the rough lanes we'd been on earlier. From there it was a mere couple of hundred yards more uphill and then it was downhill all the way to Tipperary, with a great freewheel round steep bits and hairpin bends. I was a bit wary to start with, as I now know how much it hurts to come off at speed, but soon gained enough confidence to go with the descent and I allowed the bike to reach 22mph before I pulled back to a steadier 18.

After pushing the bikes around Tipperary town centre for a while, we found a café and had lunch before setting off on the long steep climb back. It was at this point that Mike realised there was no power left in his bike's battery. Despite this, he managed to cycle a good way up under his own steam, although he did walk some of the way towards the summit to keep me company when, despite the highest power setting on the bike, I had to have a break from pedalling. My poor knees were aching from the effort I was having to put in simply to stop myself going backwards! But before we knew it, we were back with Christ the King and freewheeling all the way. It was fourteen and a half miles in all and when we got back to the campsite all we were fit for was to flop into deckchairs and enjoy the sunshine.

Bessie's mileage since leaving home: **108**

Points of interest

- Bessie is a Bessacar motorhome on a Fiat Ducato. She's about seven metres long, 3.3 metres high and comes complete with lounge, double bedroom, shower room, flushing toilet and mini kitchen with sink, running hot and cold water, fridge, freezer, microwave and a cooker with hob, grill and oven.
- The bikes are Kalkhoff electric bikes with eight gears, three power settings and belt drive. They have a range of about 120-150 miles on the lowest setting but that drops dramatically if you use maximum power to help with cycling uphill or into the wind.

County Cork

Blarney

Thursday, 11th May

We woke up early and stayed in bed for a while, drinking tea, listening to the dawn chorus and watching the sun rise over the treetops. The promise of yet another glorious day. The caravan park is surrounded by a thick growth of mixed trees and so it attracts a wide variety of birds. We were watching blackbirds and a song thrush hunt for worms on the grass beside our pitch. At this time of year they sing from before dawn until after dusk, their rich tones often joined by the sweet, poignant sound of a robin. Another regular visitor here is a hooded crow, a species that you would by highly unlikely to see in England or Wales.

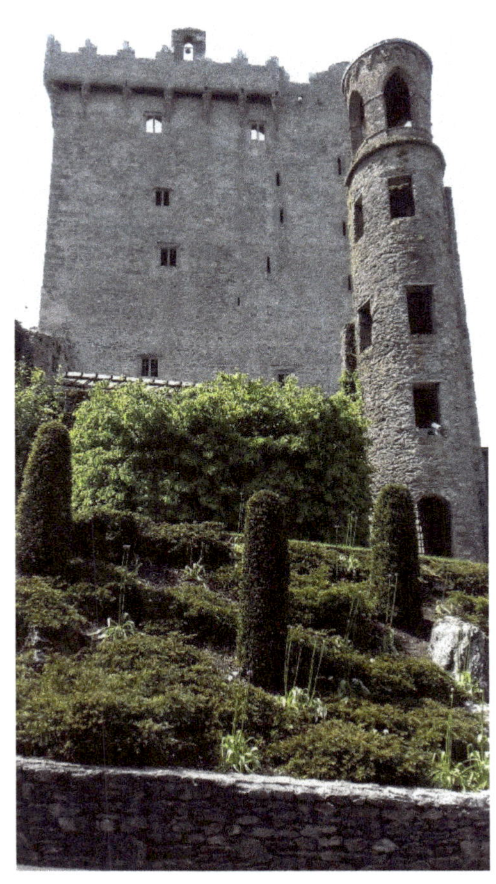

Blarney Castle

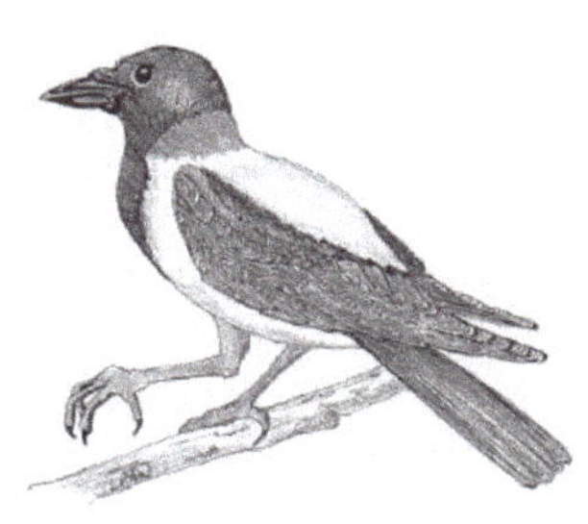

The site is in the grounds of an old mansion that was burnt down during The Troubles in the 1920s. The current owners bought the place in the early 2000s, replaced the derelict old building with a house for themselves and have clearly worked hard to transform the land to the idyllic place it is today.

We were away by 10 am and were soon on site at Blarney, all set for a visit to the castle. Admission was €15 for adults (€14 if you book online in advance) but for wrinklies such as ourselves it's €12 (€11.50 online). It was well worth it, if only for the exquisite grounds, but of course the big attraction here is the Blarney Stone.

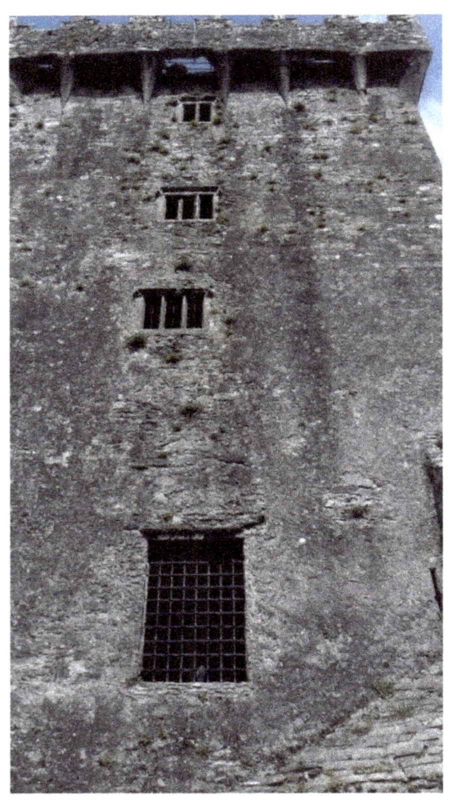

In my ignorance I'd thought the stone would be a big old granite lump in the middle of a field, similar to the standing stones that are so much a feature of the Welsh landscape. But no – it is much more challenging than that. First you have to struggle up the 100 slippery steps of a spiral limestone staircase to the top of a tower. I have huge feet and was anxious the treads were too narrow for me to negotiate the tight turns without stumbling and causing a domino effect onto the queue of fellow pilgrims behind me.

Then comes the tricky bit, although, to be fair, the procedure is a lot less hazardous now than it used to be, thanks to modern health and safety precautions. Even so, it takes a bit of courage, not to mention physical dexterity. First you have to lie on your back with your head hanging down a stomach lurching drop in the walls' cavity, with only an iron grating between you and certain death a very long way below. Then you slither on your back until your shoulders are now also over the gap. This enables you to get close to the outer wall of the castle, where the mythical stone is embedded, at which time you are exhorted by the burly man hanging onto your body to *tip your head back and kiss the stone*! Reminder to self: in future do your research first!

See the bit of blue sky poking through the hole at the top of the battlements in the picture? That's where the Blarney Stone has been embedded since 1446.

If you're interested in finding out more about the Stone's origins, visit the castle's website: www.blarneycastle.ie

I made Mike go first and was so transfixed – or do I mean scared? – that I forgot to photograph him. Then when it was my turn he couldn't work the camera on my phone and so neither of us has a record of the occasion.

All in all, it was a highly entertaining experience and we are delighted that we now have the legendary gift of eloquence – or blarney (not to be confused with baloney)!

Here are some pictures of the castle gardens, including The Seven Sisters. According to legend, a King of Munster had seven daughters and two sons. The sons were killed in a battle against a powerful clan chief. Oh his way back to the castle, the king's victorious army passed a druid's circle, consisting of nine stones. In his grief the king commanded his men to push over two of the stones in memory of his fallen sons, leaving the seven sisters standing, where they remain to this day.

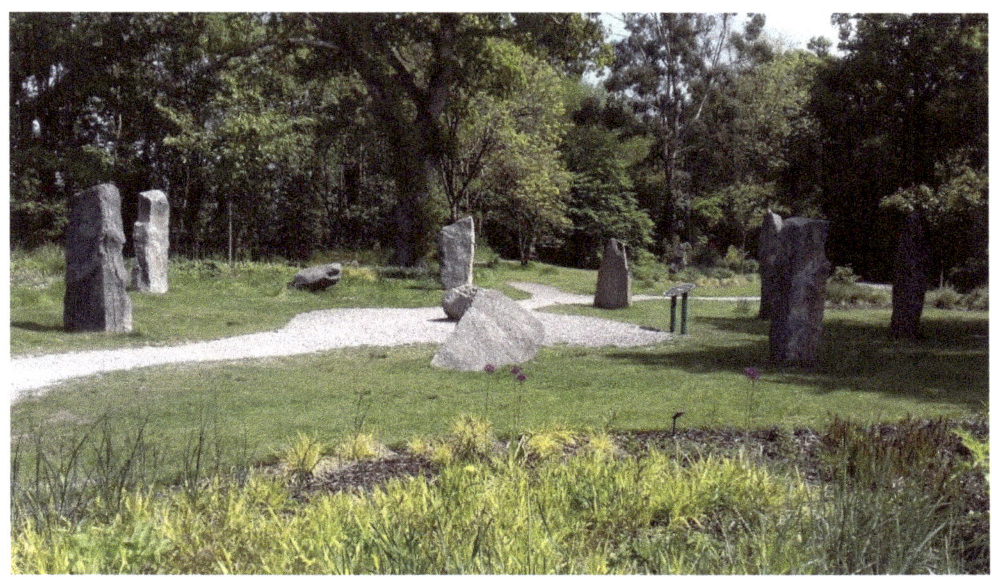

The Seven Sisters

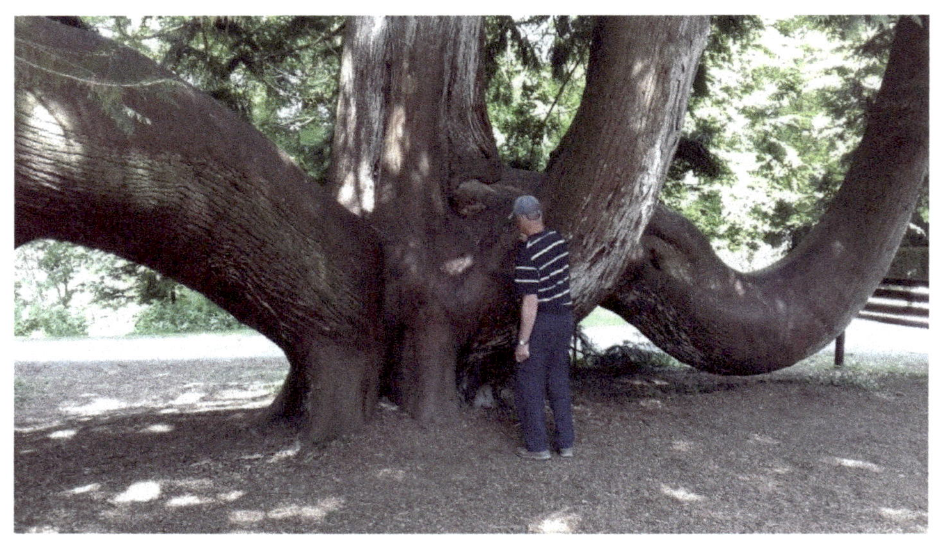

An amazing tree: Thuja plicata

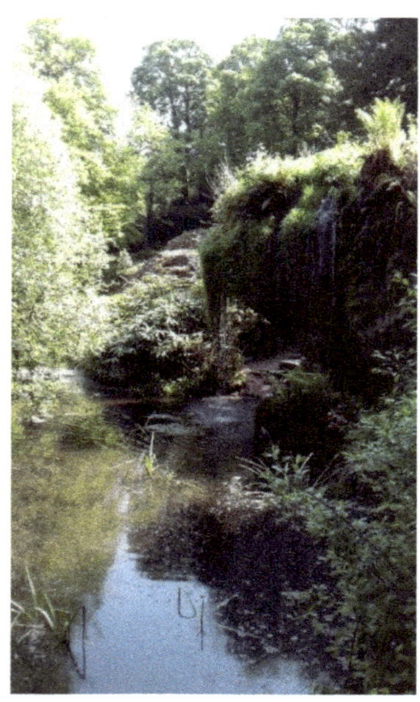

Waterfall

Today's mileage: 60

Kinsale and Garrettstown

Friday, 12th May

It was back to our sailing roots this morning as we arrived in Kinsale. Mike and I had a memorable meal there many years ago during one of our early sailing trips to Ireland in *Cevamp,* the yacht built by his father that became the star of my first book, *Cevamp, Mike and Me.*

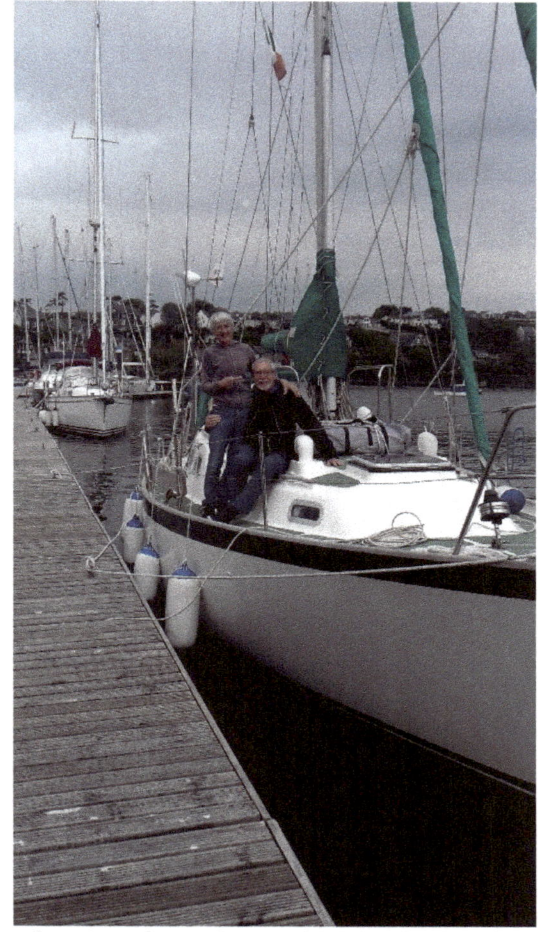
Captain and crew: Dave and Faye on Green Jacket

Today we'd arranged to meet up here with Dave and Faye, who had sailed round from Waterford. We had coffee on board *Green Jacket* followed by a stroll around the historic old town, then it was back on the yacht for lunch. Thank you, Faye.

***

The Battle of Kinsale on Christmas Eve in 1601 was the final campaign in England's conquest of Gaelic Ireland, also known as the Nine Year War. It is also famous for being the longest ever march into battle. Led by the Earl of Tyrone, Hugh O'Neill, and the Earl of Tyrconnel, Hugh O'Donnell, the brave Irish defence against the English ended in defeat – the Irish army had already walked 300 miles in appalling wintry conditions and by the time they reached Kinsale they were in no fit state to fight. I remember learning about the battle for A-level – no, not history but English, funnily enough.

One of our study books was *Making History* by the Irish writer and dramatist Brian Friel, whose play tells the story of the final days of the war.

The town is bursting with history, all of which is readily available on-line so I'm not going to go into it now, and it's also well-known for its thriving, cosmopolitan restaurant quarter.

Our wanderings took us past Desmond Castle, which has had many lives since it was built in 1500 by Maurice FitzGerald, 9th Earl of Desmond. Originally the customs house for the port of Kinsale it has also done duty as a prison, an ordnance store and, during the Great Irish Famine, as a workhouse. In the 1930s it was declared a national monument and these days it is an international wine museum.

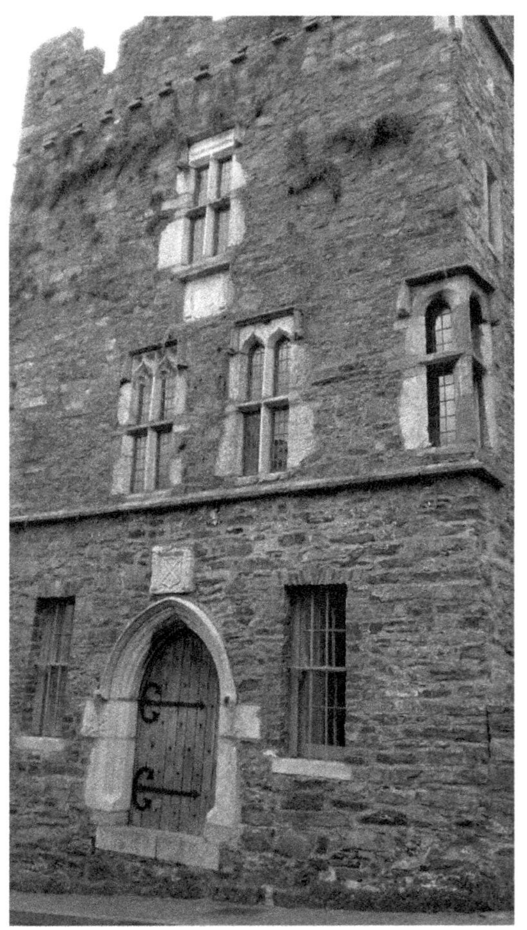

Desmond Castle

Strolling down a side street we were fascinated by the ironically named Mansion House. None of us had ever seen a building that looked less like a mansion. No sooner had we finished giving our opinions on its colourful exterior and wondering about its past, than we came across the equally ironically named Giant's Cottage.

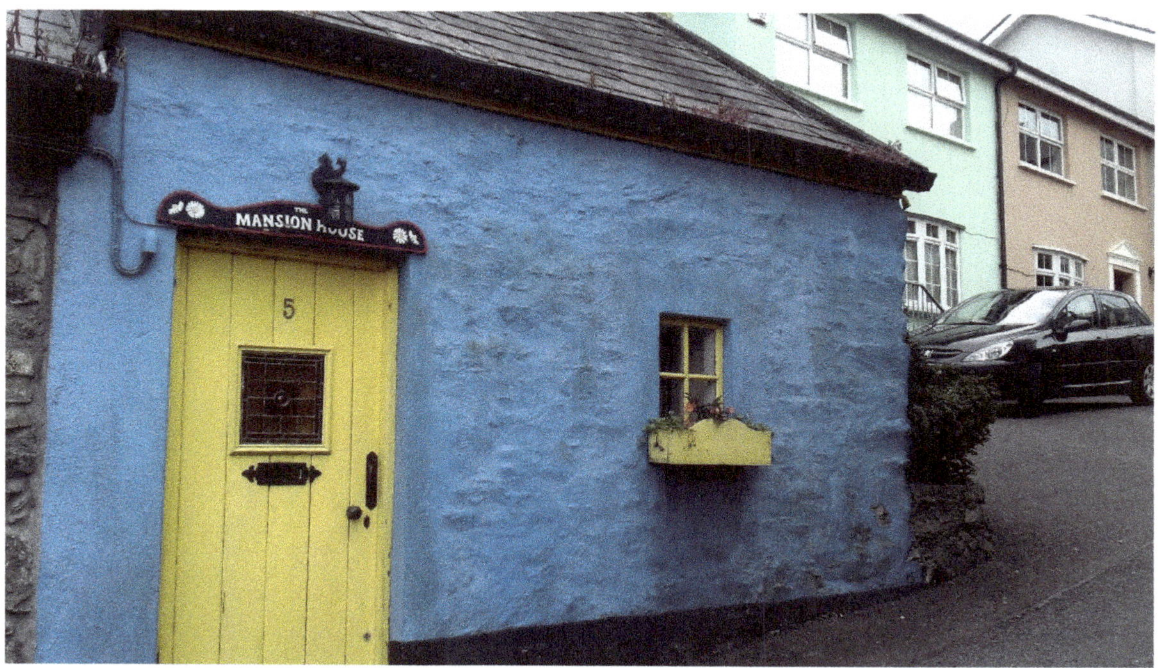

Why, I wondered, should a cottage that small be given such an inappropriate name? The reason soon became clear. It was once the home of Patrick Cotter O'Brien who was the first person in medical history to grow to the height of eight feet. His main claim to fame was as a circus attraction but his career was short, as was his life. He died in 1806 at the age of 46, from what is believed to have been the effects of gigantism. According to Wikipedia, he left the grand sum of £2,000 to his mother, along with a request that his body should be entombed within 12 feet of solid rock to prevent exhumation for research. This request appears not to have been granted as one of his arms is preserved in the Medical Museum at the Royal College of Surgeons in London. His 'giant boots' are on display in Kinsale Museum.

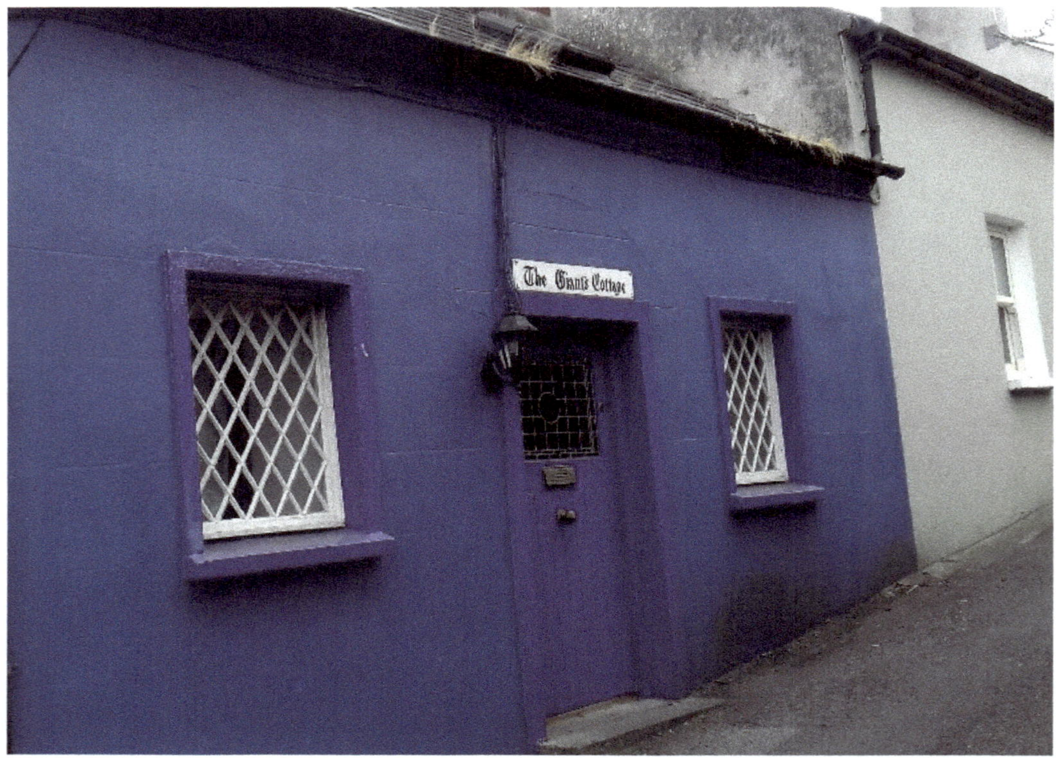

On leaving Kinsale, a short drive around the coast brought us to Garrettstown House Caravan Park, in the grounds of a huge, crumbling, early 18th century mansion that will one day be restored and returned to its former glory as a family home. It's a massive project, requiring great vision and an even greater pit of money. Its current owner, like all the Irish people we've met so far, is a knowledgeable historian, an entertaining orator and something of a philosopher.

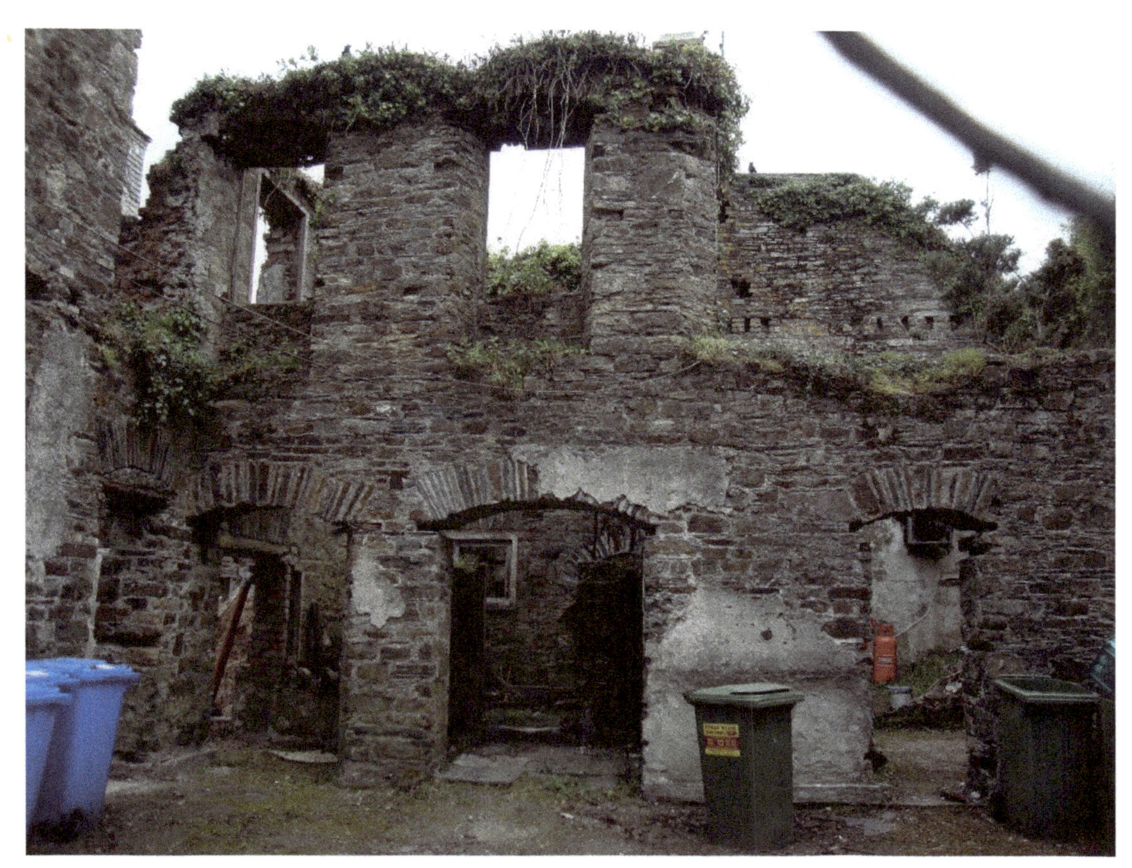

Garrettstown House – currently home to families of rooks and jackdaws

Today's mileage: 32

County Kerry
Sneem

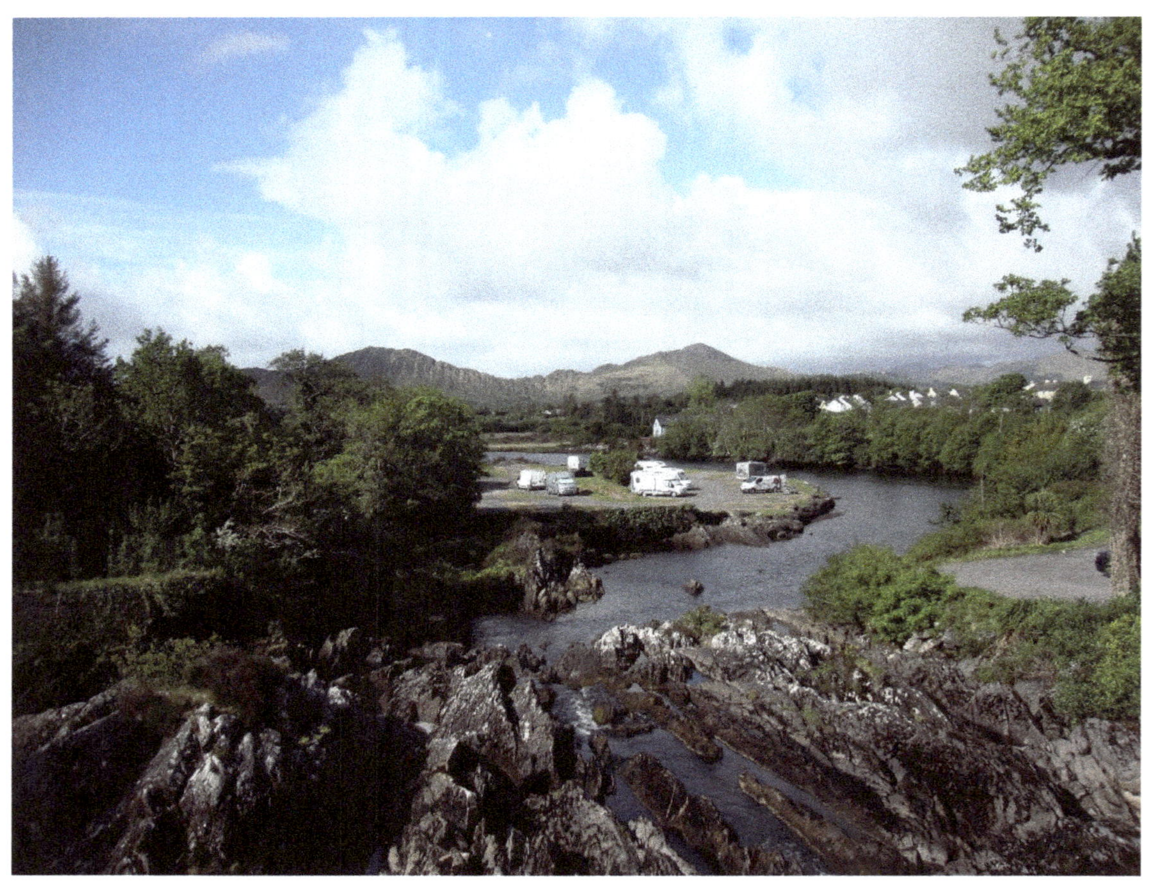

Sneem Aire

Saturday, 13th May

The journey from Garrettstown and along The Wild Atlantic Way took us through winding country roads, past sea and estuaries, over the Caha Mountains and down the other side, passing Clonakilty, Skibbereen and Bantry Bay, with a couple of stops on the way for coffee and, later, lunch.

Our first coffee stop was Molly Gallivan's Visitor Centre and craft shop, with a scenic lay-by opposite, known as Druid's View. The 12 foot druid after which it is named, represents the first settlers to the region 6,000 years ago. Clad in copper, it was carved from the trunk of a Monterey cypress, and is the work of two artists from West Cork, Anthony Cornforth and Peter Little.

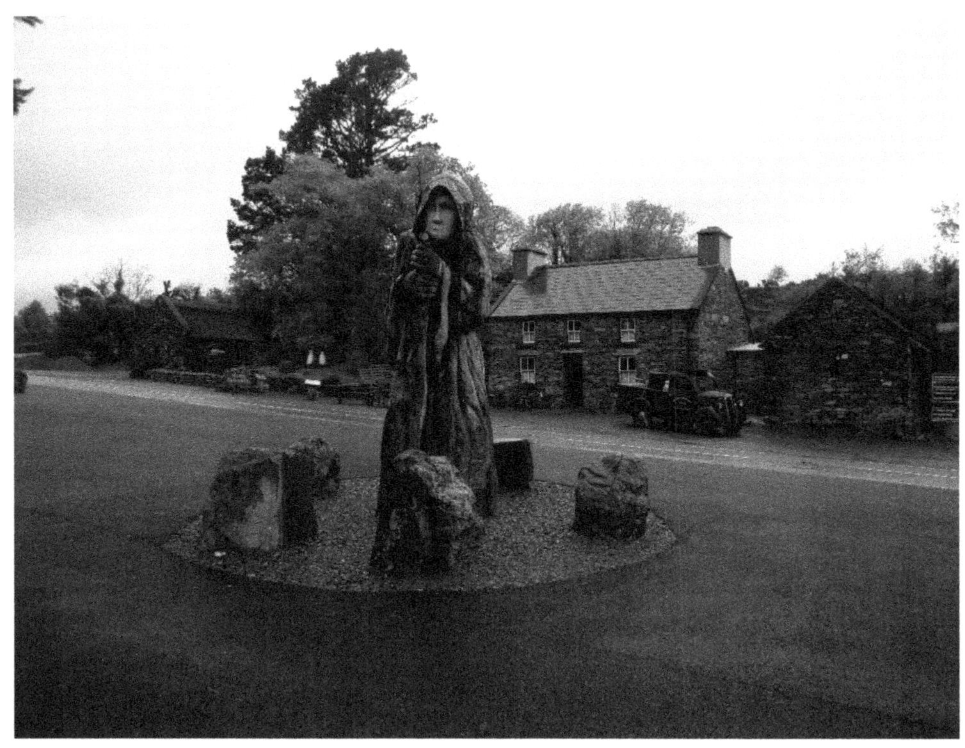

The Druid, with Molly Gallivan's shop and café in the background

The afternoon saw us picking our way through a litter of Ring of Kerry tour coaches that were parked haphazardly around the village of Sneem, and making our way to Sneem Aire, also known as Goosey Island Motorhome Park.

***

Crouched below the Caha Mountains with the River Sneem running alongside, the parish of Sneem has a population of 800 but local people are heavily outnumbered by tourists, including many Americans, who descend on it during the holiday season. The few shops (predominantly selling Irish knitwear and knick-knacks such as four-leafed-clover-ornaments, Guinness tumblers and garish leprechauns) are filled to overflowing with crowds of souvenir hunters but a few hundred yards from the bustle of the village centre you're in the peace of the riverside, where we settled for the night.

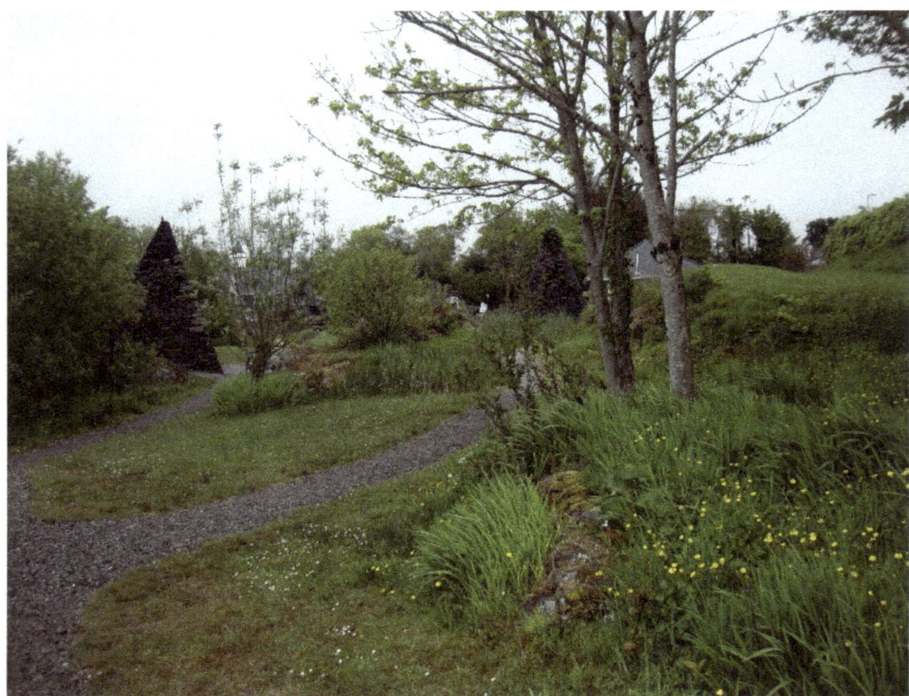

'The Way the Fairies went'

We went for a circular walk along the river and back into the village, which appeared to have its own suitably rustic character – an elderly, white-bearded man posing for photographs with his equally white-bearded billy goat. He made me think of Joe Grundy from The Archers: anything to bring a bit of extra cash. There is also a bronze sculpture of a real-life hero of Sneem. Steve 'Crusher' Casey was born in the village and was one of only two Irish wrestlers to become world heavyweight champion. He died in 1987 at the age of 78.

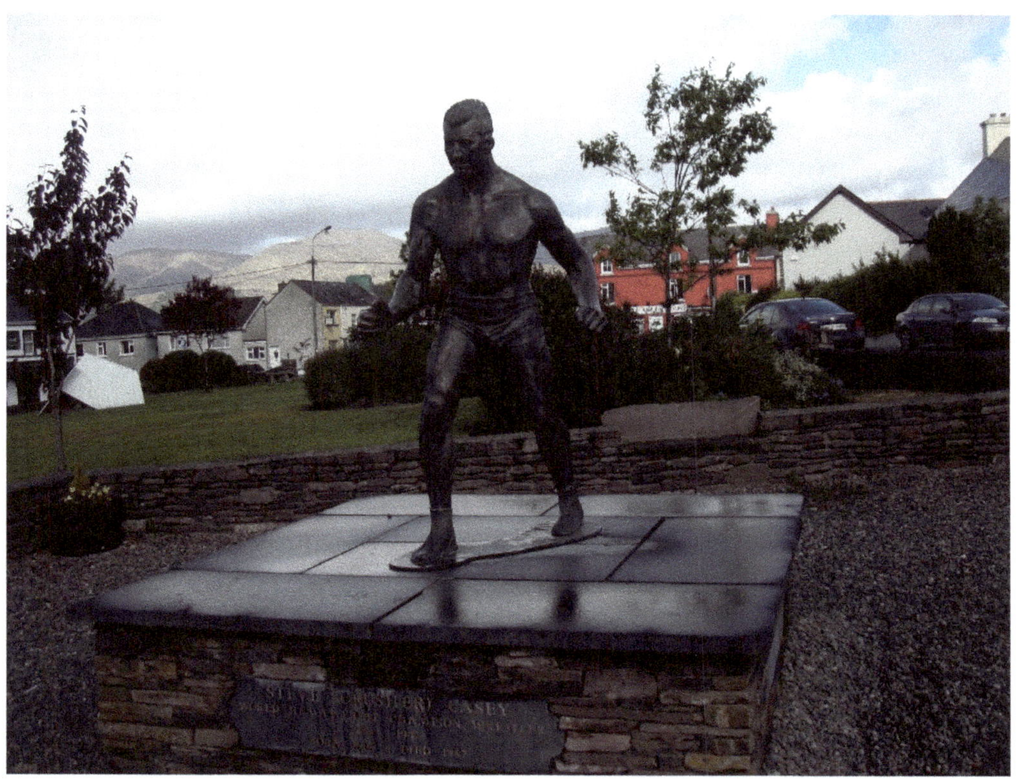

Steve 'Crusher' Casey – world heavyweight champion wrestler

We also passed a neat terrace of new, nearly finished houses, bearing a For Sale sign proclaiming they were now being offered at seventy per cent of their 2007 prices. Clearly they were built during the period of rapid economic growth during the late 1990s and early 2000s, when Ireland became known as the Celtic Tiger. This period of expansion, fuelled mainly by EU and US funding and investment, eventually fell victim to the financial crash of 2007, and the houses, along with developments in other parts of the country, have stood unsold and empty ever since.

Houses in this part of Ireland are a constant source of fascination for Mike and me. Many are eye-poppingly grand and elegant, on huge plots with no real architectural style common to any of them. Especially popular are sprawling, ranch-type bungalows, with arched terraces reminiscent of Spanish villas. But then every so often you see tiny whitewashed dwellings with a window either side of the front door and often with a thatched roof. Some of these are traditional roses-round-the-door cottages but others have been abandoned and left to fall derelict, sometimes in the gardens of the grander houses that have been built to replace them.

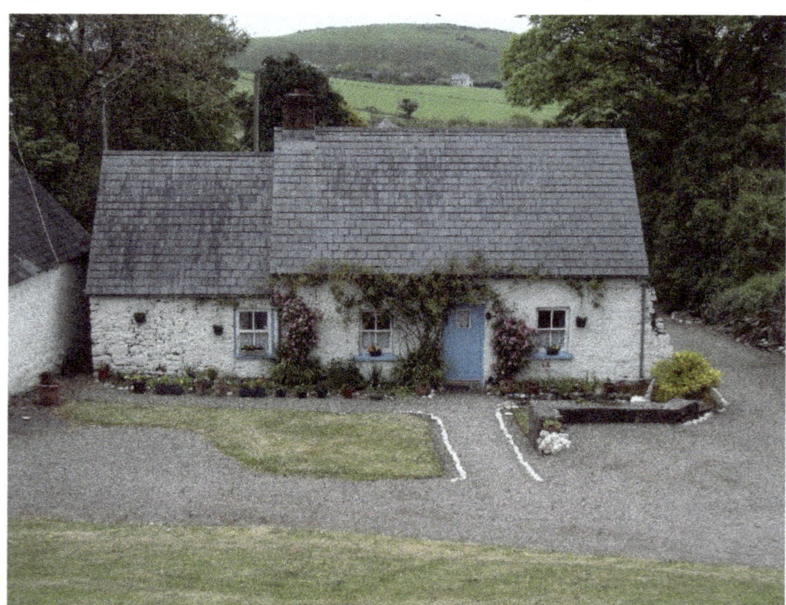

Traditional Irish cottage

We enjoy seeing the Irish names of towns and villages and the way even many of the English translations still have a foreign ring to them. Here are a few, in English:

Garranfula

Boharcogram

Coomnahora

Knockaunnaglashy

Moingaphuca

Reennanallagane

Borris in Ossiry

Illaunstookain

MacGillycuddy's Reeks

Today's mileage: 104

Glenbeigh, Dingle Bay

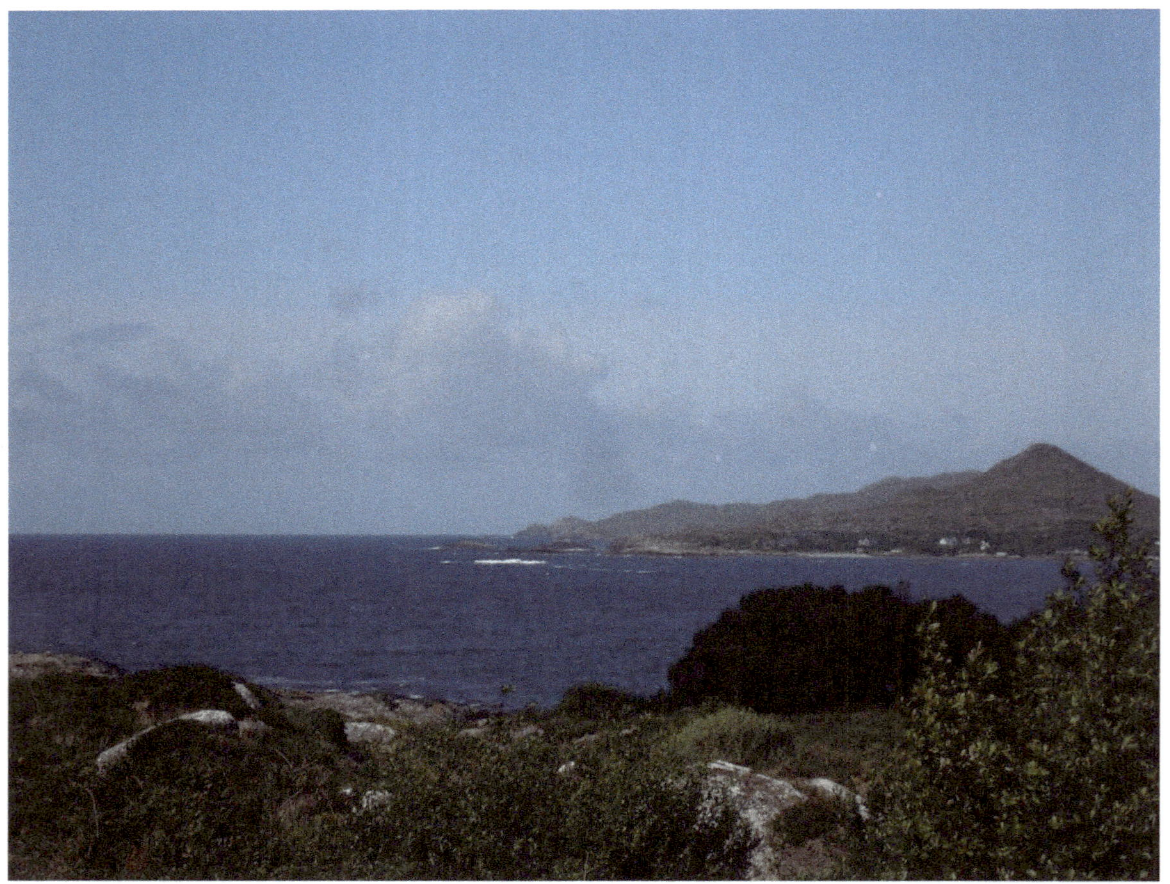

The Kerry Coastline

Sunday, 14th May

The county of Kerry makes you realise why Ireland is known as the Emerald Isle. Its lush green fields are full of glossy Kerry cattle, including the most adorable calves imaginable. You also realise, as you travel around, what it is that brings so many tourists to this part of Eire. The scenery, from coast, inlets and estuaries to rock, scrub, boglands and range after range of ancient creased and wrinkled mountains, simply takes your breath away. Even though Mike was doing all the driving yet again today, he was still able to take most of it in and made the comment 'every corner you go round opens up another panoramic view'.

The roads, even the major N-routes, vary in quality from smooth and well surfaced to bumpy and potholed. Some stretches, as in France, are long and straight while others snake their way through miles of bends, prompting another wry comment from Mike on the stretch between Waterville and Cahersiveen: the Romans certainly didn't come this way!

At one point we spotted a couple of young women hitch-hikers, laden with huge backpacks, so we took them as far as Waterville. They were French and having finished their studies were spending time touring Ireland. They were thrilled when Mike spoke to them in his best schoolboy French and I was filled with admiration at him trying, especially as I knew he'd failed it at O-level twice at school.

We were heading for Glenbeigh on the north coast of the Iveragh Peninsula, and a night at Glenross Caravan and Camping Park. We were looking forward to enjoying Kerry's International Dark Sky Reserve later, but first we tackled the four-mile Reennanallagne circular walk, to give ourselves an appetite for dinner. Glenbeigh is an interesting town in Dingle Bay, with an interesting history and a tradition of horseracing on the sands each year.

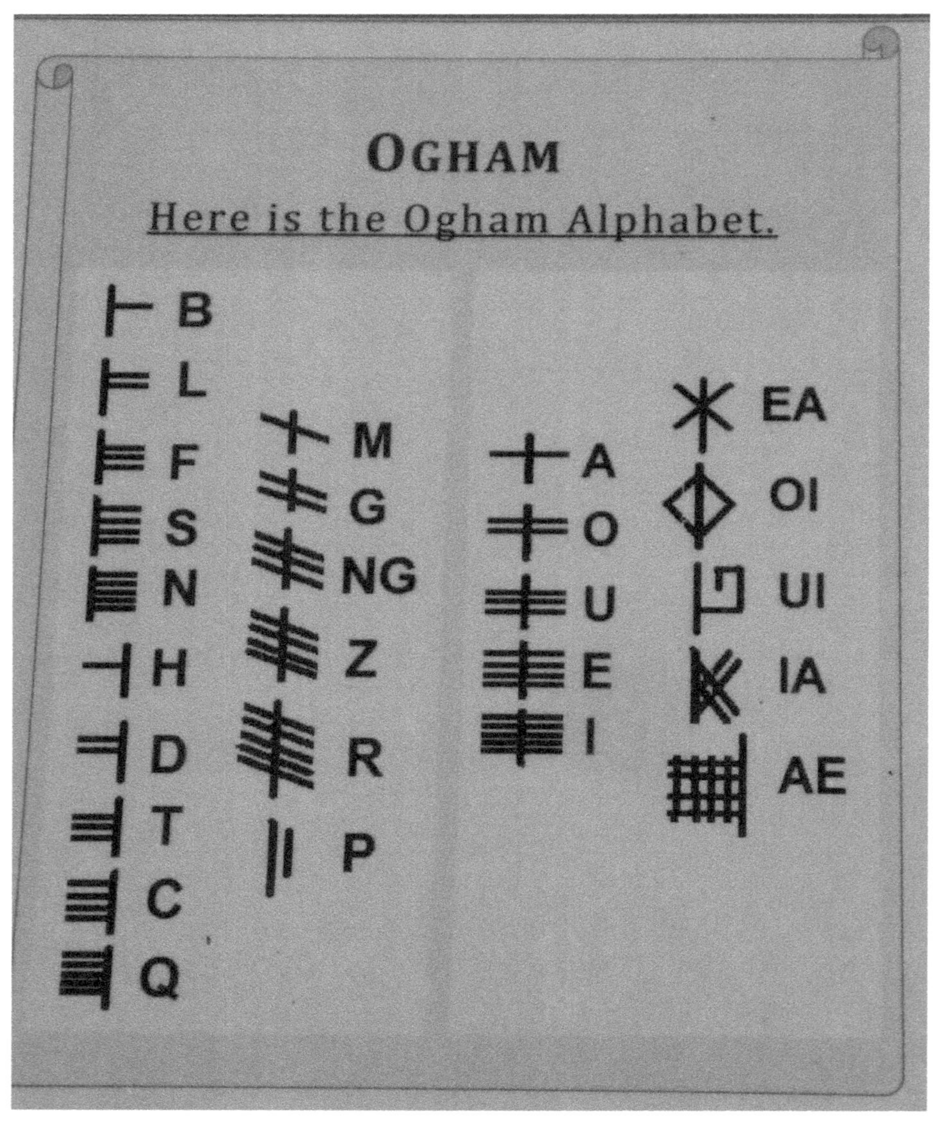

The ancient Ogham alphabet was used to write the Irish language in Medieval times. You read it from the bottom up

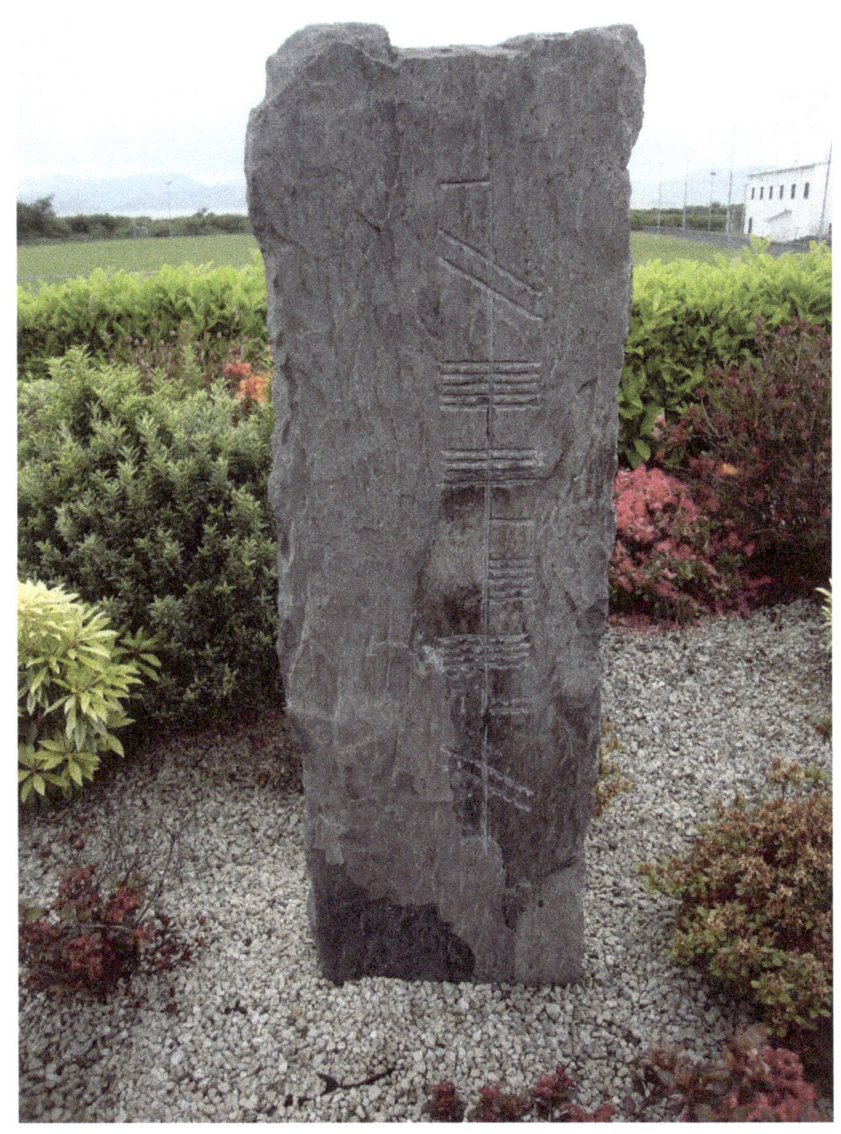

*Now see if you can decipher the words on the standing stone**

Sad to say, our plan to stay up late and gaze at the stars was scuppered by a huge dinner of roast Irish beef, Aunt Bessie Yorkshire puds, roast potatoes, carrots, broccoli and cauliflower, followed by apple crumble and custard. After that little lot, all we wanted to do was sleep. So we missed the show!

* Answer: Glenbeigh

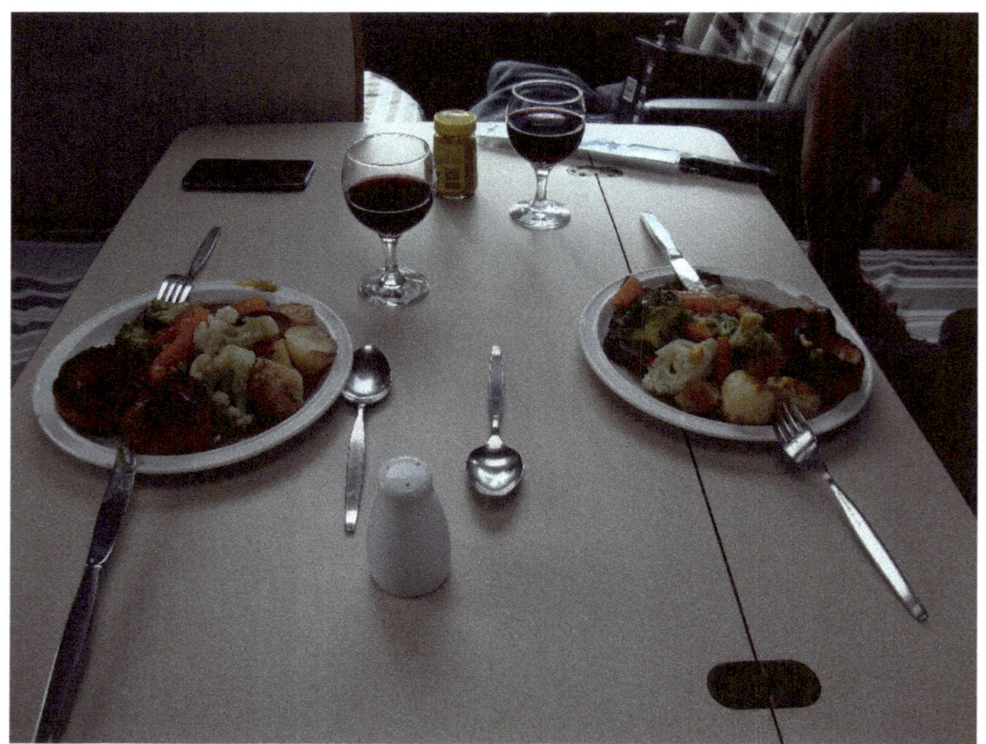

Sunday roast

Today's mileage:50

County Limerick

Curraghchase Forest Park

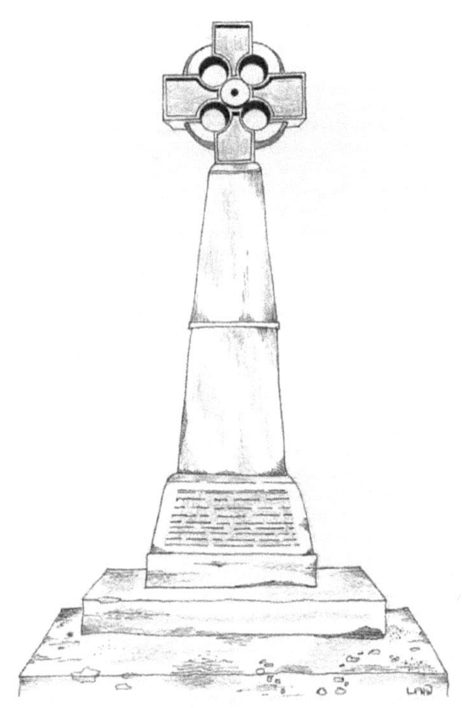

(Curraghchase Forest Park is near Kilcoran, close to the banks of the Shannon, a few miles from Limerick)

Monday, 15th May

On leaving Glenbeigh we soon realised what a mecca for tourists this part of Ireland is. Within ten minutes eighteen huge coaches had come trundling past us from the other direction and yes, okay, we are tourists too. But no way could either of us endure a coach touring holiday, where you have all your stopping points arranged for you and having to share the 'must see' spot with hundreds of other people at the same time, not to mention the local characters who pitch up at these sites with their donkey, their dog and their goat, to be photographed as true Irishmen and be paid for the privilege.

We are probably extremely boring people who exist in our own little bubble, but we are here mainly to see the scenery and the countryside of Ireland, picking up odd bits of culture along the way. With the exception of Blarney Castle, which was a delight, we tend to keep away from cities and big tourist attractions. I know everyone is different and there is a huge amount of art, poetry, literature and history to be found here. Indeed, I only have to go back two generations to find my own family originated from Eire. It's just that Mike and I like to 'get away from it all' and are happiest in forests, the countryside or by the sea.

Curraghchase is a truly beautiful forest. There are thousands of mature trees in its 774 acres, with an abundance of different broad leaf species. With trees, of course, come birds and their song at this time of year is magical.

Unfortunately, many of the trees here, both young and mature specimens, are being suffocated by a strong growth of ivy and although foresters are clearly attempting to deal with it, by cutting through the ivy trunks at the base of the trunks, it could be too late for many of them. I discovered that contrary to what I believed, the reason ivy-clad trees die isn't that ivy is a parasite. It grows its own roots and doesn't 'feed' on the tree: it merely uses it as a support to grow up, like roses on a trellis. But if the ivy reaches its host's canopy, it smothers the leafing branches, destroying the tree's ability to photosynthesise, or 'breathe'. It is also possible that ivy prefers weak or diseased specimens, which is why these are the ones that tend to fall in a gale.

It's a never-ending battle for the forestry workers of Curraghchase. Even where the strong growths of ivy have died back as a result of their efforts, there are still more trails of new growth creeping along the ground and back up the trunks.

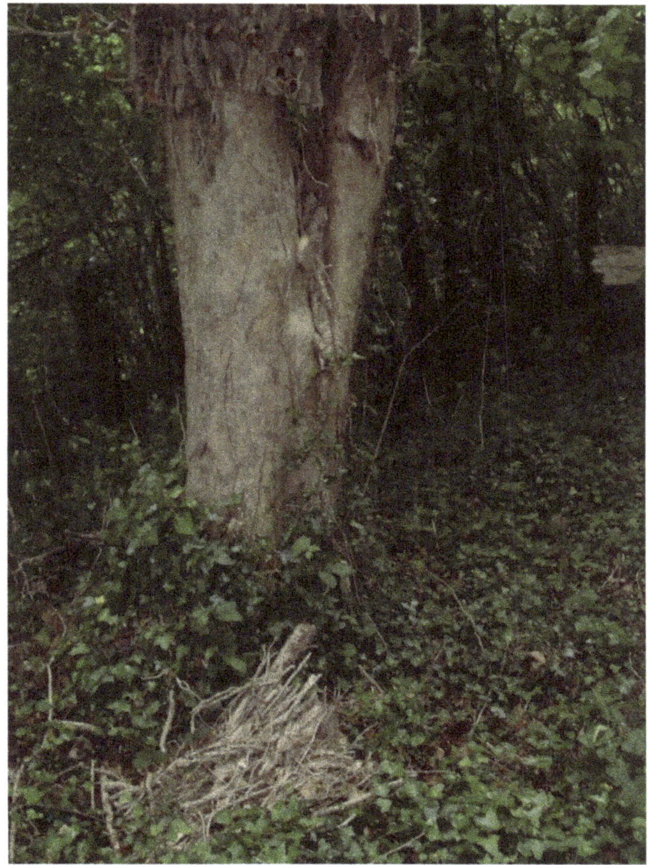

This picture shows how ivy has been cut away,
with more creeping along the forest floor and up the trunk to take its place

The caravan park itself has been neglected for many years but in 2015 it was taken over by a new, enthusiastic young proprietor, Warren Higgins, who, with the help of his dad is working hard to put it on the map for motorhomes, caravans and tents. Warren told us he has a ten-year lease on the place and we wish him every success.

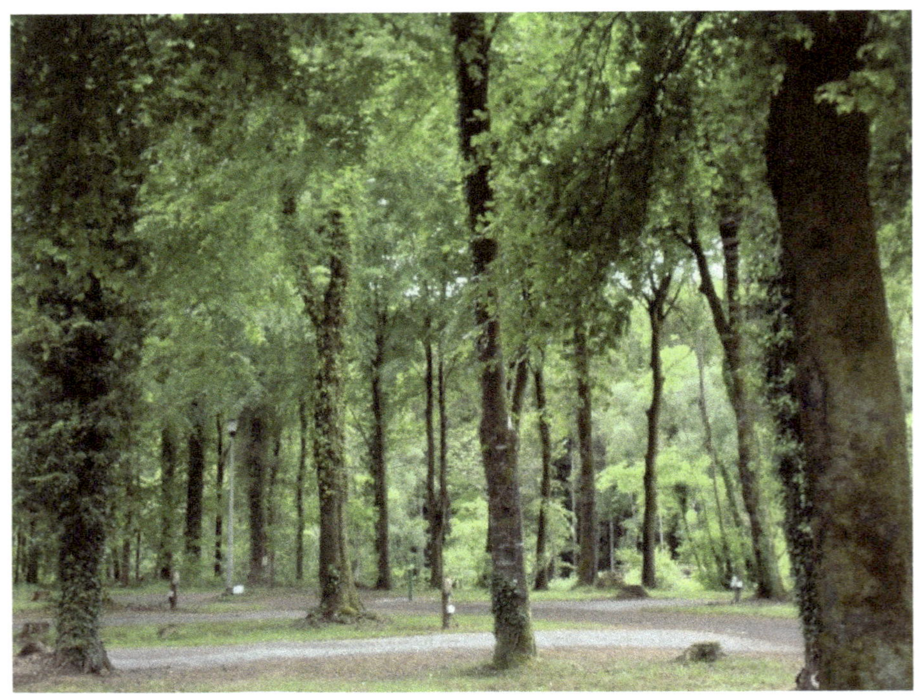

Some of the pitches at Curraghchase

We absolutely love this site, with its woodland walks and cycle routes, and were tempted to stay an extra night but after weighing up our options, reluctantly, we made the decision to move on. There are still of lot of places we want to see before catching the ferry from Belfast to the Scottish port of Cairnryan next Tuesday.

The Curraghchase Estate is packed with history and tales of hauntings, but for me the saddest thing about it is how it fell into decline. Curragh House mansion was built in 1657 by Vere Hunt, an officer in Cromwell's army, and 300 years later it was still in the hands of the same family. By the early 20th century it was the home of Robert Stephen de Vere and his wife Isabel Catherine. Robert was only 64 when he died and his widow erected a Celtic cross in the woods in his memory.

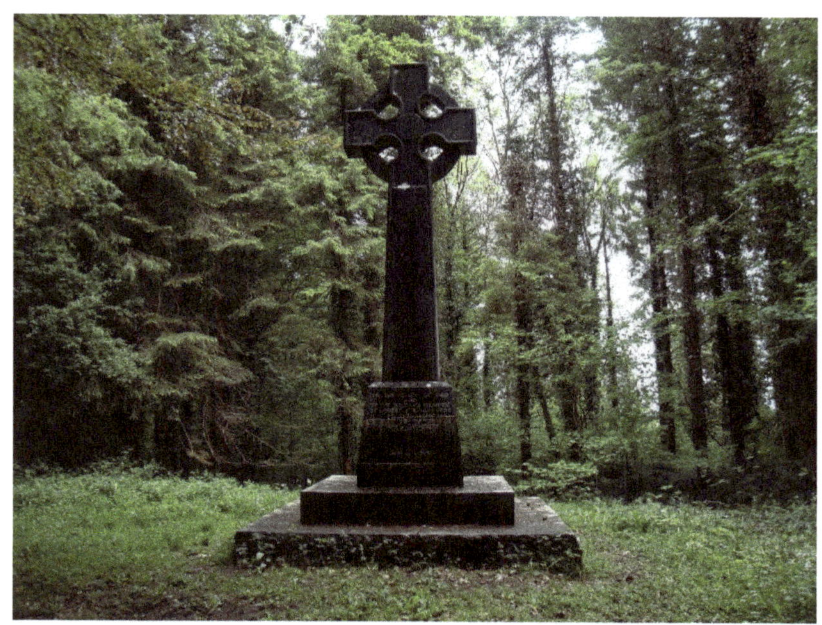

Celtic cross in memory of Robert Stephen de Vere

Then just five years after losing her husband, Isabel de Vere lost her home too, when it was destroyed by fire during a storm in December 1941.These days all that is left are the outer walls and the cellars, which have become home to lesser horseshoe bats, a protected and endangered little creature that is no bigger than a plum.

If you're interested in the supernatural you might enjoy visiting Curraghchase on Christmas Eve. Back in the late 1800s the poet Alfred, Lord Tennyson was visiting the house when he described seeing the mystical arm of a woman rise above the waters of the lake. A hundred years or so later, guests were enjoying a Christmas party in the big house when a piercing cry of torment was heard from outside, so loud it was clearly audible above the noise of a raging storm. Looking out towards the lake they saw the red, glowing figure of a woman with her arm stretched out and pointing towards Curraghchase.

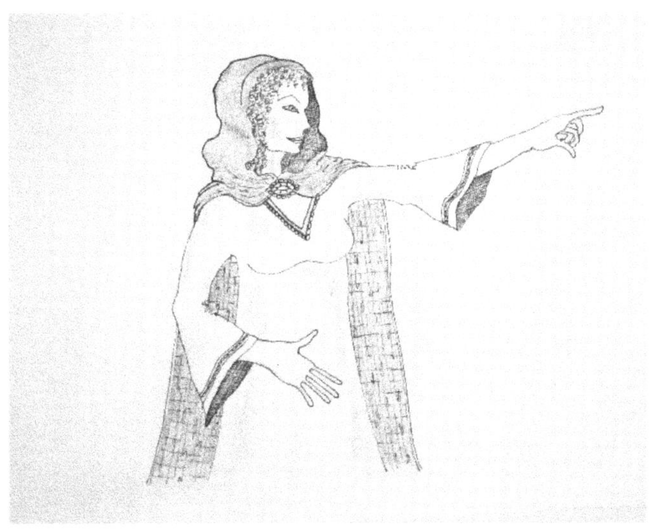

The ghost of Curraghchase (artist's impression)

Later that night a branch was torn from a tree in the gale. It crashed through a window of the house, knocking over a candelabra and starting the devastating fire that ravaged the entire building. According to legend, on every Christmas Eve since, the burning figure of a woman – the Lady of the Lake – can be seen floating on the waters of the lake in the grounds of the mansion.

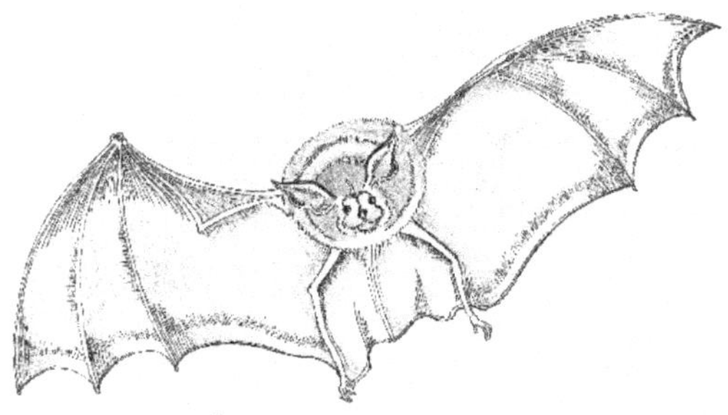

Today's mileage: 80

County Roscommon

Loch Ree and Galey Bay

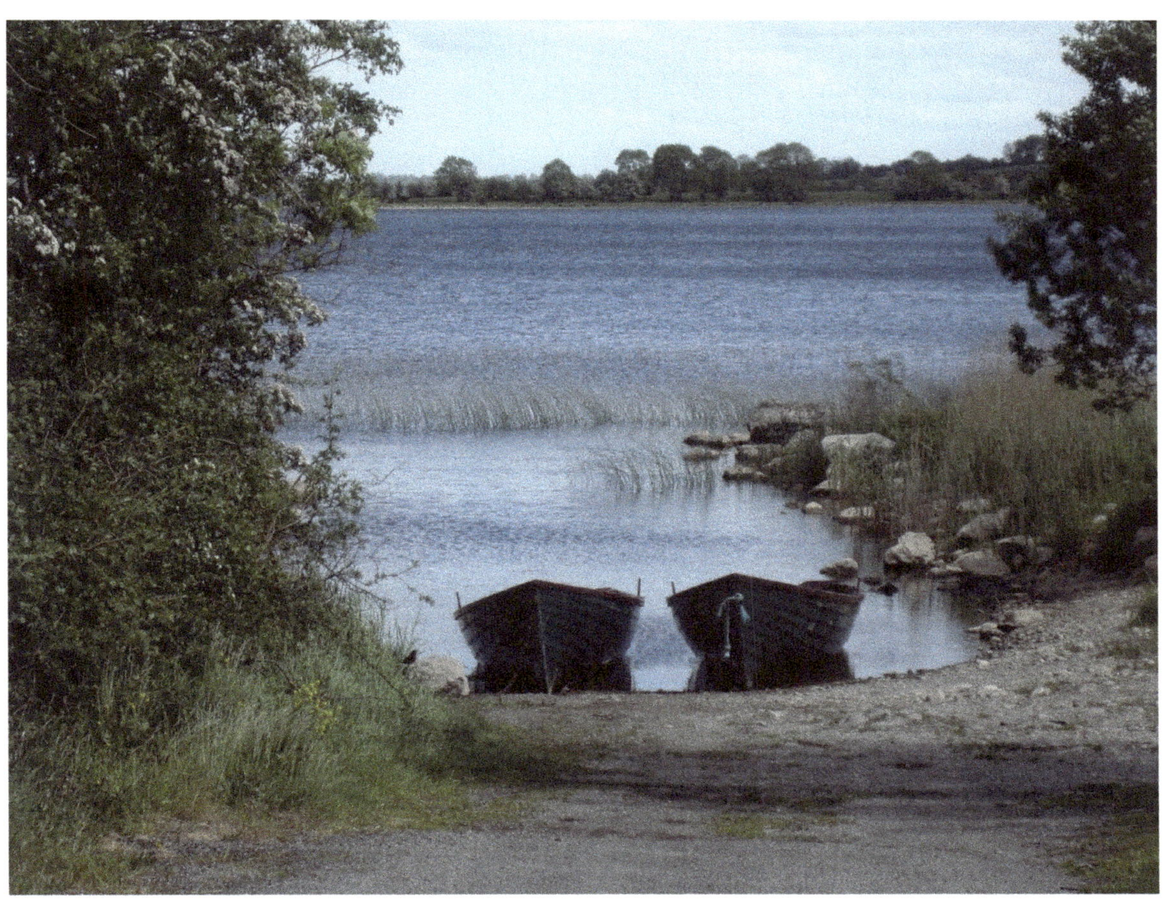

Lough Ree is in the midlands of Ireland, the second of the three major lakes on the River Shannon. It is the second largest lake on the river, after Lough Derg

Tuesday, 16th May

We drove from Curraghchase to Lough Ree via Limerick for provisions – our supplies of treats and chocolate, not to mention proper food, were running a bit low. I continue to be shocked at the price of groceries in this part of the world. Today, for example, I paid €3.50 for a small packet of chocolate Hobnobs.

Driving around Ireland you can't help but notice every town has a castle and, needless to say, all these fortresses have their stories to tell. Some are incredibly old, dating back to the late 12th century, and I think that is a big part of the appeal to American visitors, who don't have buildings of such antiquity. Many are well preserved while others are just ruins (the castles, I mean, not the Americans), but that simply adds to their charm. Another major draw for people from the United States is something I've already mentioned: the chance to search for their much-prized Irish roots. Even the great and the good fall for that one – a big attraction is Barack Obama Plaza, a motorway service station that was dedicated to America's first black president after he discovered that his great-great-great-grandfather was from the nearby village of Moneygall. Signs at the side of the road exhort tourists to *Visit Barack Obama Plaza: best place to stop off in Ireland,* not to mention the equally well signposted *Barack Obama's Ancestral Village!!!*

In 2011, a presidential visit to Ireland by Barack Obama and the First Lady gave rise to a plethora of incorrectly apostrophised O'Bama souvenirs: there were O'Bama placemats, teapots, hats, key chains . . . The president delighted a large crowd when he joked: 'Hello, Dublin! Hello, Ireland! My name is Barack Obama of the Moneygall Obamas. And I've come home to find the apostrophe that we lost somewhere along the way. . .'

On both sides of the road towards Athlone there is mile after mile of fields of black peat – under the grass of the meadows is peat, and that peat is being harvested just as intensively as wheat or oats or barley would be elsewhere.

Galey Bay Caravan and Camping Park is about a hundred yards from the shores of Lough Ree on a farm near the lough's north western tip. It's well-ordered and tranquil, and we were enchanted at how tame the wild birds were in their search for food to take back to their young. One in particular, a bold cock chaffinch, kept us amused all evening, hopping into the van looking for peckings and actually taking crumbs from my hand. He was joined by sparrows, dunnocks and a skinny robin on the grass while we sat reading, and the chaffinch even perched on Mike's foot at one point. He, the chaffinch, was still collecting food at nine-thirty in the evening.

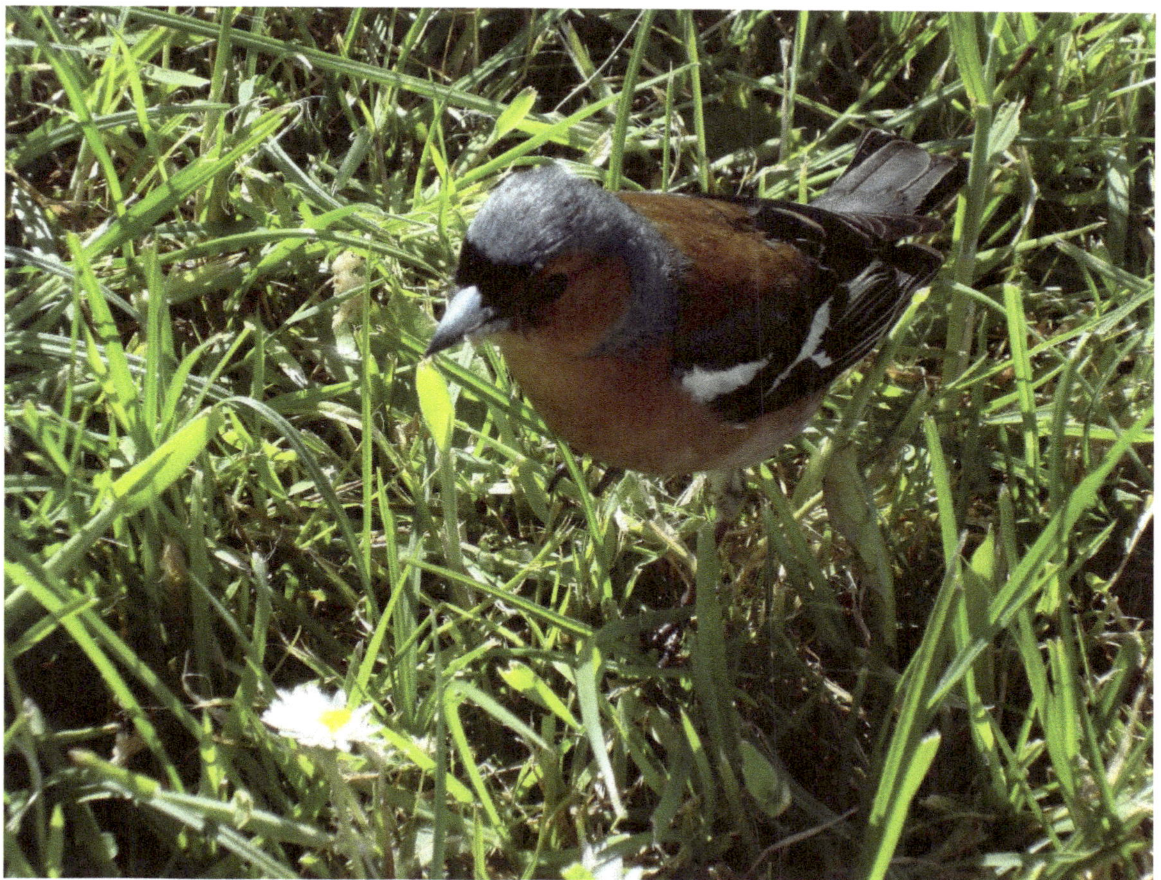

Cheeky chaffinch

As soon as we'd got Bessie hitched up to the electrics we walked down to the lough and as far round it as we could, crushing wild mint under our feet as we picked our way through long grass and over ditches. After a while the rough grassy track reached a fence and we were unable to go any further. On our way back we discovered an ancient dilapidated tower, covered in ivy. It turned out to be all that is left of the 14th century Galey Castle, former home of the O'Kelly Clan. What a brilliant setting for a story this place is.

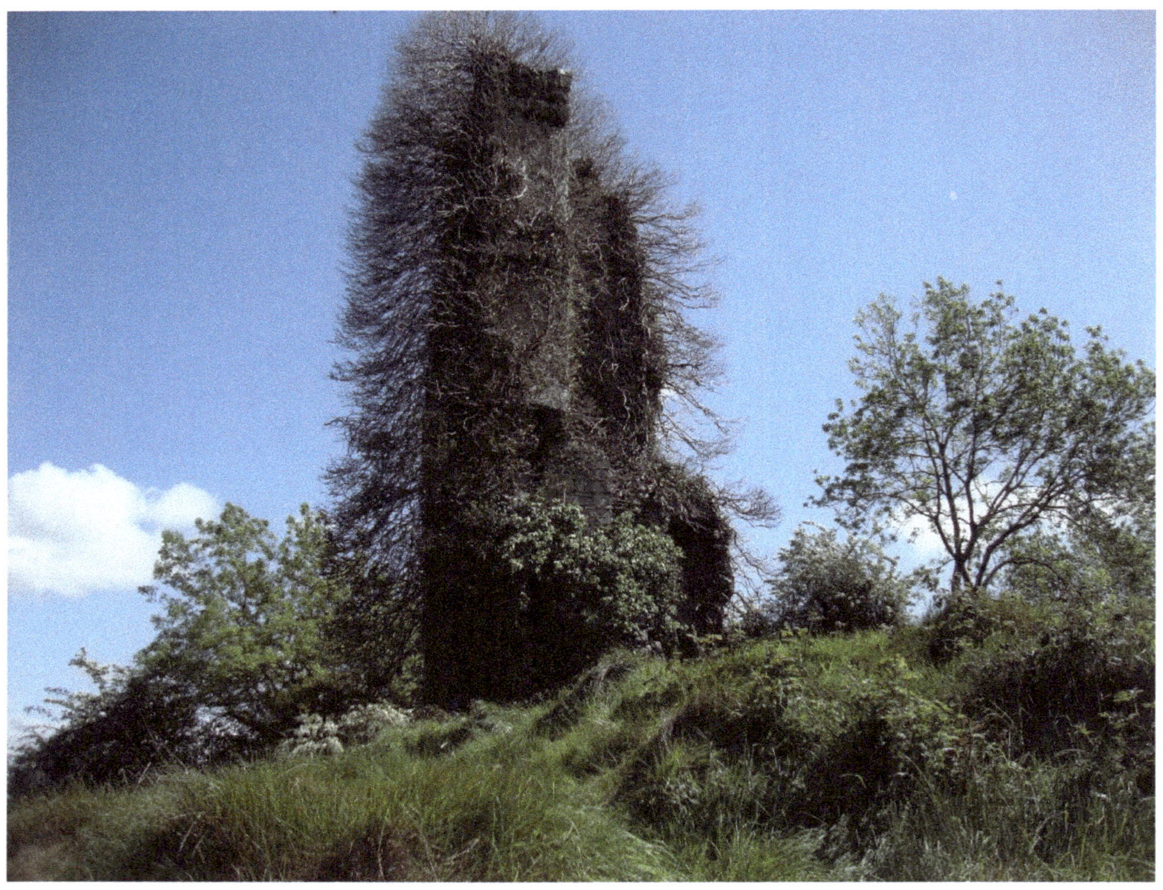

The remains of Galey Castle

A dark and peaceful night under the Kerry stars.

Today's mileage: 121

County Sligo

Strandhill

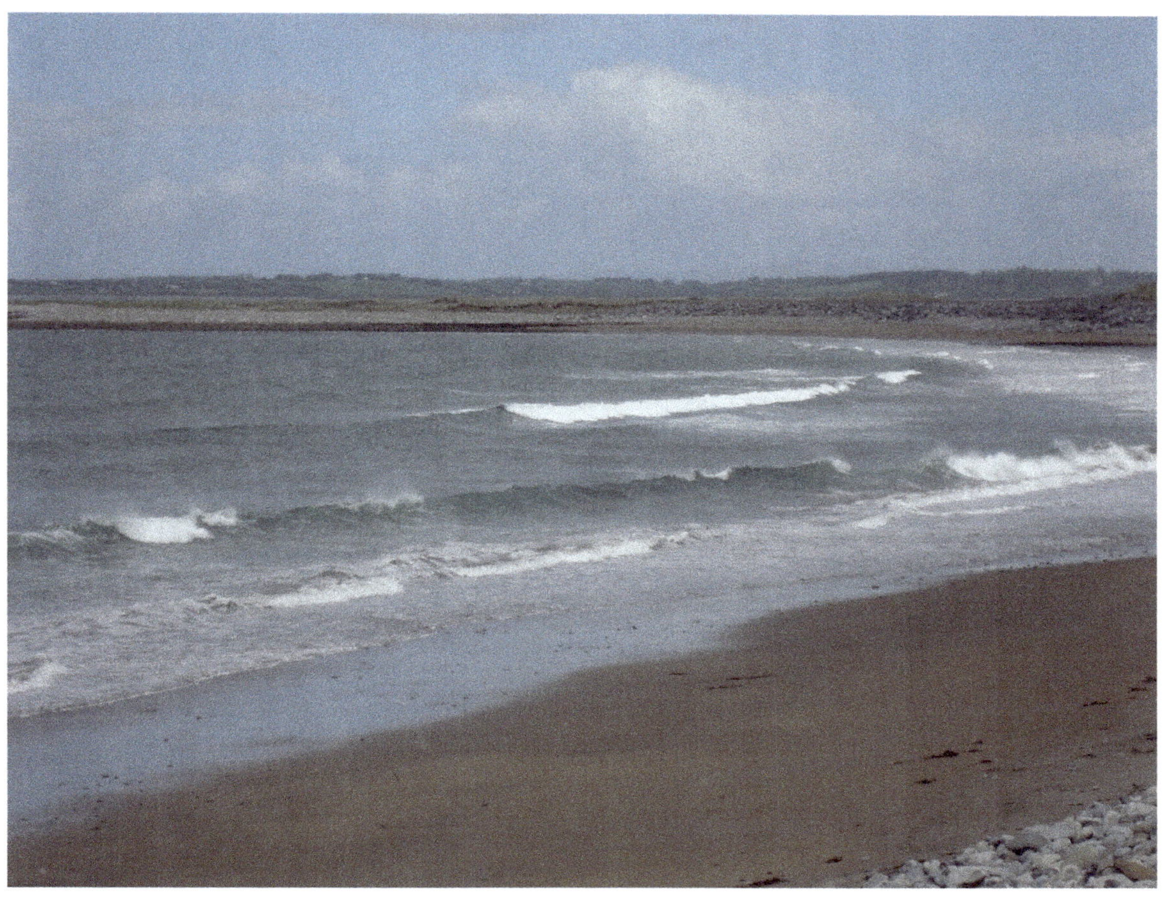

Strandhill Beach

Wednesday, 17th May

Today's route was notable for its hawthorn hedges and bushes. They bound the fields and fill the hedgerows and, laden with blossom, they look as though a giant sieve full of icing sugar has been shaken over them.

Strandhill Caravan and Camping Park is almost on the beach and today it is taking the full brunt of a cool south westerly breeze. Away from the sea, behind the site, is Knocknarea Mountain and the town of Sligo is on the other side of the bay. The big sandy beach is edged with huge marram grass covered dunes, which are under protection to help stave off the effects of erosion, caused as much by human activity as by the effects of wind and waves. We walked for a couple of miles on the beach, where we spotted a ringed plover, and then cycled the four miles or so to Cummeen Strand. This forms the causeway to Coney Island, where the estuary is a feeding ground for ringed plover and hooded crows, hunting for small crustaceans, worms and other invertebrates in the soft wet sand.

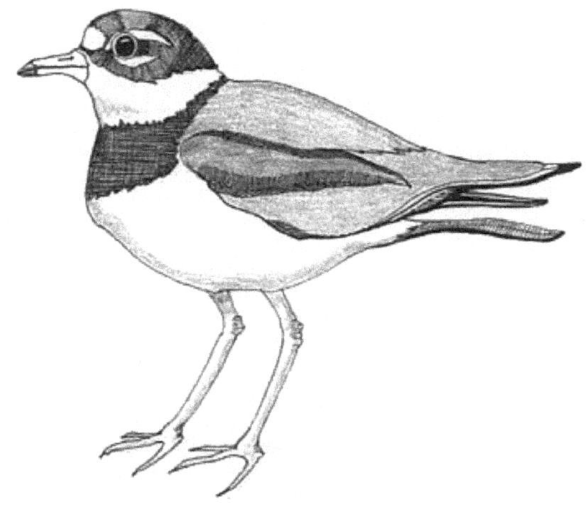

Ringed Plover

Coney Island used to be full of rabbits, hence its name, and Coney Island in New York is said to have been named after it, in a nod to the tens of thousands of Irish people who migrated to America between the 1920s and 1930s. I don't know how much truth there is in that, but it's a nice thought. The path of the two-mile causeway, which goes under water when the tide comes in, is marked by 14 stone pillars that were built in the mid-1890s and, from the road, are easily mistaken for channel markers. At least, they were by us erstwhile sailors.

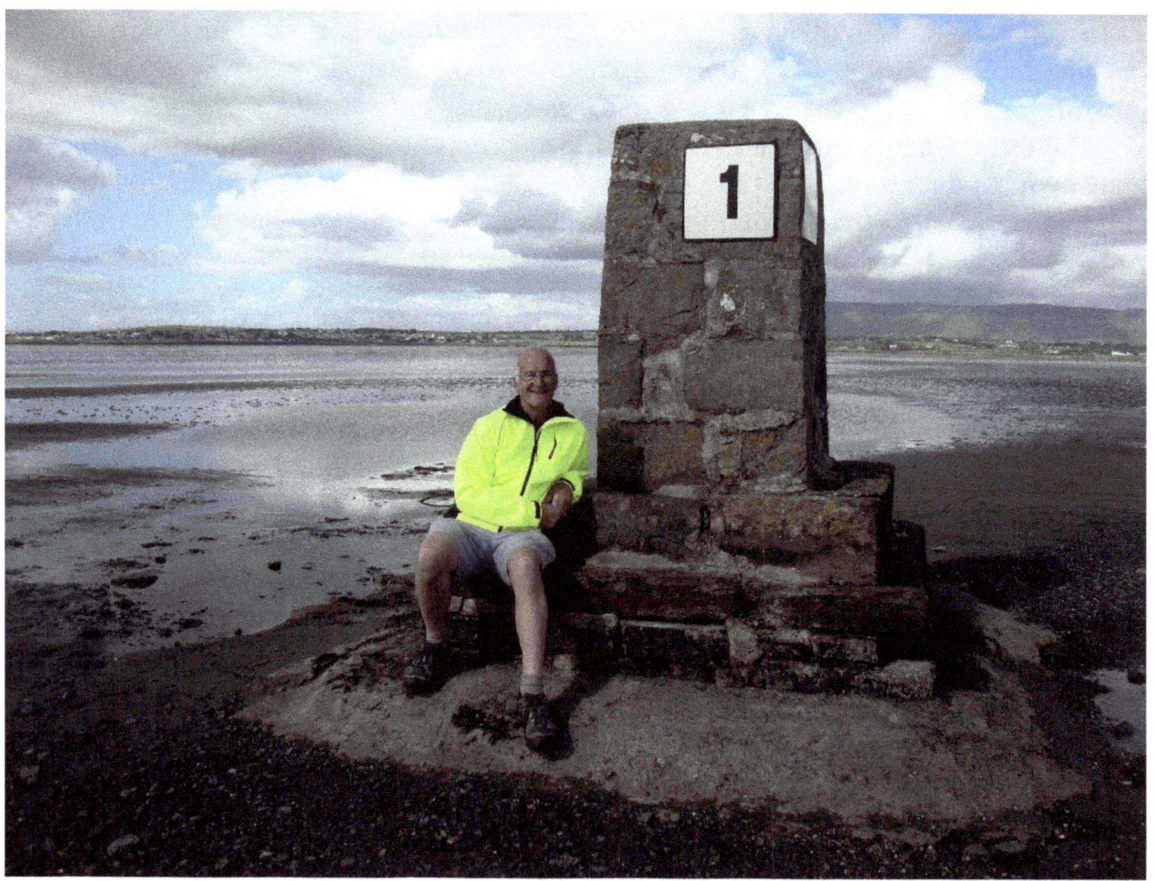

Mike at the first of the causeway's 14 marker pillars

Although it was only just after low water and we would have had plenty of time, we decided against crossing the causeway on our bikes because of the risk of salt damage to the bearings. In any case we were wearing entirely the wrong footwear for walking through the saturated sand and I didn't fancy it in bare feet either: I have a strong aversion to slimy creatures attaching themselves to my naked flesh!

Irish petrol stations all have amazing Tardis-like supermarkets, many with on-site *Cuisine de France* bakeries. This is a temptation we are unable to resist and our morning coffee stops are an *homage* to *pains aux raisins* and *pains aux chocolat.* Waistlines expanding. If the smell of baking is difficult to resist, the tantalising aroma wafting from a restaurant on the strand was impossible, and we elected for fish and chips in a beach-side café tonight. It was a disappointing experience. The fish was cobbler, allegedly and according to the menu 'to save the cod' (to save them spending out more-like, we thought), the batter was oily and the chips were hard. The Pinot Grigio was nice and cold but arrived in a glass little bigger than a thimble. The bill was just under €35 – a high price for a mediocre meal. From now on we will continue to do our own cooking, and eat on board Bessie.

On the approach road to the caravan park is a sports ground, where this notice to spectators caught our eye. What a good mantra.

Today's mileage: 64

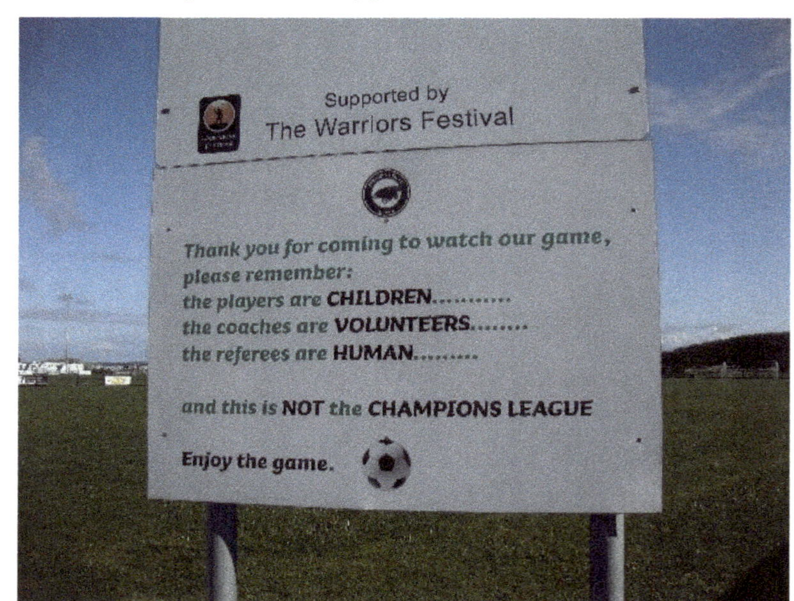

Fair play off the pitch!

County Donegal

Killybegs

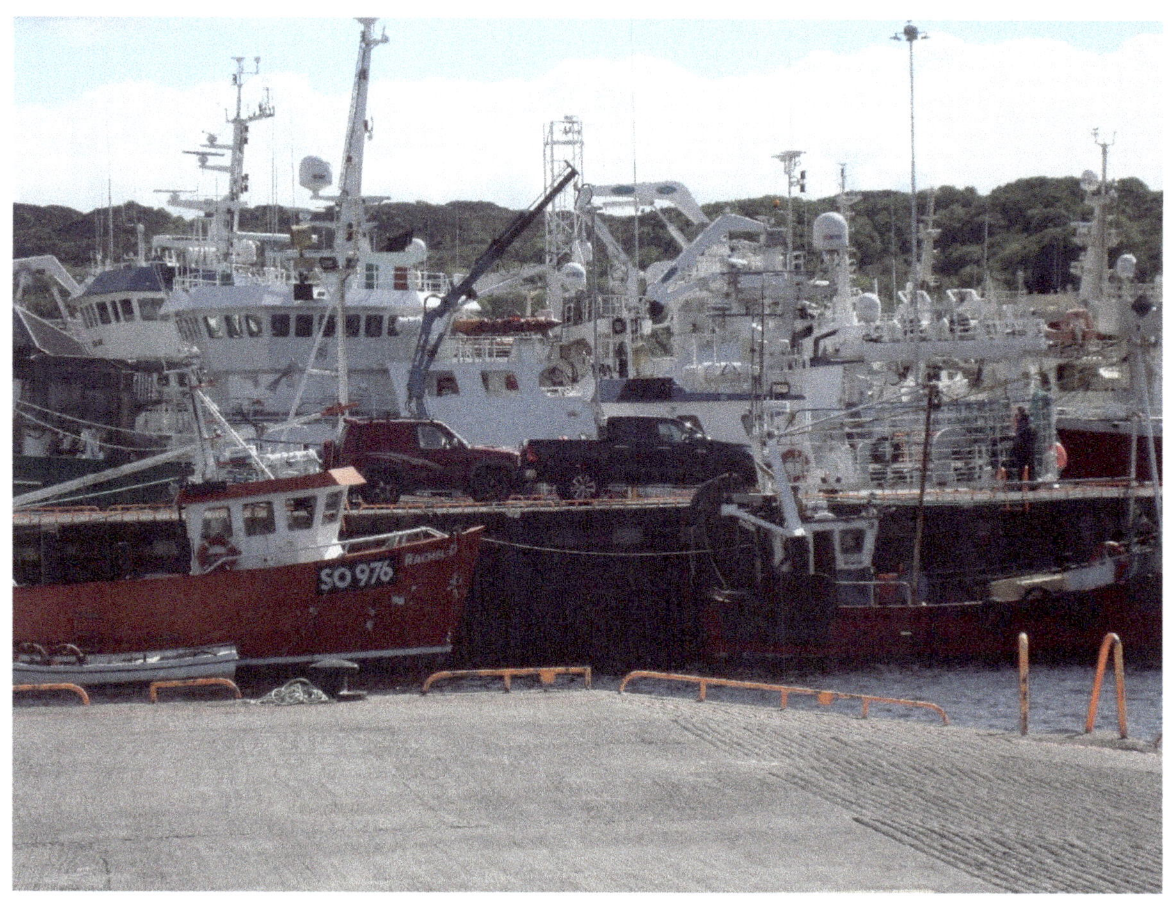

Killybegs Harbour: Ireland's premier fishing port

Thursday, 18th May

Ireland is full of superlatives. The biggest, the best, the oldest . . . it seems every town and village has something to boast about. But when it comes to Killybegs Holiday Park the claim rings true. It's *The World's Best Kept Secret,* according to *The Lonely Planet* travel guides.

We drove into the town expecting to see nothing more than a picturesque harbour and were surprised to find a big port crammed with trawlers and other fishing vessels. But not only is it *Ireland's Premier Fishing Port* – it also welcomes cruise liners. The one dwarfing the harbour today was the *Astor,* a German ship en route to Dublin. Later in the afternoon we watched from the shore as she made her way regally, and carefully, through the islands before disappearing into the haze.

At first, as Bessie threaded her way through the narrow roads of Killybegs, we thought the reason for the *'best kept secret'* reputation for the holiday park was that it was impossible to find. We missed the sign to start with and did a second circuit of the town before we spotted it. The road then took us past the fire station and through an industrial estate. We were not impressed and considered turning round and going elsewhere. But soon the grey buildings of the factories were behind us: we drove a short distance up a hill, through the entrance gates to Killybegs Holiday Park and then stopped sharp. What we saw took our breath away. We have seen some spectacular scenery since we've been in Ireland but nothing quite as exquisite as what lay before us now. The old saying 'a picture paints a thousand words' is probably true, but not one of my scores of photos of the view from here will ever succeed in portraying the real thing in all its splendour.

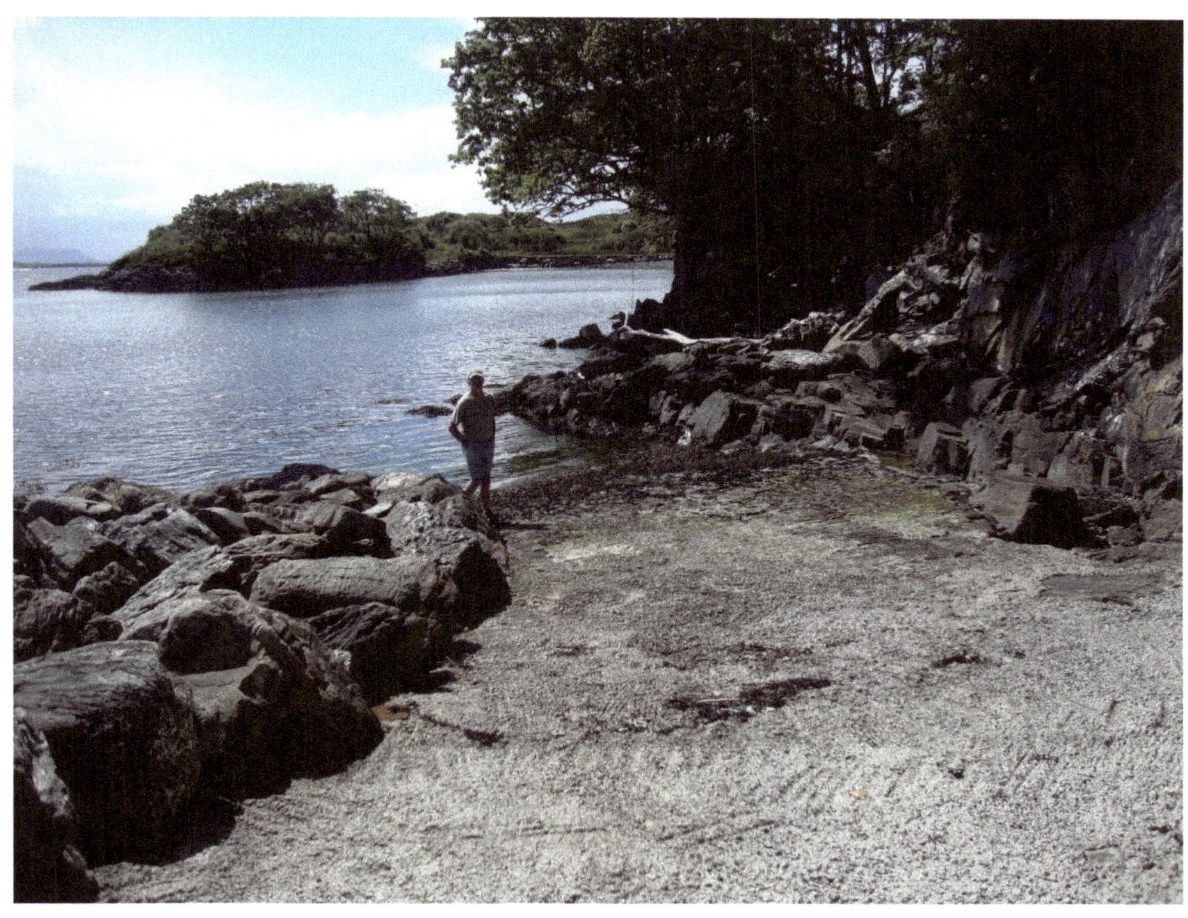

The path to the beach

The site overlooks Donegal Bay and is on top of a steep hill. The seaward side of the hill has been cut into terraces by the current owners, with half a dozen pitches for motorhomes and caravans on each terrace. Terrace number two is grassed and for tents. Each pitch has its own water tap and electricity hook-up, and there are two toilet blocks. These are in Portakabin-type buildings and win the accolade for being the most immaculate showers and toilets we have so far come across in our travels.

Everything here is perfect, including the weather. We donned shorts and had a walk down the track to the private beach, where we felt as though we were in the Caribbean: warm sun, azure sky, turquoise water. There are even benches set at the side of the track to ease the way back up, and the pebble beach has been levelled off to make the surface easier for weary walkers.

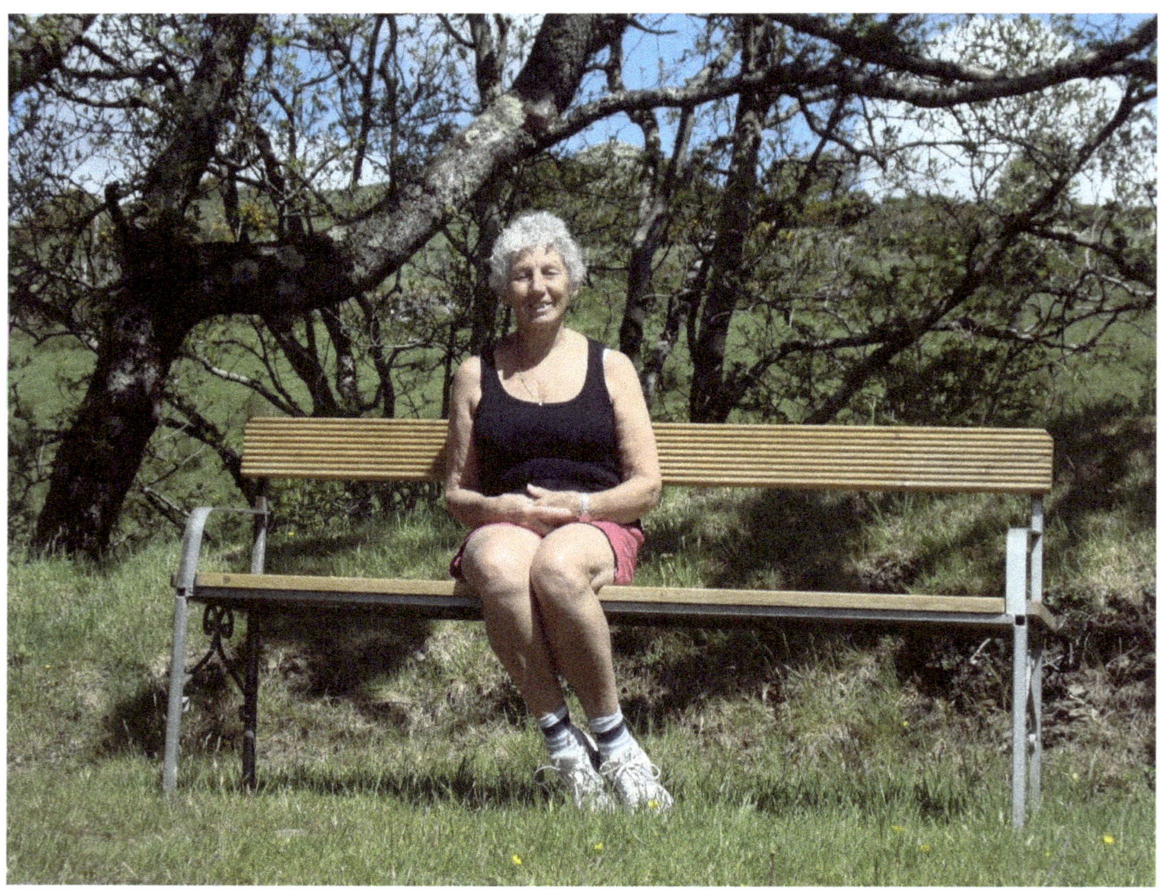

Jackie's Princess-Diana-at-the-Taj-Mahal pose. Shame about the knees!

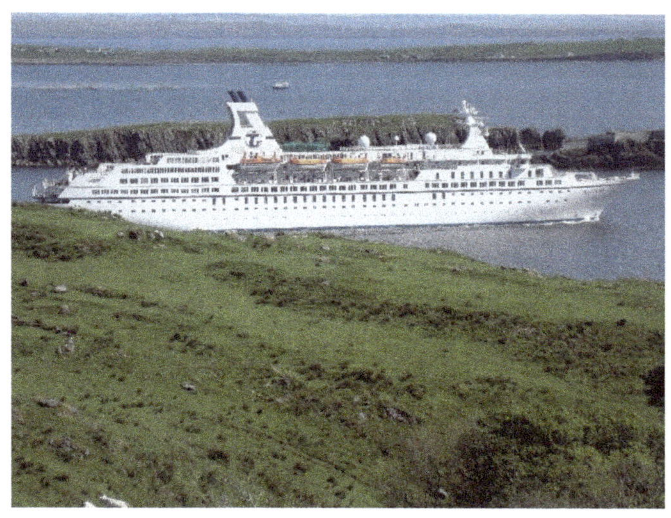

The cruise liner Astor sets of for Dublin

If you never go anywhere else in Ireland, it has to be Killybegs Holiday Park.

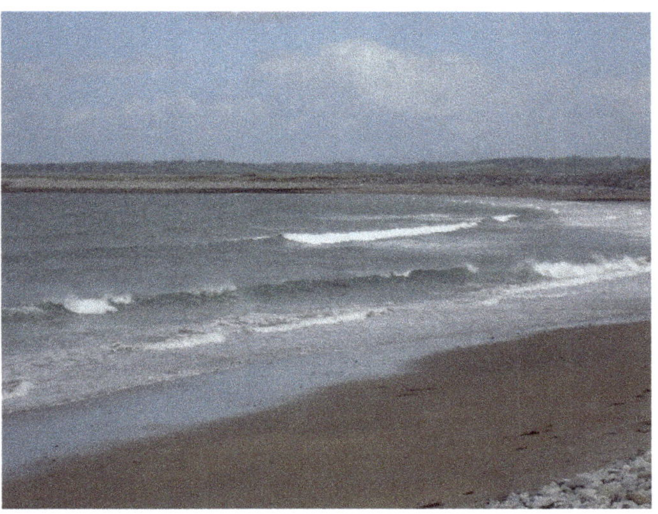

The terraces provide sea views for every pitch

Today's mileage: 66

Slieve League and Dungloe

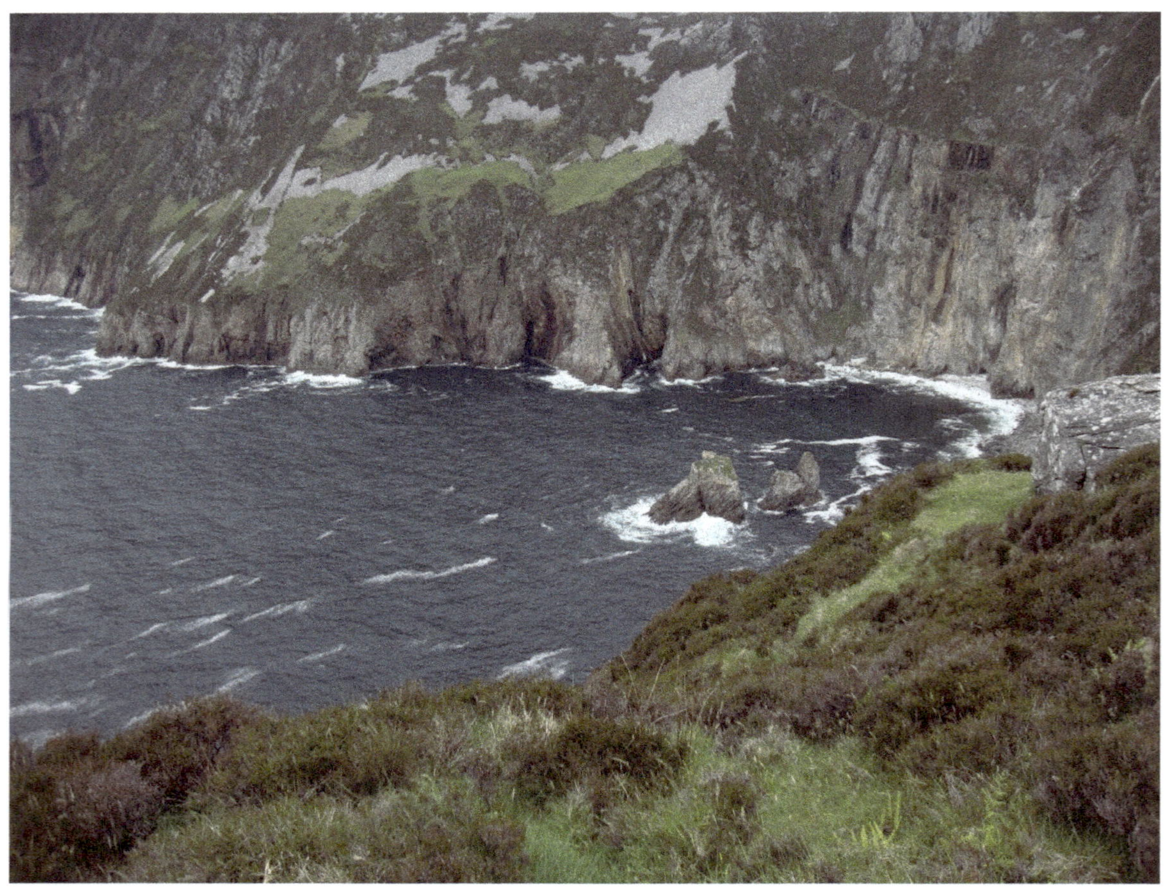

Slieve League cliffs

Friday, 19th May

The big attraction for us today was Slieve League on the Wild Atlantic Way in County Donegal. At just over 600 metres the mountain of Slieve League, also known as Leag or Liag, boasts some of the highest sea cliffs in Europe. It's a good uphill mile, maybe a bit more, to walk from the roomy parking area to the main viewing point of the cliffs, but the dramatic panorama when you get there makes it well worth the steady uphill tramp. It is also possible to drive up if the walk doesn't appeal, or if you aren't physically able to do it. From there, if you're particularly energetic, you can continue up a grassy track to the top of the cliffs, from where the landscape is certainly equal to the effort of getting there.

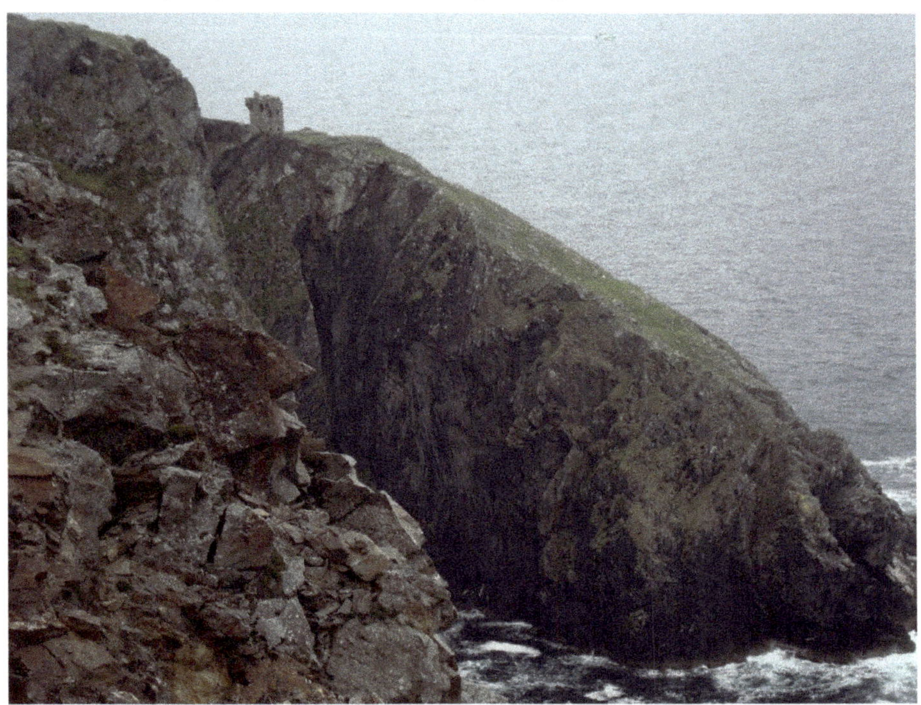

An early 19th century signal tower, built to look out for signs of a French invasion, perches on the cliffs high above the sea.

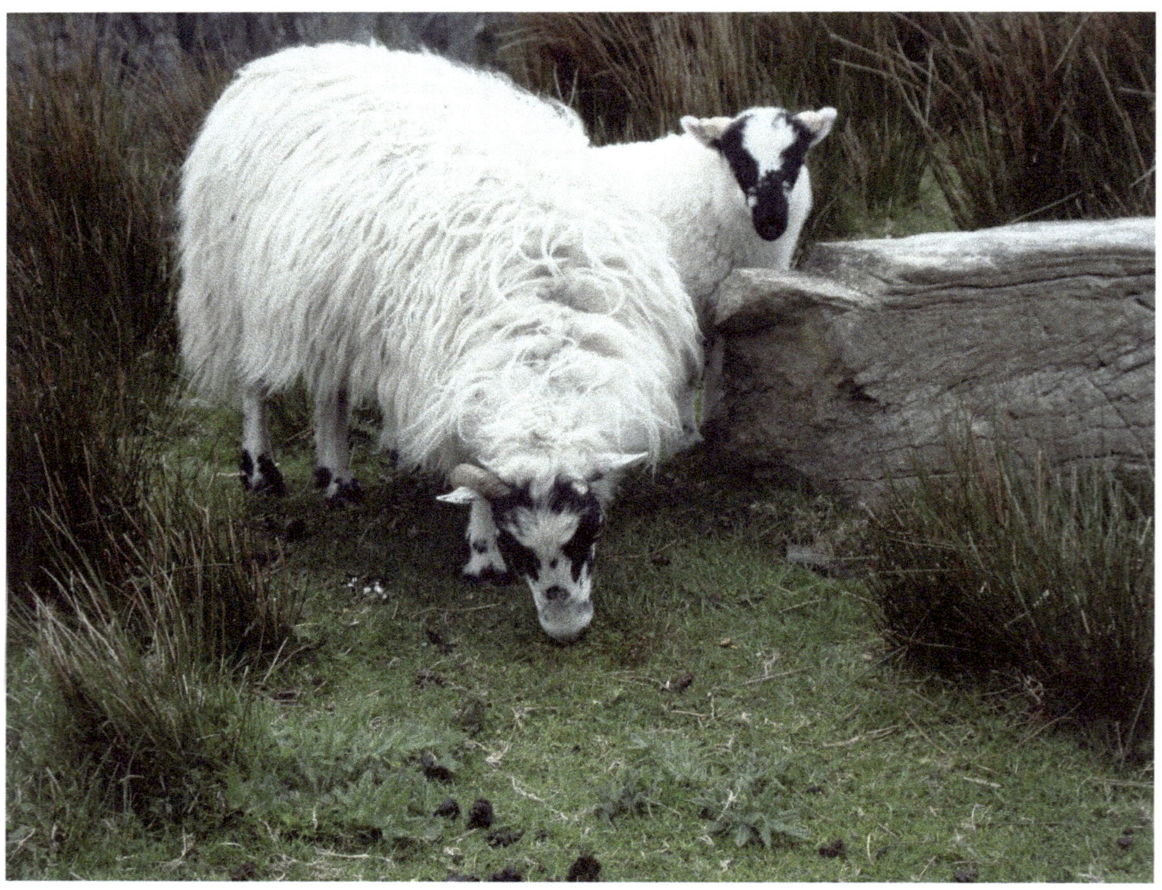

The hills are dotted with Scottish Blackface sheep, a hardy variety that is well suited to the harsh conditions of the sea-facing mountains.

The drive from Slieve League to our next overnight stop at Dungloe was notable for what we have come to recognise as typical Donegal landscapes, with rugged, heather-covered lumps of mountains, dry stone walls, loughs, rivers and switchback roads. As we'd noticed on previous days, much of the land is boggy and blackened where peat is cut from ditches, rolled and laid out to dry. Because the ground is unstable up here in bogland, the telegraph poles are supported like yacht masts with strong steel cables to keep them upright. We stuck to minor roads all the way to

Dungloe and, as long as you take it steady, they are navigable in a motorhome. It's mainly a long, downhill stretch the nearer you get to Dungloe. We had a brief stop on the way down and enjoyed the pure sound of a cuckoo.

Dungloe Touring Caravan Park is situated in the centre of the town and yet is a haven of quiet and tranquillity. It's a small site with excellent amenities for caravans and motorhomes, and is a good base to stay for a few days to visit the surrounding area. As well as a pretty riverside walk there are some good traffic-free cycle paths leading from the town, and we noted that Dungloe is also part of the Donegal Cycle Route.

Two things to look out for at Dungloe: midges and the cat. Midges – we all know about them, and the allegedly proven properties of Avon's Skin So Soft Body Oil Spray. I brought three bottles with me, knowing how likely we are to need them when we get to Scotland. Unfortunately I bought the wrong variety. You need the Woodland Fresh fragrance. Otherwise it doesn't work. Believe me. I know!

As for the cat – the campsite has a friendly black cat. It picks its way over to you, the epitome of feline elegance, meowing and winding itself round your ankles. But be warned. Don't pick it up. I did. It snuggled into me for a couple of seconds then spun round in my arms faster than a dervish, lashed out with its front claws and caught me on both sides of my face. I think I look like a Red Indian (am I allowed to say that?) in full war paint. Mike says I'm a drama queen and they're just minor scratches. He's right. My face is now so tanned that they don't even show.

Today's mileage: 62

Knockalla, Portsalon

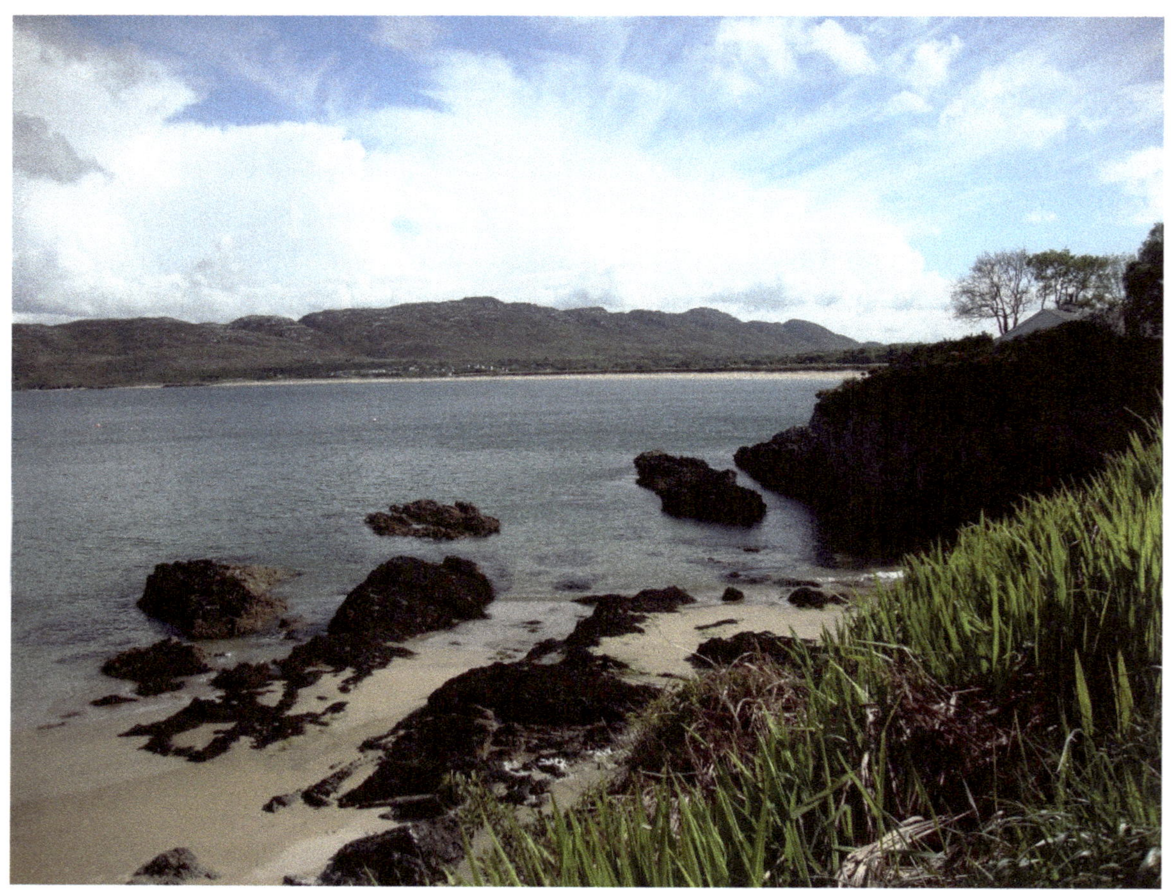

'The Second Most Beautiful Beach in the World'

Saturday, 20th May

Mike and I really do have to start planning our cycle rides and walks a little better. It is no use setting out 'for a little walk' only to find three miles later in hot sunshine that we wish we'd brought drinks, sweets and some cash to buy a beer or an ice cream. Especially a beer. We've been in Ireland for 11 days now, and still haven't had an ice cream or, more to the point, a Guinness. And by the time we'd finished this afternoon's three miles, we were gasping for a drink. Especially when we knew we still had to walk the three miles back. And even more especially when we got chatting to a friendly Australian couple who asked us to join them for a beer. How we wanted to! But we had to decline because, as usual, we'd misjudged how far we would walk and had come out without any money. We couldn't not stand our round. So we walked the three miles back again, faster than we went, spurred on by the thought of the bottle of cool white wine waiting for us in Bessie's fridge.

The walk in question took us about a mile from Knockalla Caravan and Camping Park, where we've pitched up for the night, to Ballymastocker Bay and two miles along the beach from there to Portsalon. Time for another superlative: according to The Observer magazine this is *'the second most beautiful beach in the world'*. The *'most beautiful'* is reckoned to be somewhere in the Seychelles, so the competition is stiff. But Ballymastocker does take some beating.

The drive from Dungloe to Knockalla shows off Donegal at its best, with the usual mountains, loughs and boglands full of freshly cut peat. The landscape here is very different from Kerry: equally as arresting but in a different, less picture-postcard way. Donegal is often described as Ireland's forgotten county and Mike and I love it. The coastline is even more spectacular than Kerry's, with inlets, islands and towering cliffs, while the heather-clad mountains are rather less verdant and more craggy, not dissimilar to parts of the Scottish lowlands. Mike, who has a thing about tractors, was fascinated by those we saw in the boggy peat fields: huge solid machines with double wheels to stop them sinking into the soft wet ground.

On the way we stopped to gaze across Sheephaven Bay. This was where, a few years earlier, whilst sailing single-handed around Ireland, Mike had one of his 'adventures'. The yacht's engine overheated because the impellor had jammed and he had to sail into Sheephaven bay to pick up a mooring in strong winds, with no engine to help manoeuvre the boat.

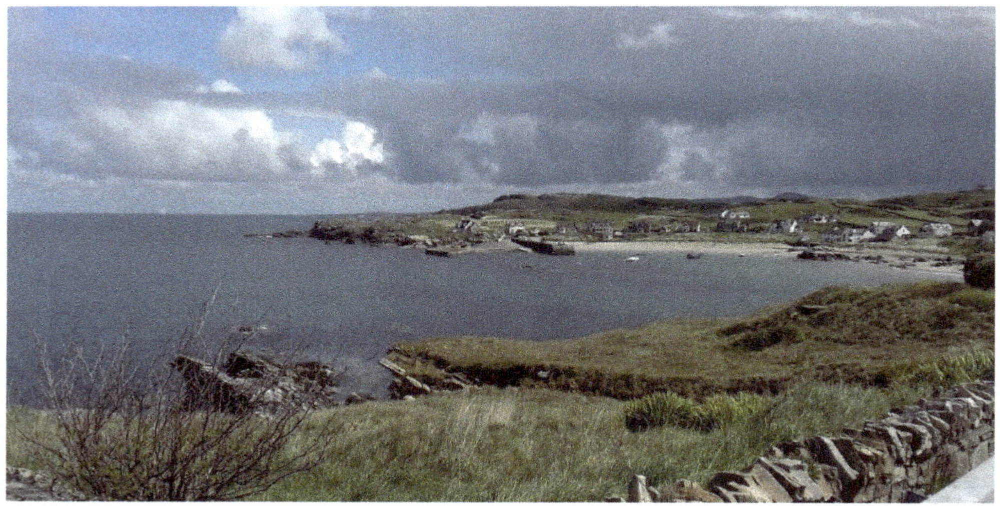

Sheephaven Bay

The caravan park at Knockalla is immaculately maintained with gorgeous surroundings and great showers. However, it's huge and mainly for static holiday caravans. If it's small and intimate you're looking for, which is what we like, this probably isn't for you.

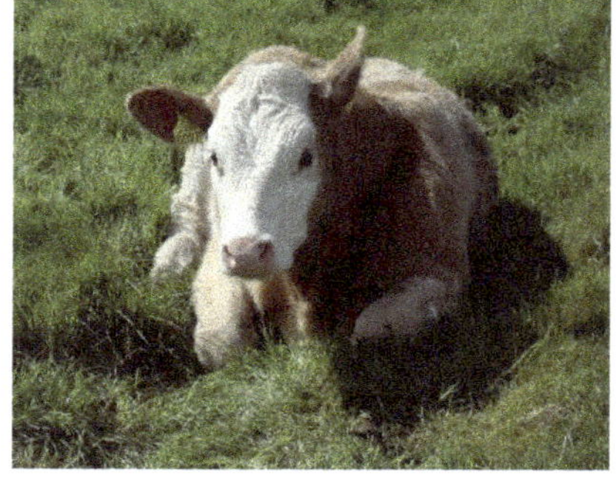

Adorable calf

Today's mileage: 59

Malin Head and Quigley's Point

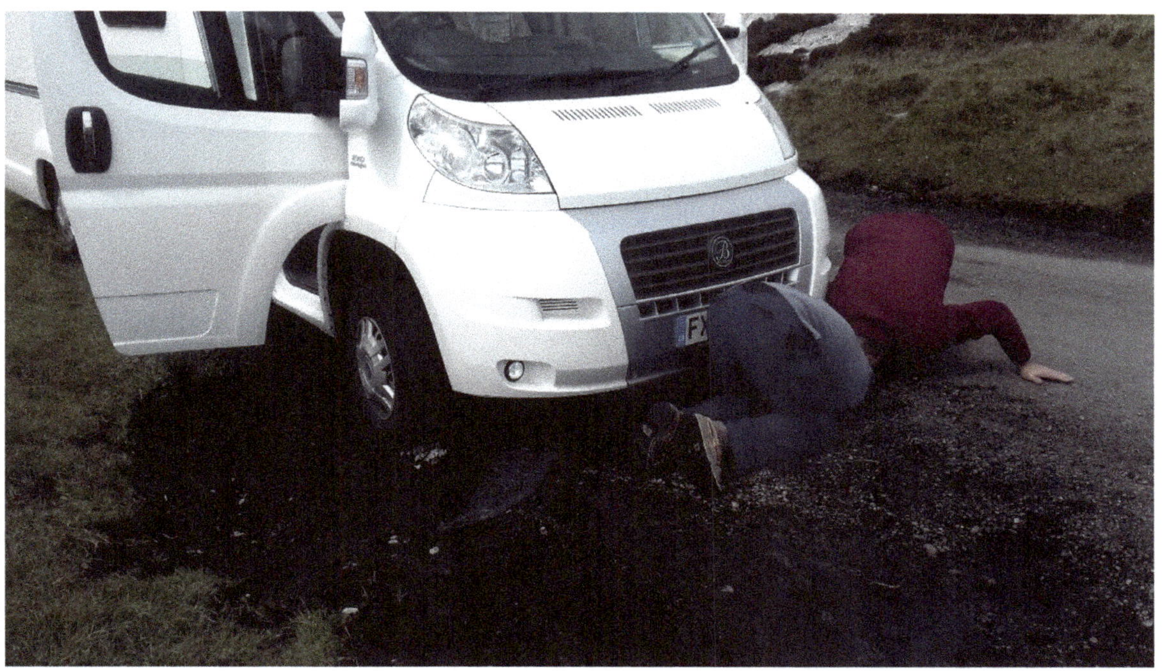

Sunday, 21st May

Mike and I have always had what we call holiday adventures, whether sailing, scuba diving, skiing or even camping. These 'adventures' may be what normal people call disasters. So far this trip we haven't had any. That is until today. Malin Head, the island of Ireland's most northerly point, will now be added to our list.

Bessie is quite a big vehicle. To get an idea of her size, think paramedic ambulance, then add on a bit of width, a bit of height and quite a bit of length. We, or rather Mike, chose to take the local road up to Malin Head. This 'local road' turned out to be a single, one vehicle-width carriageway, with edges that fall away into boggy ground. I wasn't even driving and I was stressed. But Mike, in whose driving and navigational abilities I have total faith, was comfortable he could get up there. There is, or so we believed, a turning circle at the top.

Yes. There is. BUT it was chokka-bloc full of cars. And as we got nearer the top, we found the road was lined with diggers and dumpers, excavators, bulldozers and other bits and pieces of heavy plant. And I don't mean vegetarian. These machines are clearly there to widen the road and possibly incorporate a few passing places, of which there are currently none. We made it very nearly to the top. But then realised there was nowhere for us to go, nowhere to turn round and, just to add to the fun, a number of other vehicles trying to drive down.

Mike edged Bessie over to the right-hand verge, where she sank into thick, black, peaty bog. And not only got stuck, but went in even deeper. I got out to see what was what. We couldn't go forward, as the front offside wheel was spinning and unable to get a purchase, and we couldn't go back because there was a big boulder against Bessie's rear chassis. The big boulder was there because Mike had put the gear into reverse instead of forward, and I only managed to stop him from crashing right into it by banging hard on the Bessie's rear end and yelling STOP! STOP! This was also quite stressful. We got the slip mats out. To no avail. I went and got some old towels, to see if they would help form a surface on which the tyres could grip. They couldn't. All that happened was that the wheels continued to spin in the mire, spraying black watery mud all over me.

Just then three angels appeared – two men in overalls and a bewitching young woman in full make-up and looking gorgeous. These angels had the most glorious bit of kit we could have wished for in the circumstances. A bright yellow, mud-spattered Land Rover with a power winch on the front. And with their help we got Bessie back on the road.

These pictures tell their own story – no captions needed.

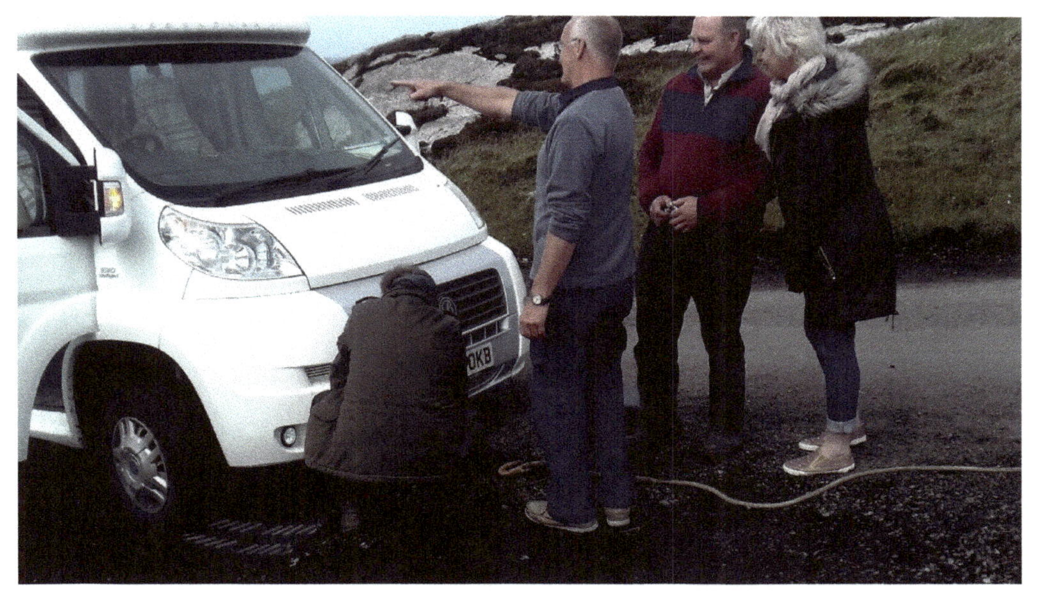

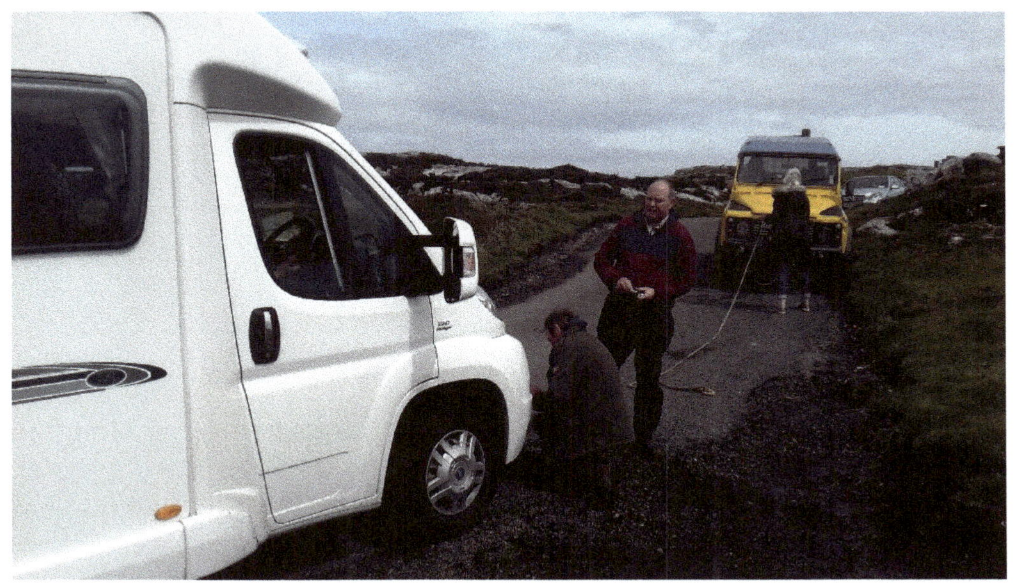

Mike still had to get Bessie turned 180 degrees, in incredibly difficult and still stressful circumstances, in an area that was jammed full of cars and had no spaces.

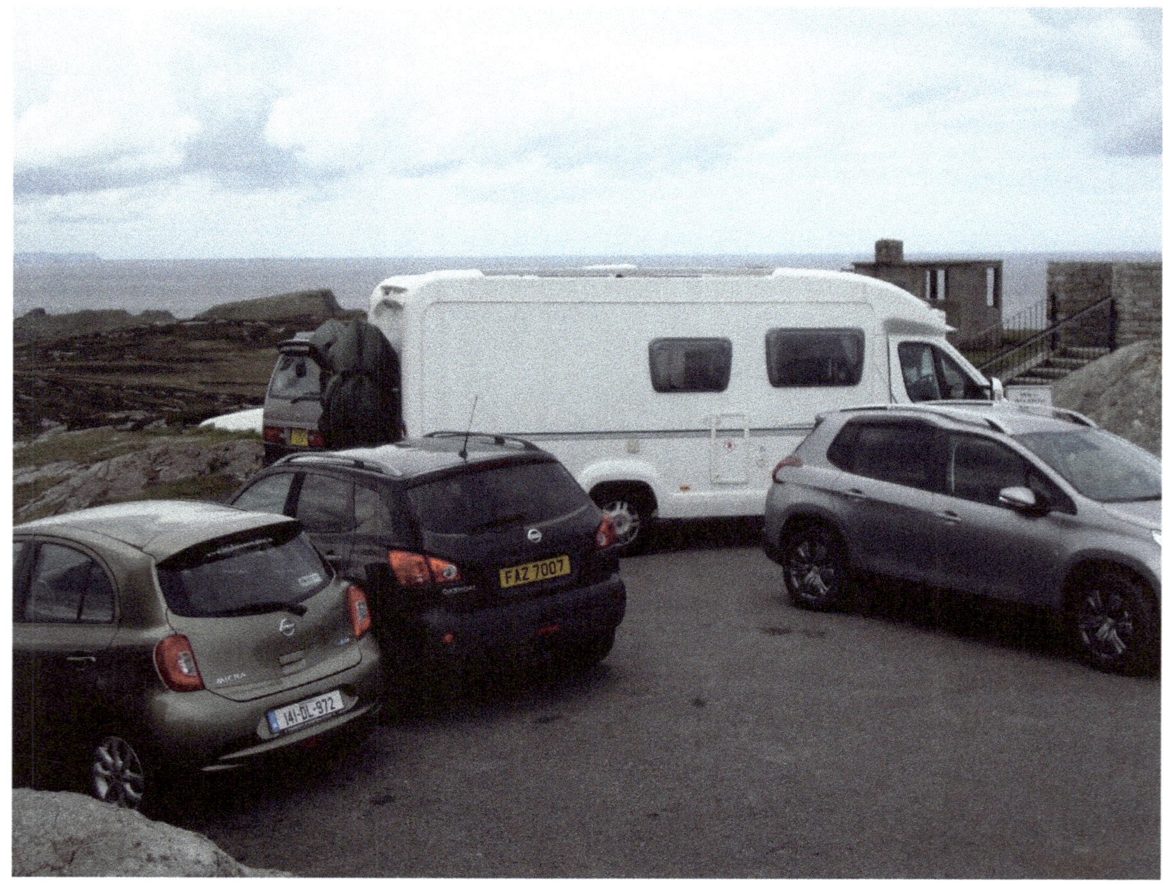

Trapped

After being barked at for attempting to inject humour into the situation – big mistake – I decided discretion was probably the better part of valour, and made myself scarce. Eventually, a space appeared a bit lower down the track and Mike was able, with great skill and delicacy, to reverse down and into the space, to turn round and head back the way we came. Phew!

'At least I now know where to find the tow-hook and tool box' was all he said.

From Malin Head, whose glories we didn't have the chance or, to be honest, the inclination to savour after our traumatic half hour, we drove to Foyleside Caravan Park at Quigley's Point, overlooking the Foyle estuary. This is another site that caters mainly for static caravans but there were more than enough pitches for motorhomes too. If you could get in:

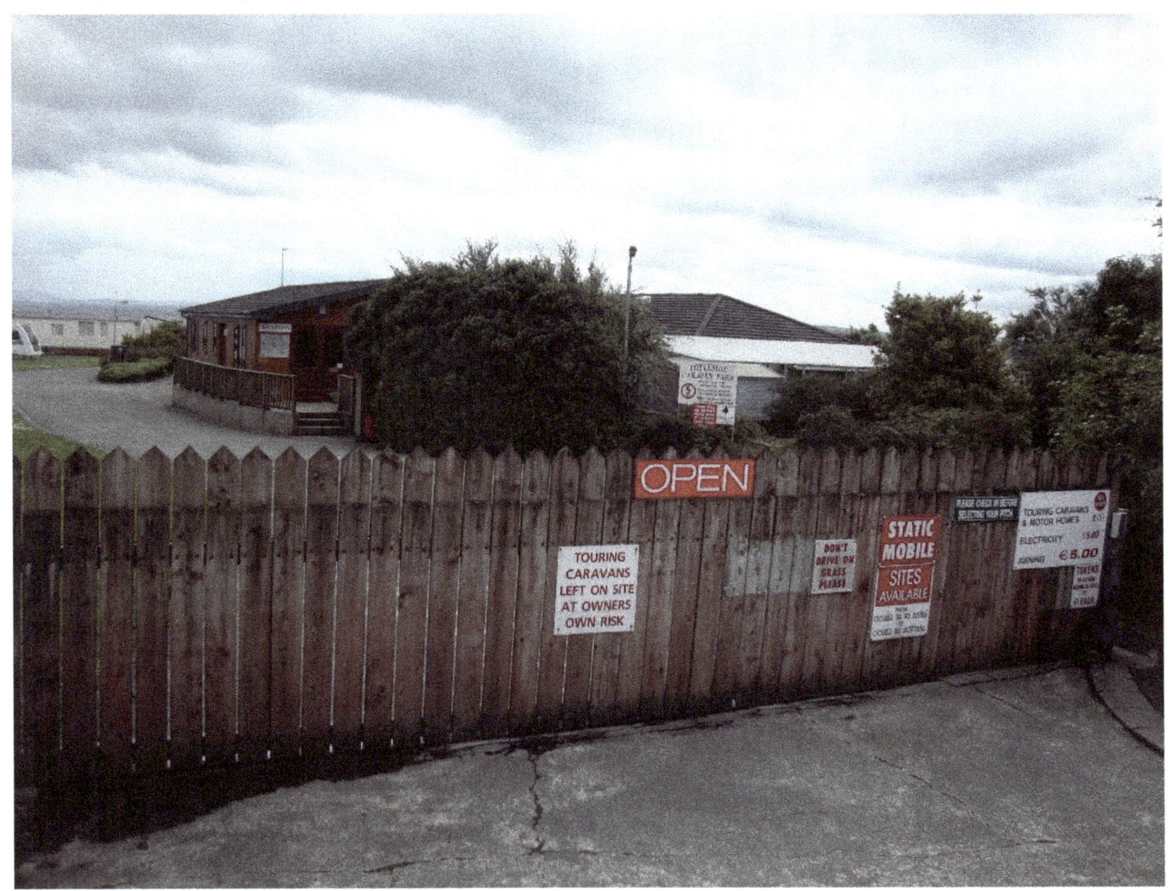

Well it says OPEN. But to our eyes the gate looks firmly CLOSED!

There was a small paddock in front of our pitch. It was home to a few Jacob and other sheep – the biggest I have ever seen. Despite spending a considerable amount of time on-line, researching sheep breeds, I still haven't a clue what they are. My best guess is Polwarth, which I believe is an Australian breed. If anyone knows, I'd love to hear from you.

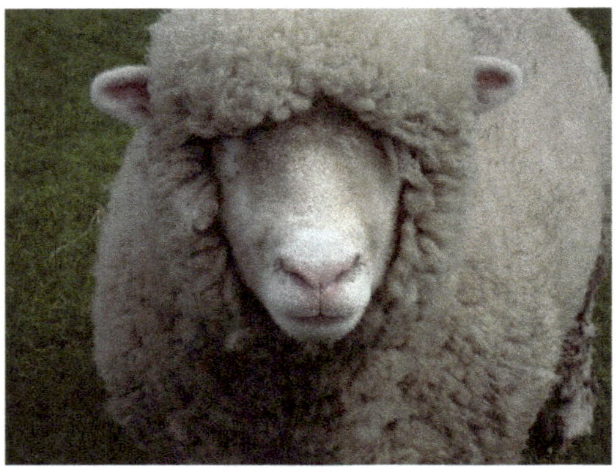

A 'can't-see-my-way' sheep

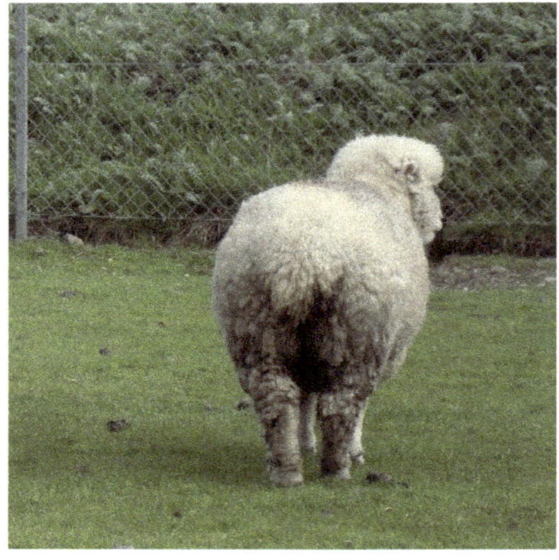

Does my bum look big in this?

The route from Malin to Foyleside went through more country roads and mountain passes, with sheep grazing on the verges. This always worries me. What if one suddenly jumps out in front of us? Or a lamb skitters across the road to get to its mother? Sheep are among the animals that, if they are hit or killed by a vehicle, have to be reported to the owner or, in the owner's absence, the police. The other animals that this law applies to in the UK are dog, horse, cow, pig, goat, ass and mule. We didn't see many of them.

By the time we got to Foyleside we were still in the Republic of Ireland but Northern Ireland was clearly visible across the water and when it got dark the lights from Londonderry and the docks lit up the night sky.

Shortly after arriving we got chatting to a couple of men who were staying on the site. One was a staunch Loyalist, the other was from the south. Their differing attitudes were marked. The Loyalist was very outspoken: strident even. He was all for Brexit, Theresa May and keeping the UK intact and was adamant that a united Ireland would be 'a very bad thing indeed'. Nicola Sturgeon, he claimed, is 'the UK's biggest threat' and is backed by what he alleged are terrorists.

On the other hand, the southerner, looking distinctly uncomfortable at this unequivocal imparting of opinions, only wanted to share his Guinness with us and enjoy a bit of the craic!

Today's mileage: 98

County Antrim

Ballymoney

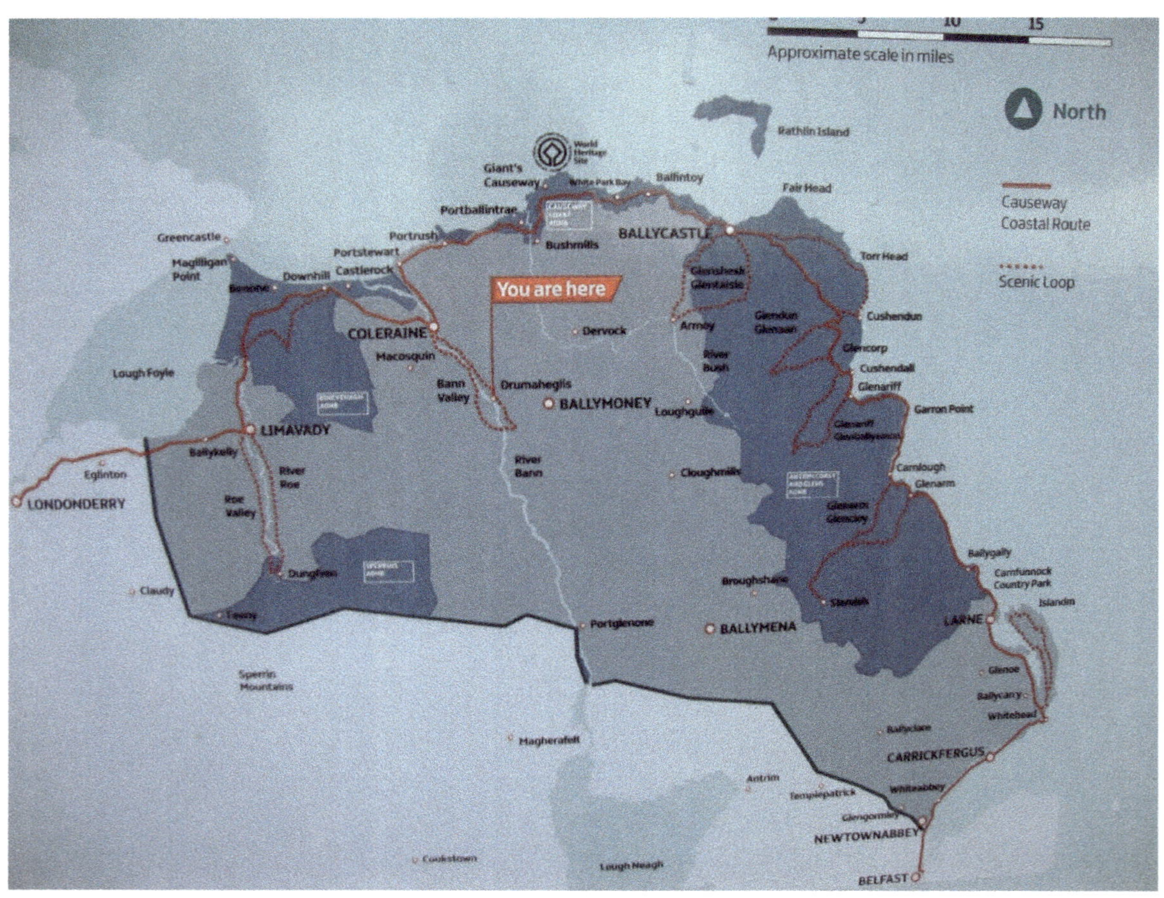

Our last night on the Emerald Isle is in Northern Ireland – red marks the spot!

Monday, 22nd May

Tomorrow we drive to Belfast to catch the early evening ferry to Cairnryan in Scotland, for the second leg of our extended tour in Bessie. For our last night on the island of Ireland, though, we are hunkered down at Drumaheglis Marina and Caravan Park. This is a picturesque and well-kept site overlooking the River Bann, near Ballymoney, Northern Ireland. We got to know Ballymoney quite well on our way to the site too, as we drove around in circles – many circles – trying to find it. But it was worth the effort and the, let us say, frustrated exchanges between driver and reluctant navigator! There were a number of empty pitches looking over the marina and river but when we arrived the wind was gusting around in circles so we plumped for a spot under the trees away from the water's edge.

This is a superb site with excellent facilities and a great extra: picnic tables dotted around, each with a metal support attached for a disposable barbecue. Not that it's barbecue weather today. But we do have steak, sausages and burgers in the freezer, ready to whip out as soon as it is!

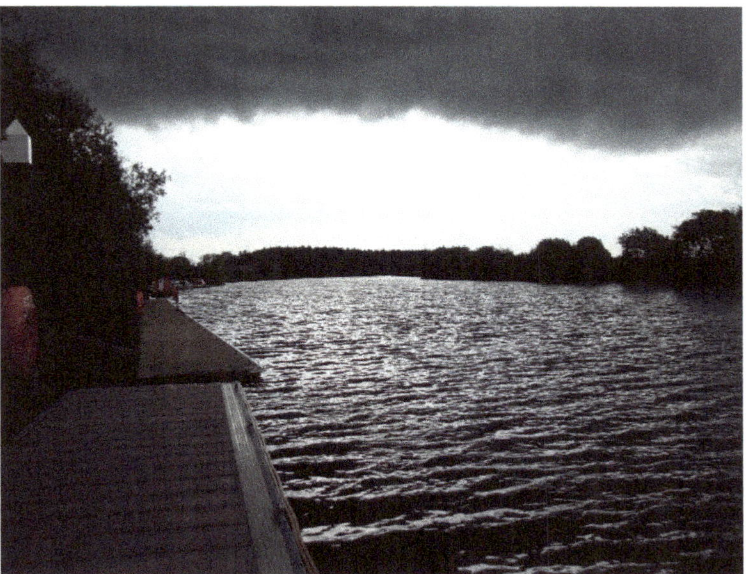

Not quite barbecue weather

It was cold and drizzly when we left Quigley's Point this morning and made our way the five miles or so into Northern Ireland. We drove through Londonderry, also known as Derry (there is a long-running dispute over which version is correct) and passed the Peace Bridge, which crosses the River Foyle in the city centre. A pedestrian and cycle route, it was opened in 2011 with the intention of improving relationships between Unionists and Nationalists in the area, the idea being that people from both sides of the political and cultural divide could travel freely from one community to the other.

There was no obvious border between north and south and we only realised we'd entered Northern Ireland when we noticed the road signs were now the same as in the UK, the schools are now primary rather than national schools, the speed limits are now in mph rather than kilometres and the signage is English rather than dual language. The price of diesel has also changed, with the price per litre rather higher in the north than in the Republic.

Much of our route this morning followed the A2, the Causeway Coastal Route, which winds its way from Belfast to Derry and is described as '*one of the greatest drives on earth'*. It is certainly worthy of the accolade, but the name doesn't have quite the same ring to it as the Wild Atlantic Way in the south.

We stopped at Coleraine for lunch in Bessie, and paid a visit to the marina. When Mike was doing his circumnavigation of Ireland in our yacht, *Jacqueline*, he had to be towed a very long way into there by sailors in two other yachts, whom he'd met during his trip. *Jacqueline's* throttle control lever had seized and Mike was unable to use the boat's engine to manoeuvre onto a mooring, so today's stop-over was a return to the scene of what could have been (yet another) disaster. 'Just one of life's little adventures' according to Mike.

Today's mileage: 78

PART TWO: Bessie Goes to Scotland

Dumfries & Galloway and South Ayrshire

Belfast to Cairnryan and Lendalfoot

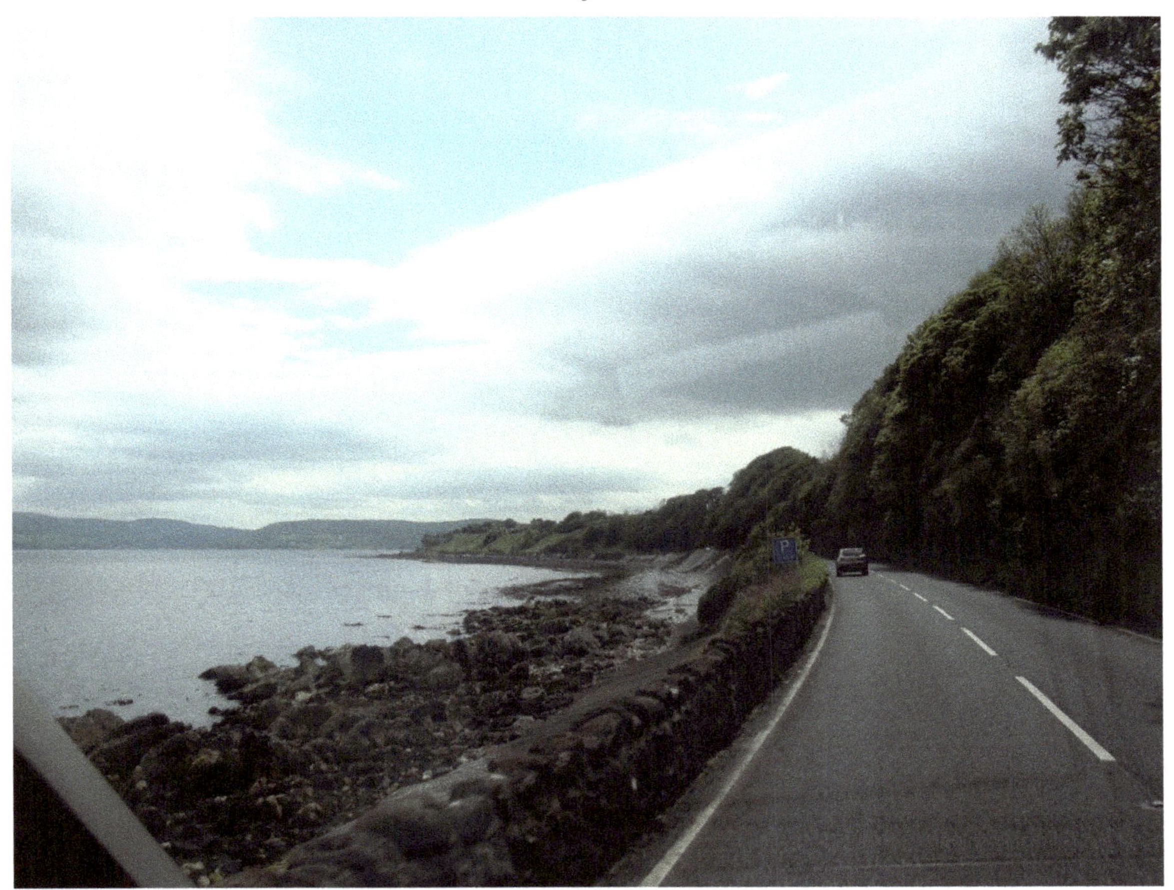

The Causeway Coastal Route

Tuesday, 23rd May

The day started well. Our early morning walk around Drumaneglis marina ended with me tripping up a concrete step, putting out my hands to save myself and jarring my still-not-healed collar bone. But what was even worse, I dropped my mobile on the step, face down, and shattered the screen. That's two this year, and still only May! The phone's still working but I don't know how long for. I've been meaning to get myself a decent cover for it and now it's too late.

We were later than usual getting away this morning but, following Mike's very detailed written route (to avoid the getting-lost-in-Ballymoney-like-yesterday) we were soon on our way to Belfast.

There was a bit of a hold-up at Ballymoney when three enormously long lorries with police motorcycle escorts had to negotiate a roundabout. The lorries were loaded with what we thought were probably vanes for wind turbines, a thought that was confirmed later when we saw a load of them in a yard next to Belfast docks.

Soon we were back on the Causeway Coastal Route, which today lived up to its claim to be one of the greatest drives on earth, up to Ballycastle. And here we found another 'greatest'. The best fish and chips Mike and I could remember ever having, at Morton's fish shop beside the marina. We have been to Ballycastle before, when sailing, so it was nice to arrive by road for a change. By the way, the tourist information centre here has the greatest toilets, too. But don't attempt the superloos on the quayside – they are impregnable!

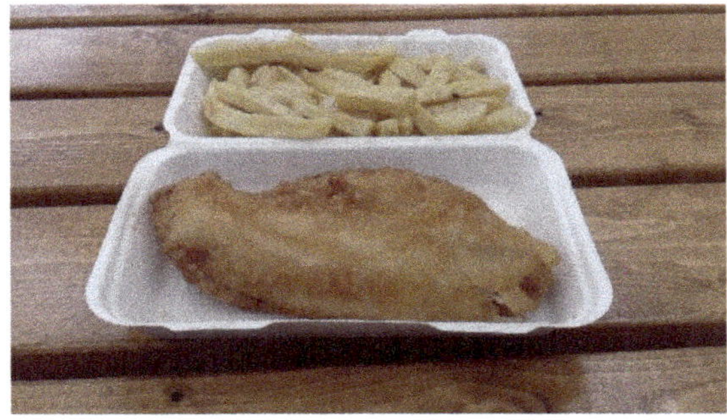

Best ever fish and chips

On the way to Ballycastle, with the Antrim Mountains ahead, we passed Loughareema – the vanishing lake. Depending on conditions when you pass by, the lake could be full of sparkling water or, as today, just a crater, on both sides of the road, of cracked and drying mud. The reason is that the lake's chalky bed has a sink-hole that sometimes gets blocked with peat, which isn't surprising given the nature of the surrounding moorland. When that happens, as soon as it rains the depression fills with rainwater and becomes a lake. Then the blockage eventually clears, the water rapidly drains away and the lake vanishes.

Today's countryside continued to delight us, in whichever direction we looked: forest and moorland, coconut-scented yellow gorse and, surprisingly, late blooming bluebells still fresh in flower to remind us of just how far north we are. On the steep downhill stretch into Cushendall the fields and mountainsides are now intensely green and as we edged past Slieveanorra Forest the road was lined with trees clad in lush new leaves.

The road hugs the coast all the way to Carlough, with just a low stone wall separating the carriageway from the beach, while towering bare-stone cliffs and densely wooded slopes adorn the other side. A delightful drive on a relatively easy road.

We reached Belfast a good couple of hours early for the evening ferry so were first in the queue but there was plenty to keep us interested – not least counting all the other vehicles as they arrived. By the time loading began at about quarter past seven I made it 25 cars, five motorhomes, nine vans, one van with trailer and around 30 lorries, one of which had a cargo of live pigs. Although the poor creatures can't help having such a strong personal aroma, they were put on the outside lorry deck, presumably to avoid contaminating the hold with their distinctive brand of porcine perfume. I, on the other hand, prefer the natural smell of pigs to the stench of diesel fumes in the bowels of the ship, but each to his own! I was amazed how quickly boarding was completed and *Stena Superfast VII* left precisely on time, at 7.30pm.

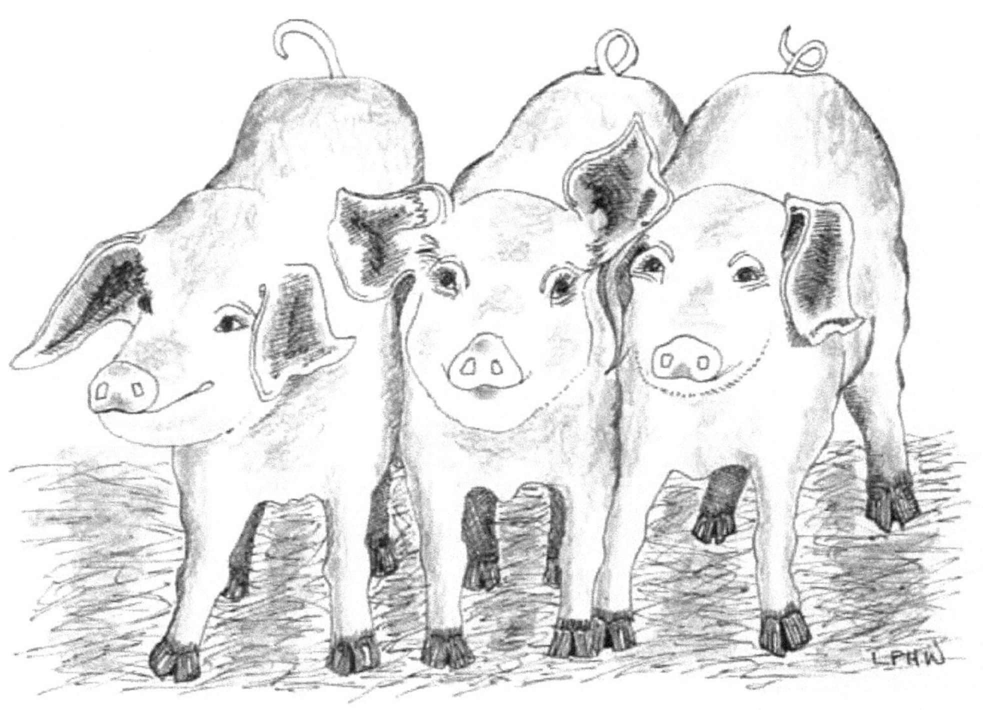

We were entertained for much of the couple of hours it took to cross to Cairnryan by one of the ship's officers. Gordon, aged (he told us) 50 next year, related the tale of how 'certain lumps of concrete' that had been ignored for decades suddenly became the subject of a fierce campaign to save them when developers wanted to take over a harbour-side site in Stranraer. It turned out that these lumps of concrete had been a vital part of Stranraer's wartime Mulberry Harbour, on which the Allies depended after D-day.

It was still not quite dark when we rolled off the ferry at Cairnryan and drove a few miles up the A77 to spend our first night in Scotland in a lay-by at Lendalfoot. From our bedroom window we had a splendid view of Ailsa Craig, an island the shape of a

Christmas pudding, that appeared to be floating above the hazy surface of the sea.

The main feature of the lay-by was a memorial to the crew of the Russian cruise ship Varyag that ran aground off the Ayshire coast nearly a century ago. The memorial relates the story, in Russian and English, of Varyag's defiance on being surrounded by 15 Japanese battleships during the Russo Japanese War in 1904. The Russian seamen defied the order to surrender and led the ship into the Battle of Chemulpo Bay off the coast of Korea, when Varyag sustained heavy damage. Because of the fear of an explosion her crew transferred to another ship and scuttled their own vessel. Varyag rolled over onto her port side and sank but was later recovered, repaired and, in an ironic twist, used by the Japanese navy before being sold to Germany as a hulk in 1920. It was on passage to Germany that she sank just off the coast at Lendalfoot.

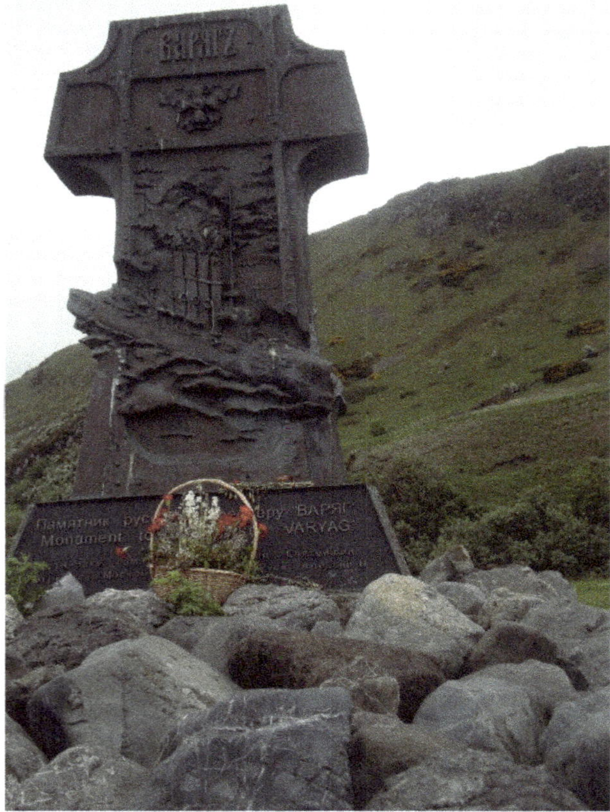

The Varyag Memorial

Mike and I have a wish-list of wildlife to see while we are in Scotland: otter, red deer, whales, golden eagle, red squirrel and, of course, the Loch Ness Monster. So far, we haven't seen any of these but we did spot half a dozen eider ducks in the shallows at Lendalfoot. This was a bonus for me, as I had never seen them before.

Today's mileage: 104

West Dumbartonshire

Alexandria, Balloch, Loch Lomond

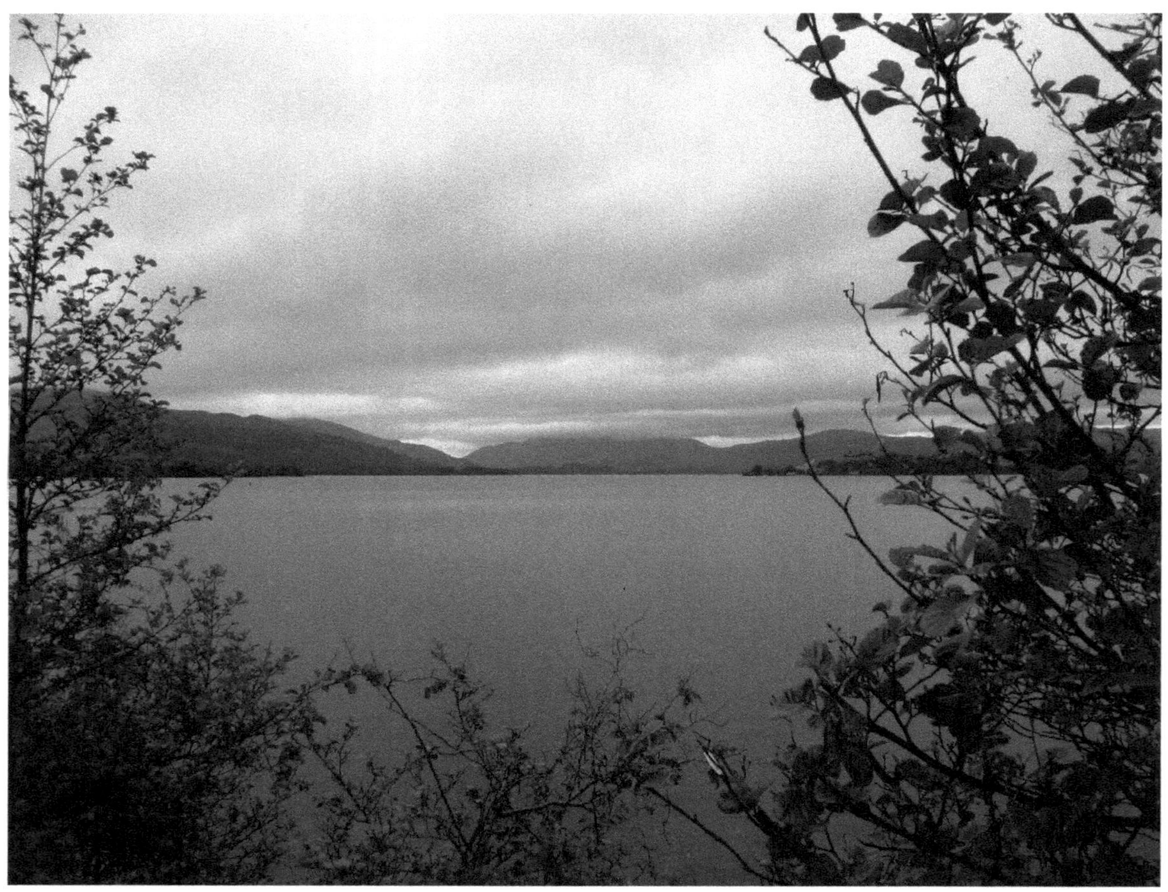

View of Loch Lomond from our overnight parking place

Wednesday, 24th May

Never before have I seen two red Ferraris, three Bentleys and an Aston Martin DB11 in the same car park. But these, and scores of other high-end marques, all with personalised number plates, currently adorn the grounds of the Cameron House Hotel in Alexandria at the southern end of Loch Lomond. All of which tells you a little about the type of hotel this is. And once tired of its glorious grounds that, incidentally, are open to anyone to walk around, guests with a bit of cash to spare could always go for a half-hour flight over the loch for a mere £119.

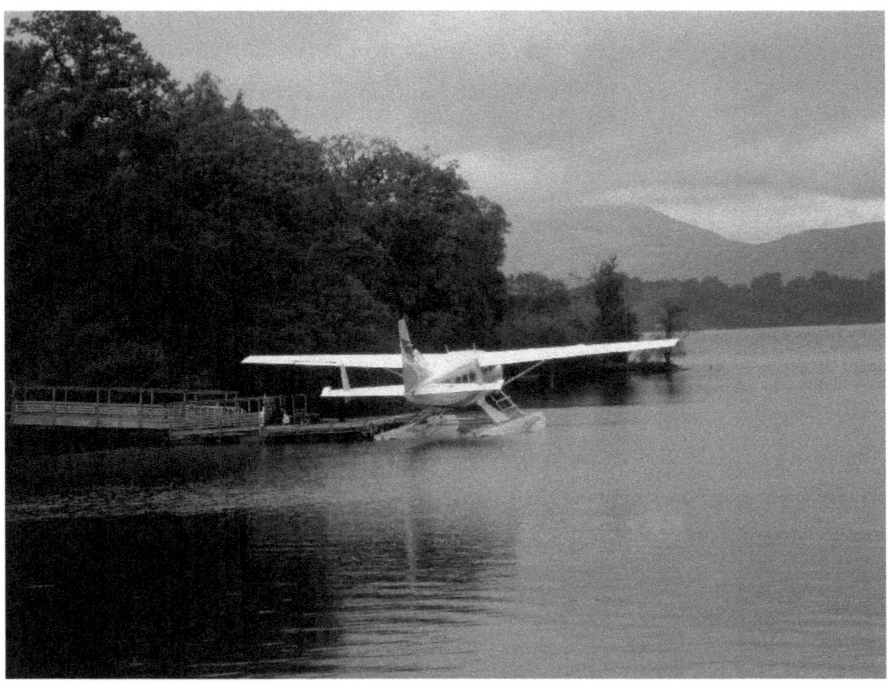

Sea plane at Cameron House Hotel – it didn't have to wait long for passengers

Mike, Bessie and I had arrived at Loch Lomond after a reasonably good drive from Lendalfoot that took us around Glasgow, over the Erskine Bridge and into what we felt was the start of Scotland proper, in terms of our intended tour. We plan to carry on from here to Fort William and the Great Glen to Inverness and then, all being well, we will drive up the north east coast to John o' Groats and along the top of Scotland. Then it will be over the Skye Bridge to Skye (where else?) and down the west coast via a ferry from Armadale on Skye to Mallaig, back on the mainland. If we have time, we will spend a couple of days taking in the sights of Edinburgh before heading south and west for home.

On our way this morning it struck me just how many places there are in Scotland that have songs about them. Here, in no particular order, are the ones that came to mind but I am sure there are others: Loch Lomond, Glasgow, Campbeltown Loch (made famous by Andy Stewart), Aberdeen, the Clyde, Loch Tummel, Loch Rannoch, Lochaber, Dundee, Doon, Skye, Maxwelton's Braes, Dumbarton and, of course, Mull of Kintyre. The lyrics for some of these songs were written by Robert Burns, the national poet of Scotland, and although some may be unfamiliar to Sassenachs such as ourselves, most Scots would recognise them all.

We left Bessie in a side road next to the loch at Alexandria and walked to the Antartex designer village on its southern shores. As well as a branch of Jenners (famous Edinburgh department store) and various fashion outlets there is a bird of prey centre, a high-trees obstacle course, an aquarium, boat trips and bike hire. All very nicely done.

Loch Lomond holds the distinction of being the largest lake by surface area in Great Britain and the second largest after Loch Ness by water volume. Today the loch is tranquil and beautiful, its bonny banks resplendent in greenery, with Inchmurrin, the UK's largest inland island, clearly visible. Towering over the eastern side of the loch is Ben Lomond, but today the ben is shrouded in cloud and not looking its best.

On the edge of the loch we saw some floral tributes tied to a tree, in memory of 21-year-old Stuart McLevy who died in a jet ski accident at the beginning of May. A tragic loss of a young life.

Today's mileage: 81

Highland

Glen Coe

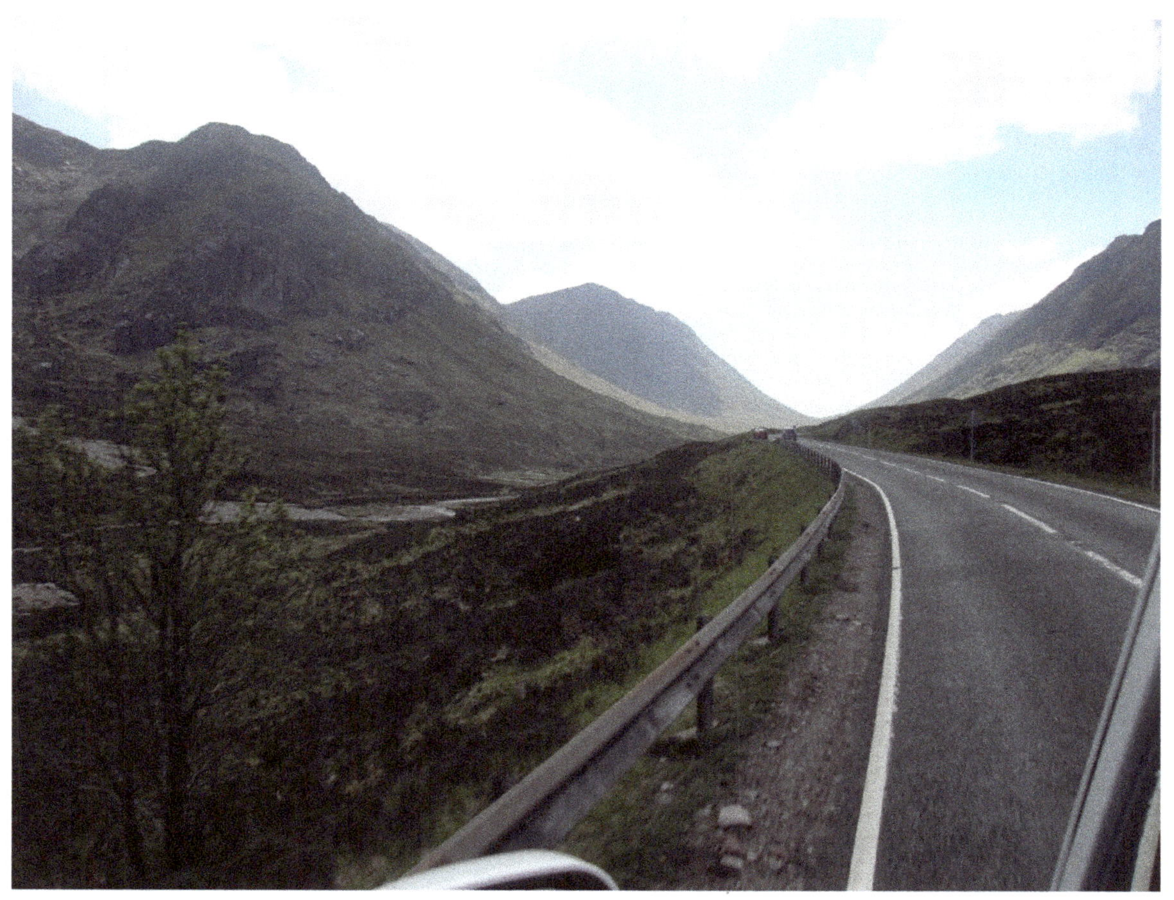

Glen Coe

Thursday, 25th May

I won't bore you with all the minutiae of this morning's trials, tribulations and fraying tempers as we attempted to find a garage that supplies LPG Autogas. Bessie's domestic gas supply, from which we cook and which also fuels the fridge when we are not running the engine or hooked up to electricity, was running low. Mike couldn't relax until we topped up, and at the moment we don't have internet to help us find out where we might get some.

Suffice it to say we drove the 20 miles back over the Erskine Bridge to Glasgow, and around Glasgow, and around Glasgow again, and around Paisley and around Paisley again until, after a somewhat bad-tempered two hours, we eventually found a Morrisons filling station with a serve-yourself Autogas pump. The in-store café provided a reviving coffee and pastry and, good humour restored, we were soon crossing the Erskine Bridge (the third time in two days) and heading north again.

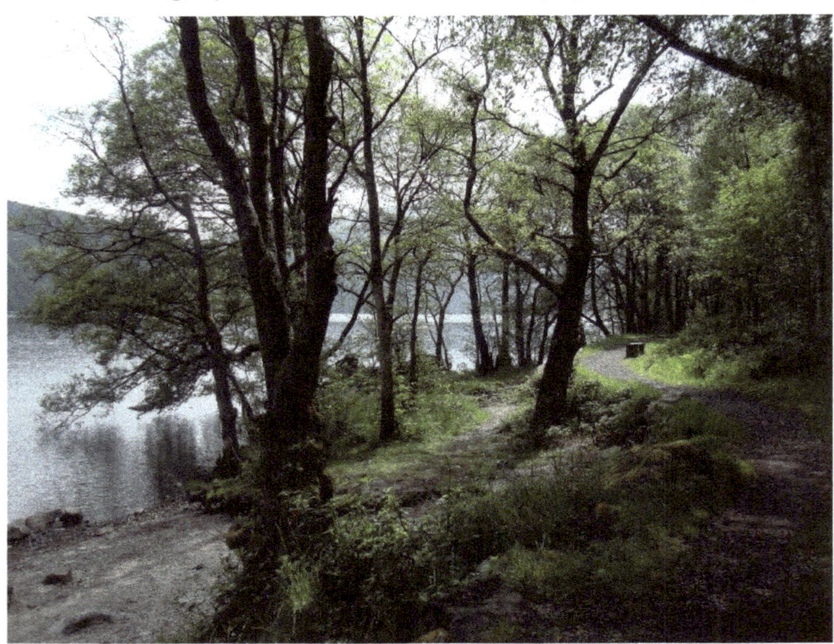

The northern shores of Loch Lomond

Our route took us back past Loch Lomond and then via Crianlarich and Bridge of Orchy to Glen Coe, with a lunch stop in hot sunshine at Tyndrum. This gave us the chance to enquire at the Tourist Information Centre whether it was acceptable for us to park overnight in lay-bys in Scotland, as we want to try to be self-sufficient and wild camp two nights out of every three. We were delighted to be told that as long as we don't cause an obstruction and there are no signs to the contrary, we are free to park for the night almost anywhere we choose. The country's Land Reform Act of 2003, also known as 'freedom to roam' gives everyone rights of access over land and inland water, providing they behave responsibly. This was a revelation to us and makes Scotland possibly the most welcoming part of the British Isles, not only to motorhomers such as ourselves but also to walkers, backpackers, campers and caravanners.

A quick word of explanation is probably useful here. Wild camping is usually thought of as spending nights under the stars and being self-sufficient in remote places or in the countryside. For motorhomers it's rather more luxurious and simply means parking up somewhere without electricity, water or washing and shower facilities such as you find on authorised camp sites. As long as you make sure you have sufficient supplies of gas for cooking and running the fridge, and enough food and water, it means you can explore more remote, unspoilt places.

I am at a loss to find the words to describe the lochs and mountains between Loch Lomond and Glen Coe. Glen follows glen, loch follows loch and big lumpy mountains are followed by even bigger lumpy mountains, fading to misty grey in the far distance.

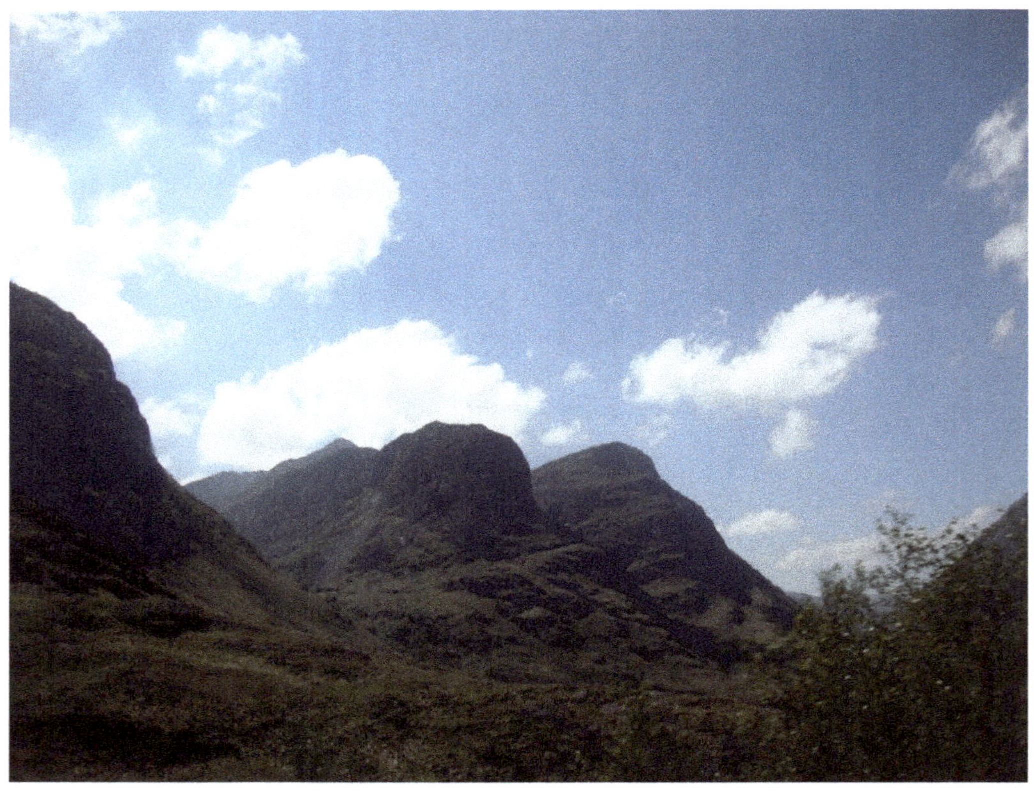

Two of the three peaks knows as the Three Sisters of Glen Coe, said to be one of the finest views in Scotland

The scenery is awe inspiring, majestic, breathtaking and sombre under the weight of history. As we drove deeper into the glen I found it easy to picture the terrible scenes of more than three hundred years ago when the Lowland Campbells slaughtered members of the Clan MacDonald of Glen Coe as they slept. I could almost see the tartan clad figures and hear the clash of their claymores, smell the blood and hear the screams of the wounded and dying as they fought for their lives on that terrible night of 16th February 1692. Scotland has a history of bloody and brutal deeds, but the most infamous of them all is surely the Massacre of Glen Coe.

As Holly Lennon wrote in The Scotsman newspaper the year before our visit:

The day is imprinted in Scottish history, not only because of the number of people who lost their lives, but because the men had enjoyed their victims' hospitality in the days leading up to the massacre.

Highlanders were regarded by Lowlanders as an obstacle in the way of the complete political union between England and Scotland. Many believed that their independence of spirit had to be broken. Most importantly, Clan MacDonald was not in agreement with Clan Campbell over their growing support of the government.

The MacDonalds of Glencoe were victims of what Highlanders called 'Mi-run mor nan Gall, the Lowlanders great hatred'. The two clans previously had troubled encounters as the MacDonalds were routinely involved in trouble with the law and neighbouring clans - one of which was the Campbells.

At the time, many Highland clans posed a possible threat to the new regime in London under King William of Orange. To secure support, it was ordered that chiefs must sign an oath of allegiance to King William by January 1st 1692 or the clans would be punished with the "utmost extremity of the law".

The Scotsman article continues:

The MacDonald clan eventually took their oath to Fort William but were told on arrival that they would have to travel some 70 miles to see a sheriff at Inveraray, in Argyll. Due to bad weather and misdirection, chieftain MacIan arrived after the deadline and as a result the oath wasn't accepted by John Dalrymple and the orders were given for the MacDonalds to be slaughtered and "cut off root and branch".

The clans lived together for 12 days before the slaughtering took place. Before then they had shared homes and enjoyed each other's hospitality.

Nearly forty MacDonalds were butchered that night, including their chief, and although some managed to escape into the mountains they were unable to survive the cruel February weather. Others '*were alerted to the coming events by merciful Campbells and managed to gather belongings to protect them from the cold and flee their homes'.*

I was married to a Scot for two decades before we agreed to call it a day, and in that time I got to know his countrymen well. One thing I learned is that the Scots have long memories – they don't easily forgive and forget. This is borne out by the fact that, to this day, you can still see signs in the Highlands bearing the words No Campbells, and I make no apology for including this once-popular school-yard rhyme: *The Campbells are coming, ye ken by the smell, the dirty wee buggers are farting like hell,* which leaves no doubt as to the strength of feeling that still lingers. On the Campbell side, though, the 18th century folk song, *The Campbells are Coming,* sings the praises of the once infamous and warring clan, and is still popular at ceilidhs and other social gatherings.

Back in 21st century Glen Coe, Mike and I were hoping to stop for a break and afternoon tea at the visitors' lay-by but it was packed out, with no room for a vehicle the size of Bessie. So we drove on, with me leaning out of the window, photographing the glen as we went. Photographs can never fully convey the height and grandeur and sheer vastness of this place, and they certainly don't compare with what you see with your eyes rather than through the viewfinder of a camera, but it's impossible not to try.

We are staying the night on a caravan park at Invercoe on the banks of Loch Leven, an idyllic setting under the huge bulk of the magnificent, and lusciously named, Pap of Glencoe. For those not familiar with the word, *pap* is a peculiarly Scottish word for breast and as the photo shows it's possibly the only name this mountain could have. Tonight, the Pap is glowing red under the intense gaze of the setting sun and is a dramatic backdrop to the site.

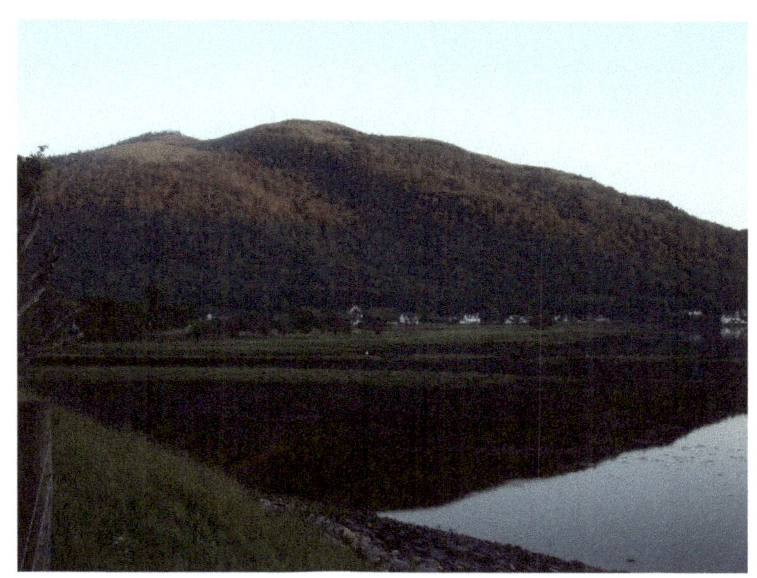

Loch Leven evening

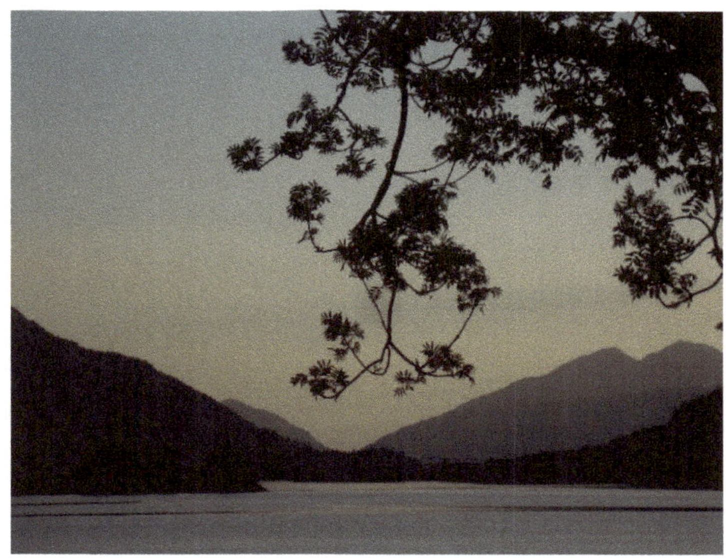

Sunset over Loch Leven

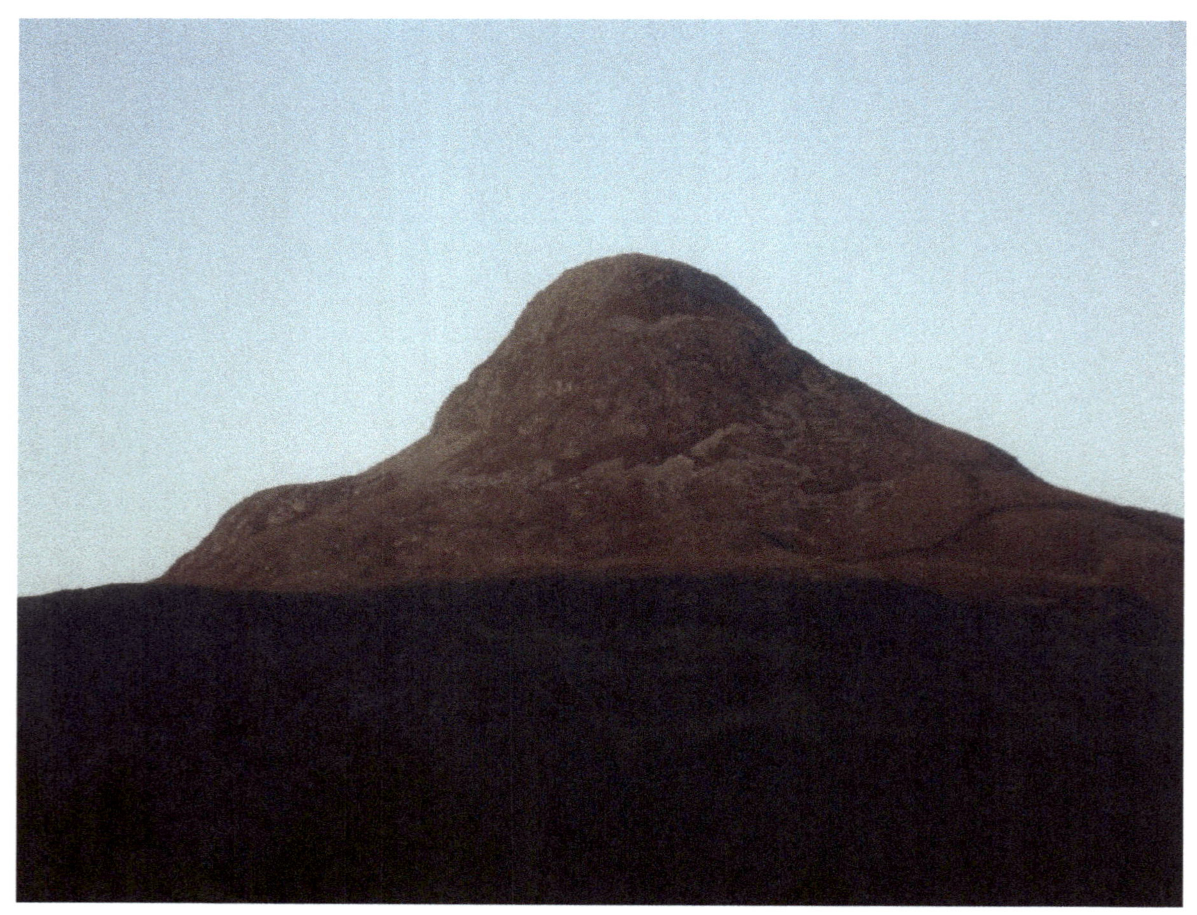

The Pap of Glencoe

Today's mileage: 121

Bunree, Onich

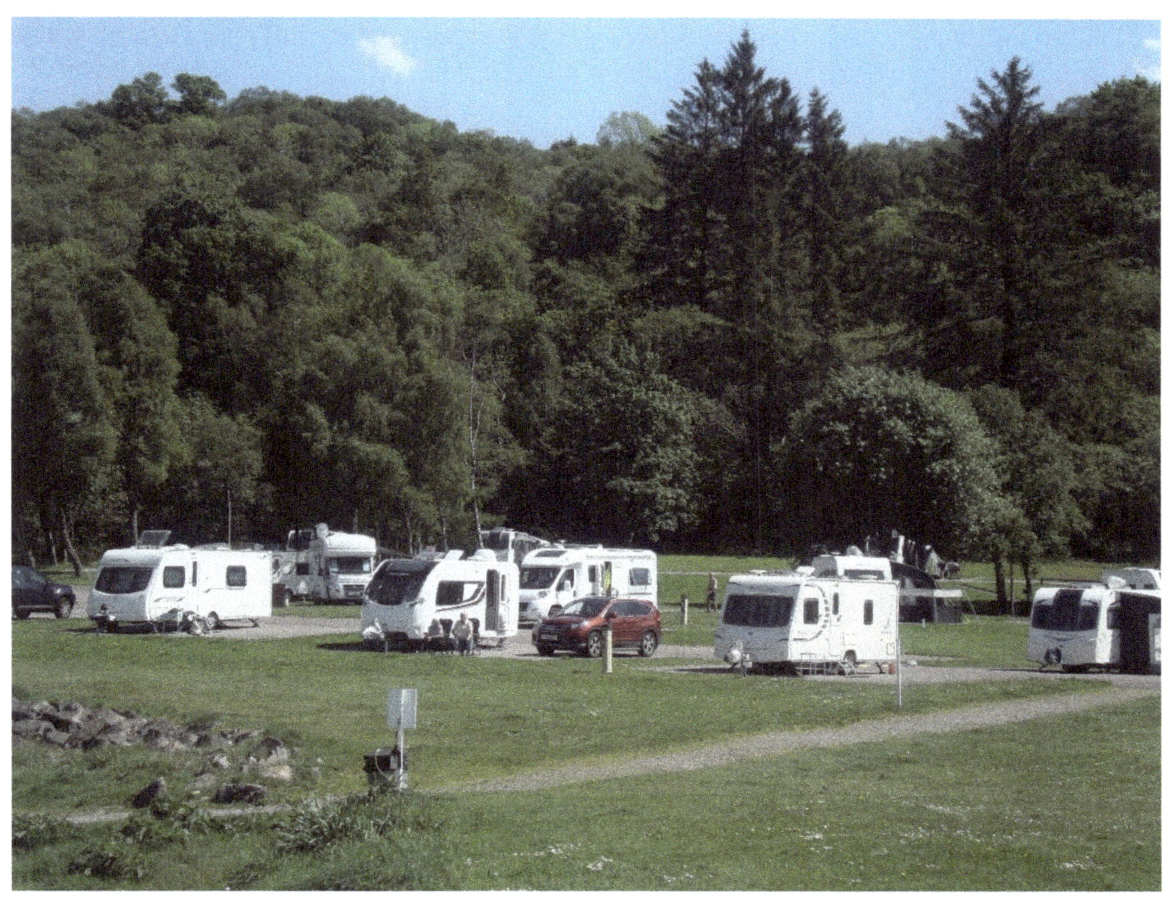

The site at Bunree

Friday, 26th May

I was woken up in the night by strange noises. It sounded as though someone was breaking into Bessie. I froze a bit then got brave enough to open my eyes. No Mike. Must be okay then – whatever it was, he was dealing with it. Went back to sleep. It turns out that Mike got up to use the loo and the red 'full' light came on. So there he was, at one-thirty in the morning, emptying, cleaning and re-disinfecting the holding tank for the toilet. It's only small and can only cope with a couple of days use . . . there must be more relaxing ways to have a holiday.

Today's destination was a Caravan and Motorhome Club site at Bunree, just south of Onich where, guess what, there is a garage selling Autogas!

This is an idyllic, tree-lined and peaceful site on the banks of Loch Linnhe. It's a bit of a memory lane place for us as we sailed down Loch Linnhe from the Caledonian Canal nine years ago on our sailing trip round Scotland. I say memory lane, but actually neither of us can picture it at all. I suppose the perspective is different from the middle of the loch, compared with how you see it from the shore.

During the afternoon the Fred Olsen cruise liner Boudicca made her stately progress up the loch en route for Fort William, but unlike her we were going nowhere and we spent most of the day in deck chairs, soaking up the sunshine – at one point the temperature exceeded 30°C – before rousing ourselves sufficiently to light up the disposable barbecue we've carted around in Bessie since August last year. It was a bit embarrassing as the wind picked up a bit and smoke from the coals billowed around all over the place, but once we were tucking into the food it made being kippered worthwhile.

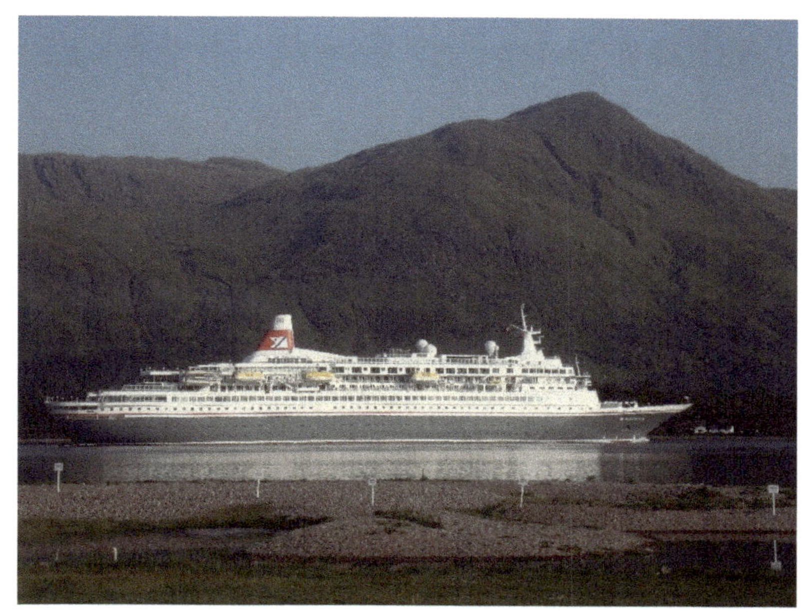

Boudicca dwarfs the loch

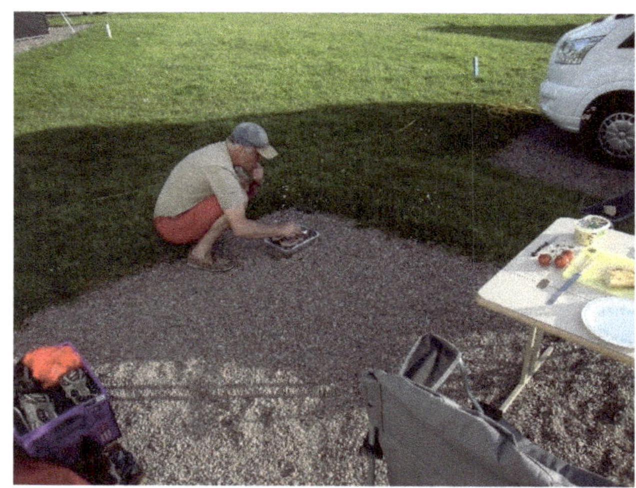

Mike lights up the barbecue

Today's mileage: 8

Fort William and The Great Glen to Laggan

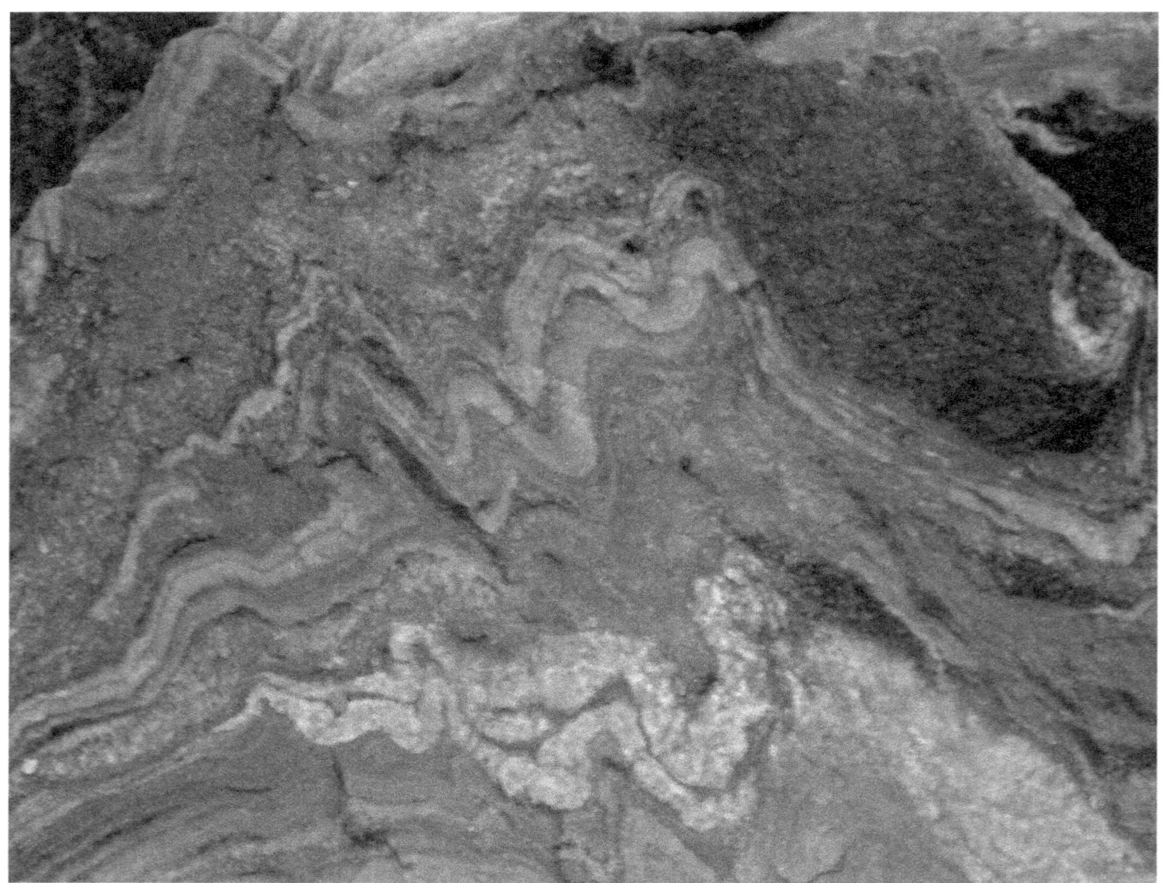

Patterns in a boulder on the beach at Loch Lochy

Saturday, 27th May

Before leaving Onich we cycled to Kinlochleven for cakes and cash. I was a bit concerned about cycling in such a hilly region. But, 'it's about five miles,' said Mike, pointing to the map. 'The road follows loch and river so it will be flat.'

Ha! It was six-and-quarter miles each way and involved several steep inclines. But it was a fine ride and the electric bikes made lighter work of the hills.

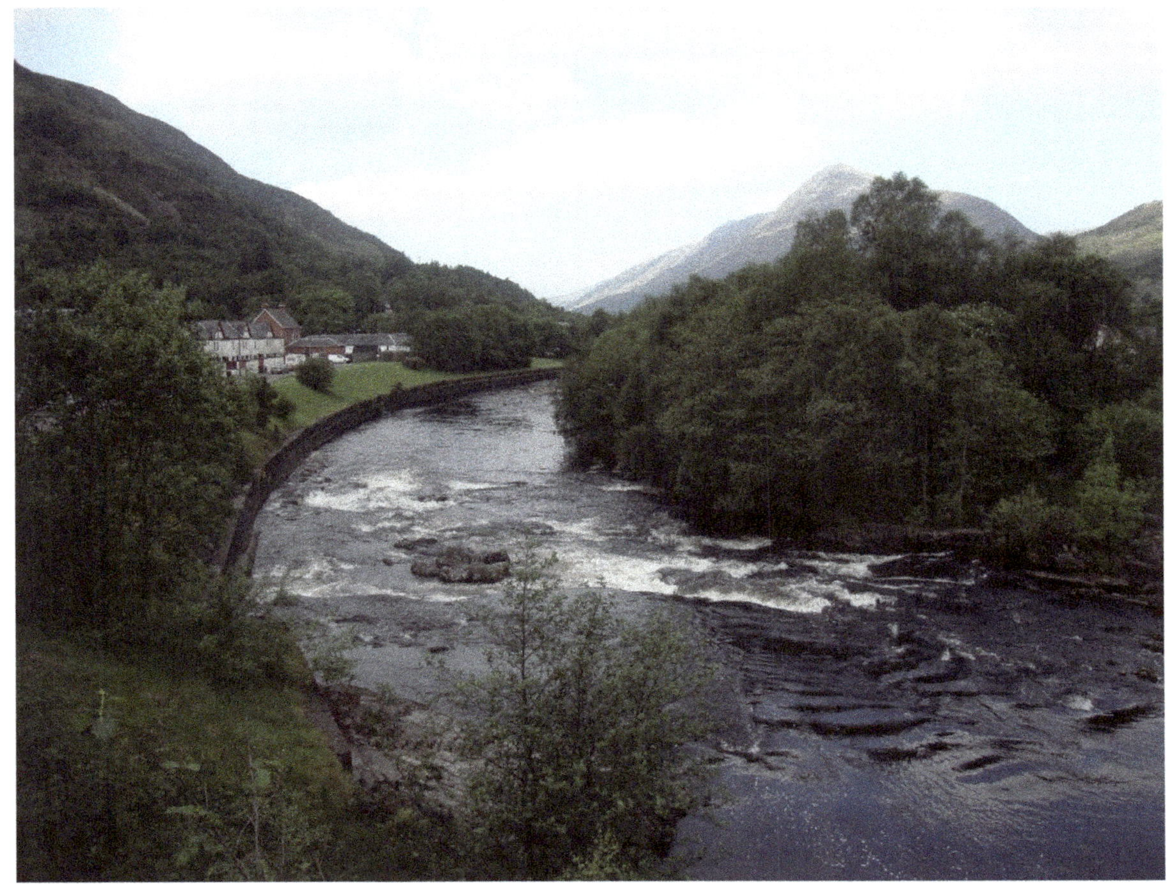

River Leven at Kinlochleven

Back in Bessie we had our elevenses, packed everything away and set off for Fort William, our first scheduled stop of the day. It is exactly as we remember it from our sailing trip nine years ago, even to the kilt-clad pipers in the town square. The only difference this time is that the pipers, in full Highland dress, were teenage girls rather than adult men.

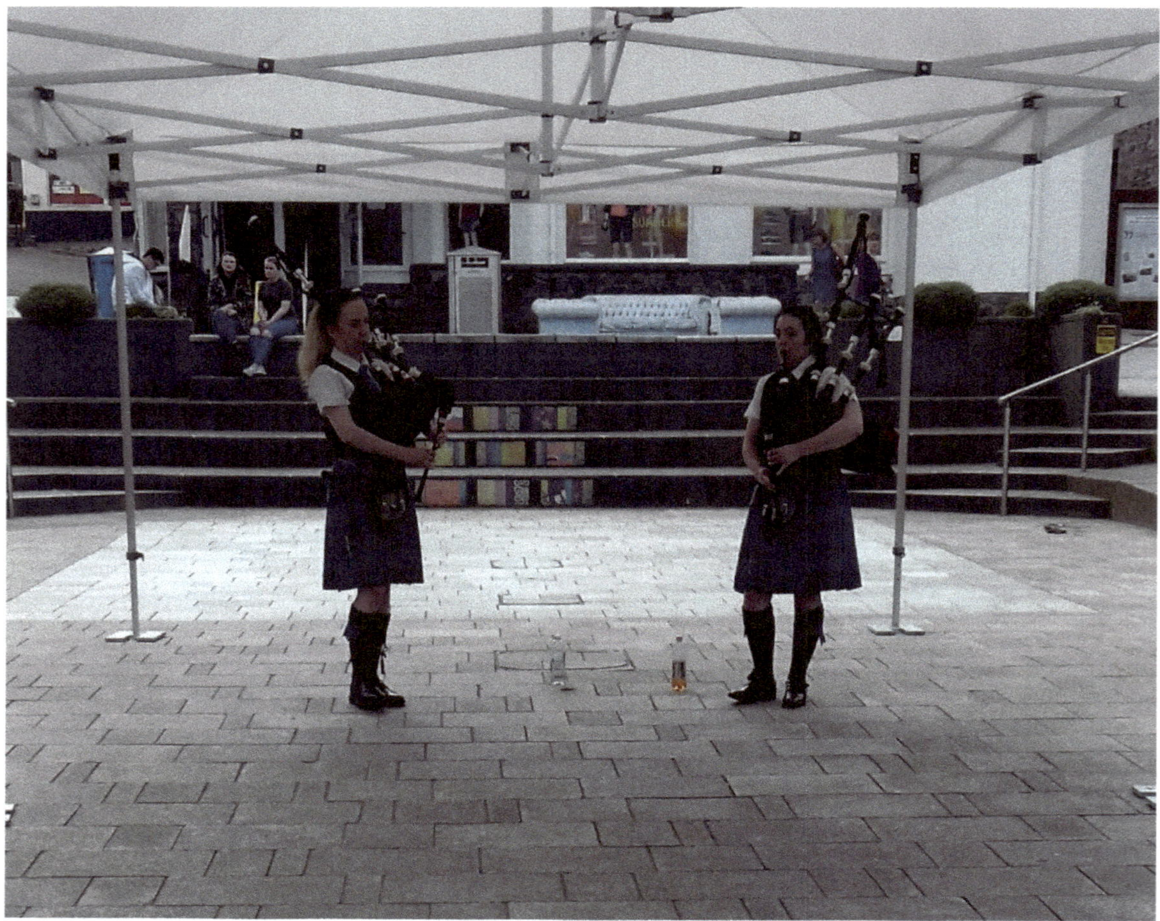

Pipers at Fort William

Although Ben Nevis is only a short drive from Fort William, we decided against a visit today. We'd climbed – or, to be accurate, scrambled up – the mountain a few years ago, and got the t-shirts to prove it, but I'm not sure my knees (or even Mike's) are up to it these days.

We are eager to see more of the Great Glen and the Caledonian Canal, which together stretch the sixty-mile length of a geological fault in the earth's crust between Inverness and Fort William. This fault is so clear that it can be seen from space, almost as a straight line. The canal, which links Loch Lochy, Loch Oich and Loch Ness, was constructed in the 19th century and was yet another great feat of engineering, along with roads, bridges and canals, by Thomas Telford.

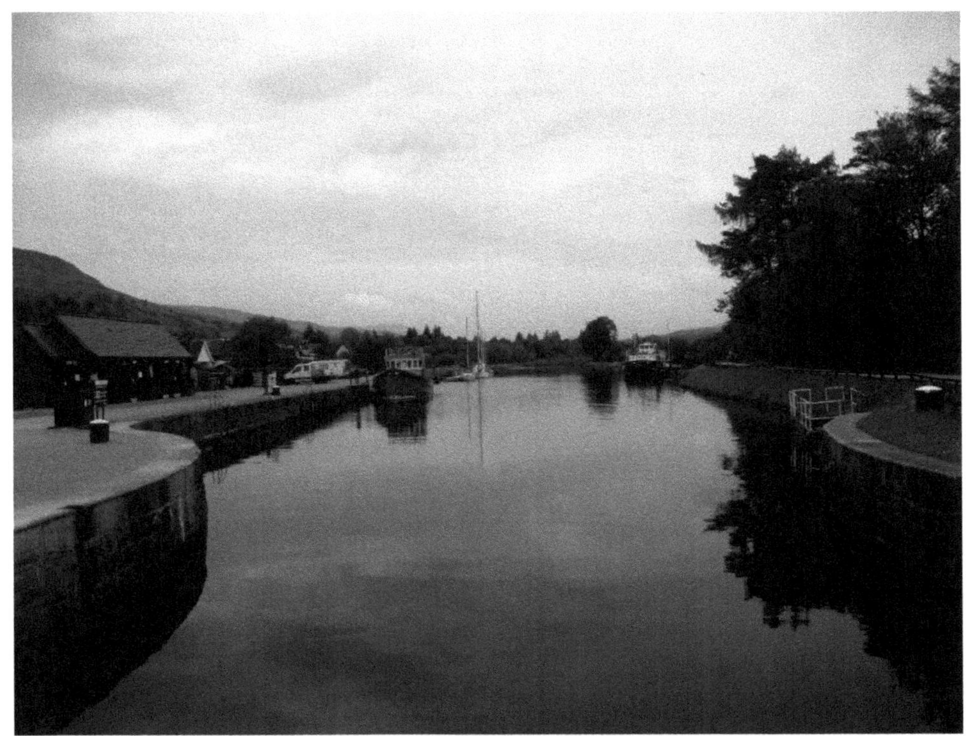

The Caledonian Canal

Mike and I also wanted to re-visit Britain's longest flight of locks this morning. This is Telford's impressive eight-lock Neptune's Staircase at Corpach, at the Fort William end of the canal, to remind ourselves of the day we sailed through from Inverness. I clearly remember the minor domestic incident that flared up that day, after a rope handling failure on my part led to the yacht nearly crashing into the lock gates. I was never any good at knots . . .

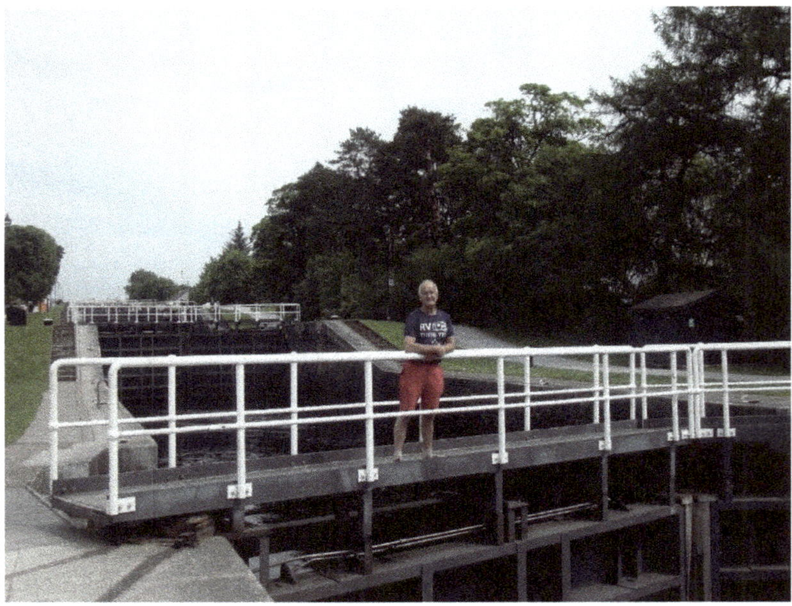

Mike at Neptune's Staircase

The start of the Great Glen Way was also the start for us today of Scotland's North Coast 500, a circular route that starts in Inverness, runs east, north and west around the coast and finally back up the Glen to Inverness. Also known as the NC500 and launched in 2015, it takes its name from its 516 mile length. It is sometimes promoted as 'Scotland's answer to Route 66' – even though it is only a fraction as long as its famous American counterpart – and takes in some of the country's most spectacular scenery. It also takes you into the notorious midgie lands of the west coast, but we'll worry about that when we get there.

Typically for us, we diverted off the 500, to pay a visit to Gairlochy, also on the Caledonian Canal, and famous for its pepper-pot lighthouse. The tiny structure, at the point where the canal enters Loch Lochy from the south, helps provide safe passage for naval vessels, fishing trawlers, cruise ships and yachts as well as the other leisure craft that populate the waterway.

Our reason for going to Loch Lochy was to see if a specific boat was still moored there. On our first visit, on the boat, we and two other sailing couples were invited for drinks on board K'ung Fu-tse (Confucius, in Chinese). A massive three-masted aluminium ocean-cruising junk, 52 feet long and weighing 28 tons, she was first launched in 1974. The boat still has the same owner but is currently being re-fitted and no longer has the distinctive and fiercely artistic hull décor of a few years ago. We were disappointed to find that Charlie, the owner, wasn't on board. It would have been nice to meet up again.

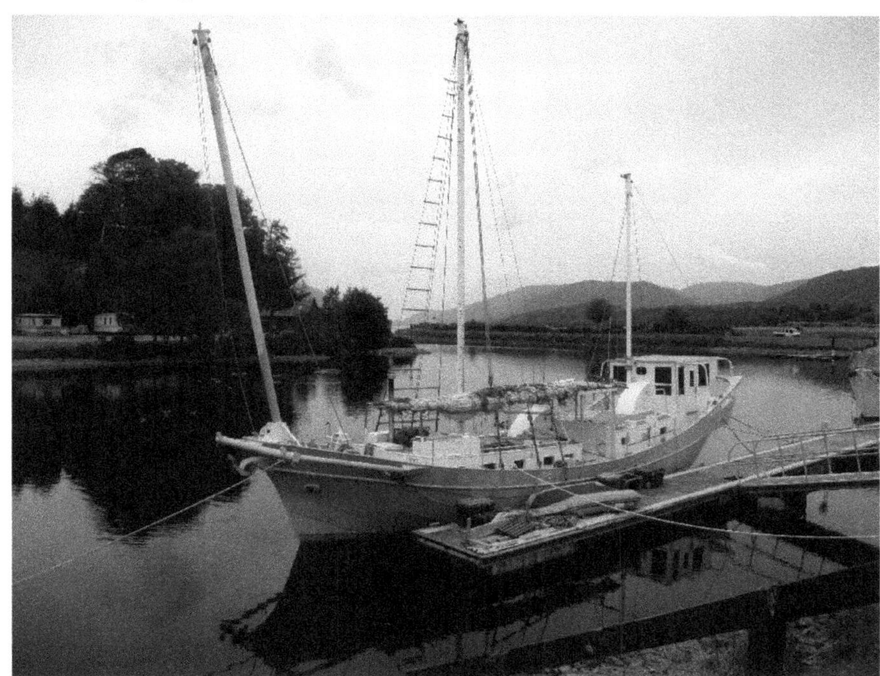

K'ung Fu-tse today . . .

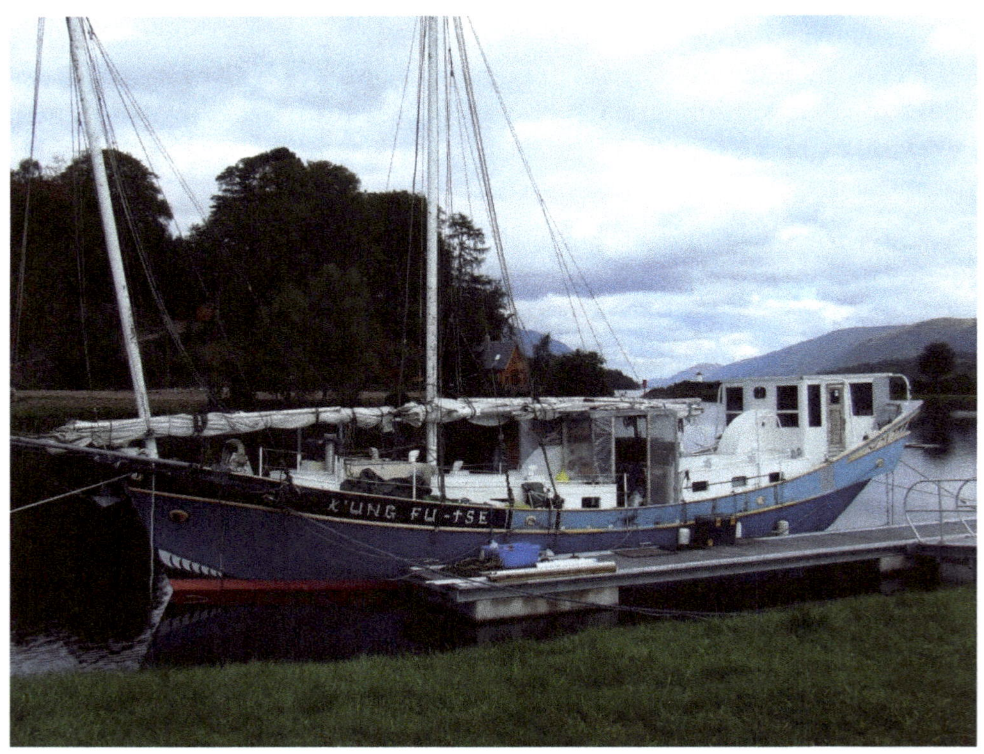

. . . and as she was the first time we saw her

A highlight of today was visiting the Commando Memorial at Lochaber, near Spean Bridge. Scott Sutherland's huge bronze sculpture of three commandos has special meaning for me as my dad, a Royal Marine in World War ll, was among the commandos who trained at Spean Bridge. The site of the memorial is fittingly bleak and moving. Next to it is a low-walled garden of remembrance with tributes to the fallen from past and recent conflicts.

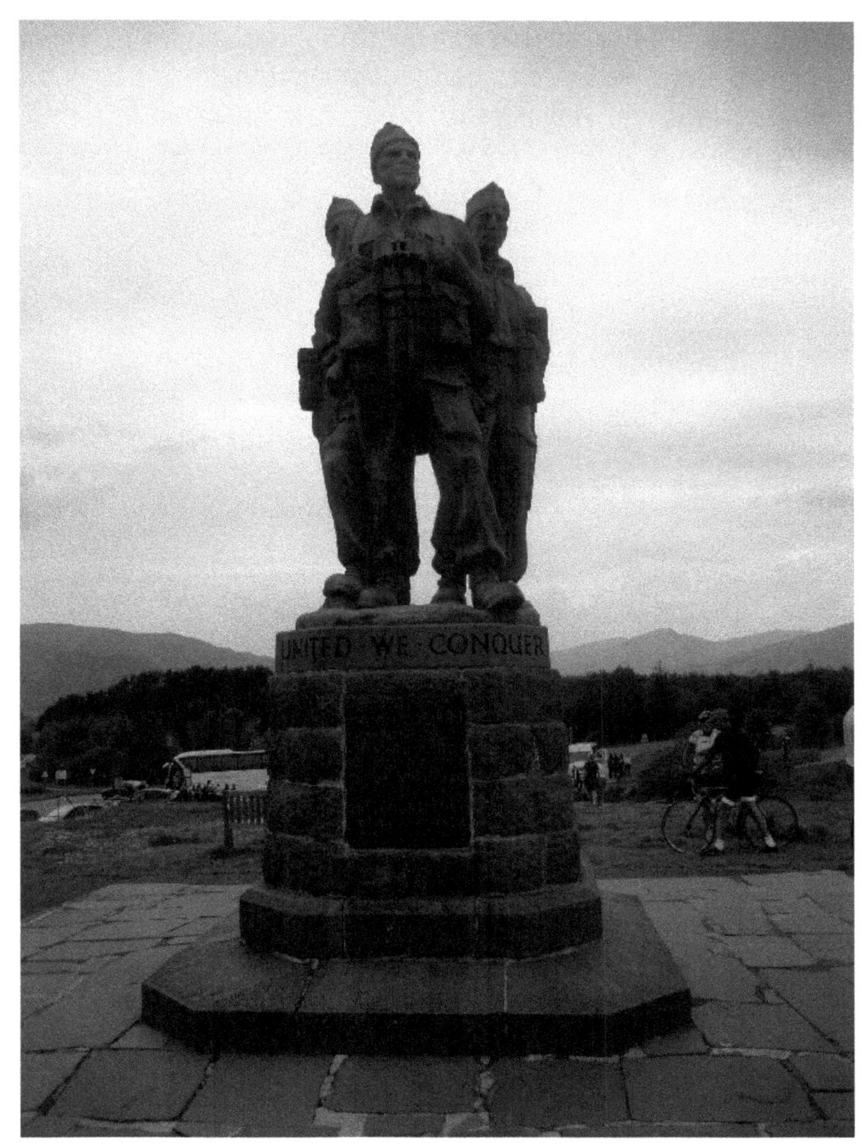

The Commando Memorial

We ended what was quite a busy day just outside Laggan in a peaceful lay-by beside Loch Lochy, where we were the only overnight visitors. I took off my sandals and had a cooling paddle, which was refreshing. Then I stepped on a wet boulder and slipped over onto my back, into the icy water of the loch, which wasn't.

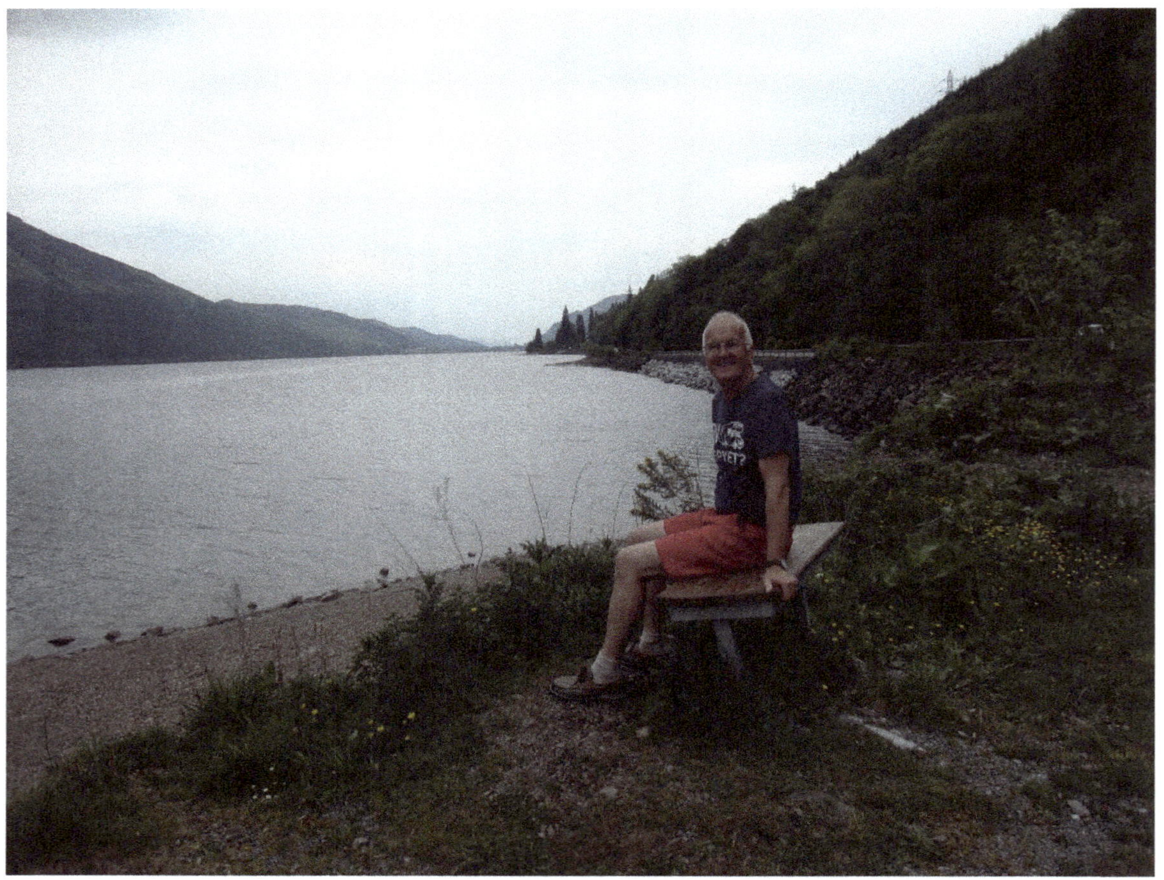

Loch Lochy

Today's mileage: 30

Loch Ness and Falls of Foyers to Dores

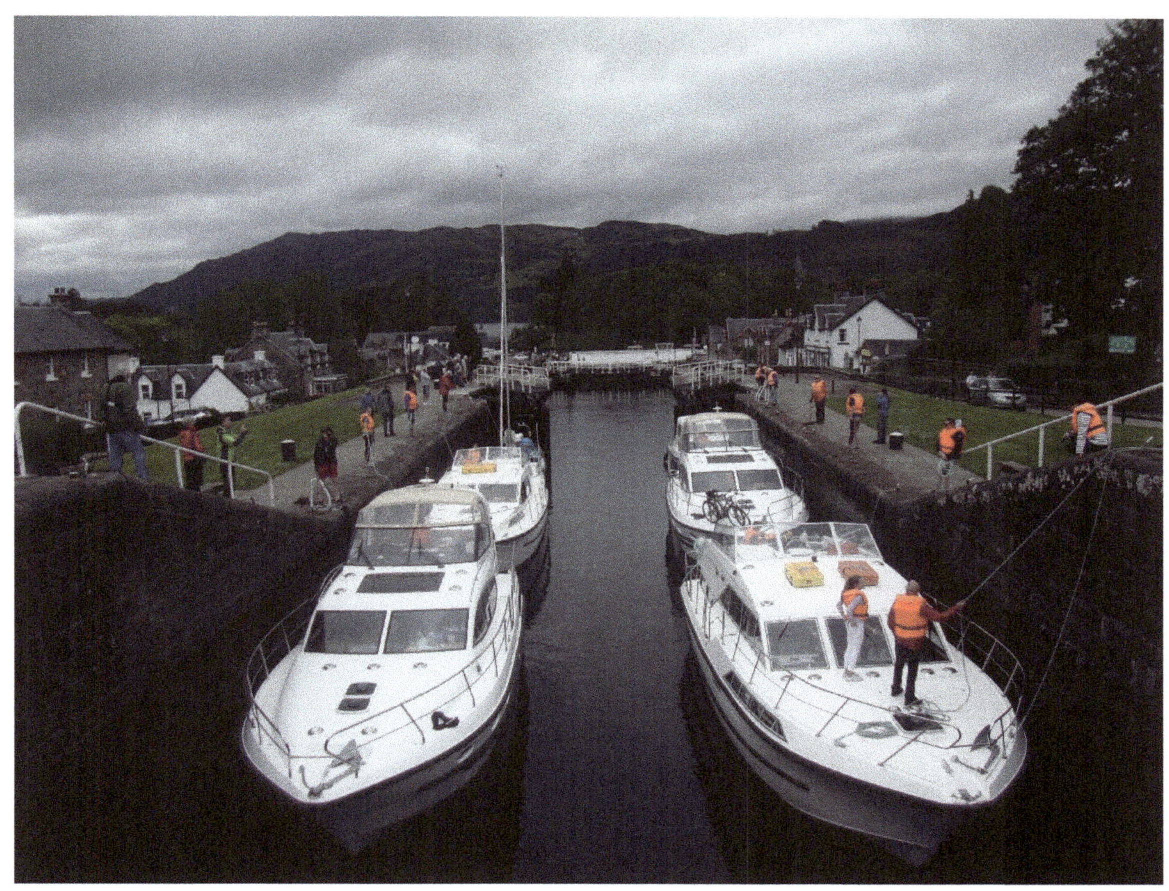

Fort Augustus

Sunday, 28th May

This morning we saw our first red stag. Grazing in a field with a few Highland calves, he was magnificent, and sporting a well-branched growth of antlers. I got quite excited and prepared to cross him off our list of must-sees, until Mike suggested he was more likely to be a farm animal than the wild red deer of my dreams.

Further into the Great Glen we came to the tourist magnet of Fort Augustus. The Nessie sculpture made from wire, that we remembered from our sailing holiday, is still there, towering above the lock, and it now appears to have given birth to a baby monster.

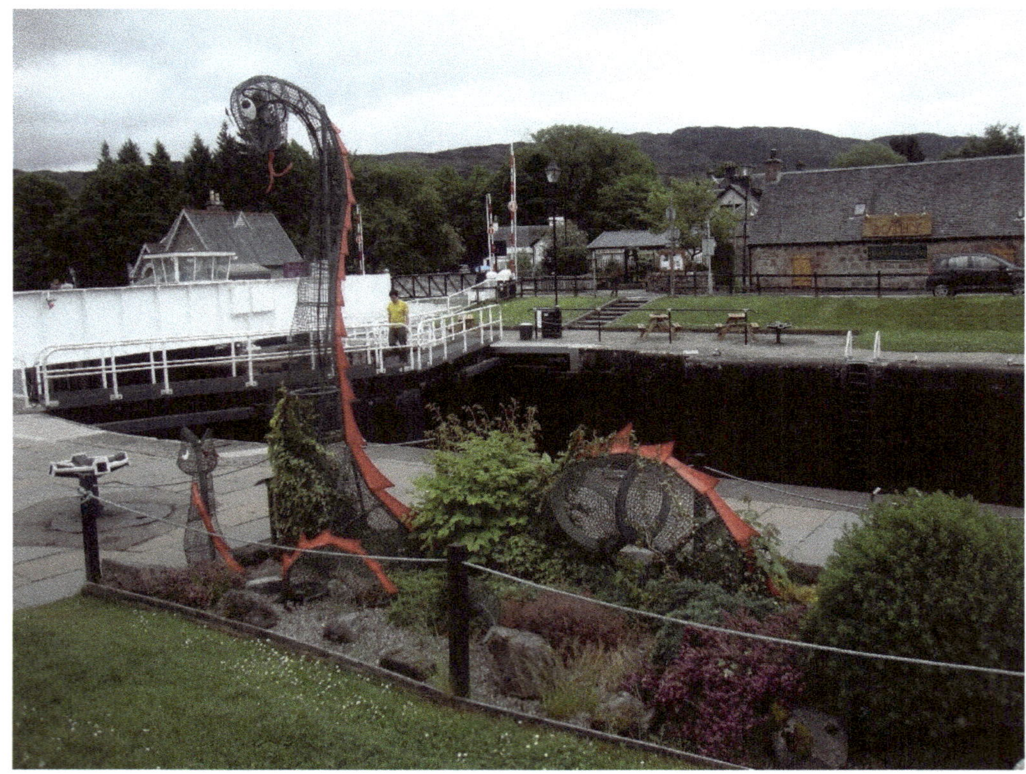

Nessie and Baby Nessie

Fort Augustus is a pretty little place, full of small shops selling a range of crafts, knitwear and knick-knacks. At the south west end of Loch Ness, it is dwarfed by the towering Cairngorms and bisected by the canal, which passes through five more locks to bring the water level down to that of the loch. We enjoyed using the closed lock gates as walkways, meaning we could go across the canal to the shops on the other side, as did many other visitors. The first time we came here I was charmed by the place but now it has lost some of its appeal for me – proving that it's sometimes a mistake to 'go back'. So we went for a walk away from the hustle and bustle, in search of 'the real Fort Augustus' and found that away from all the touristy bits and bobs, the village has a strong sense of community. I expect that outside the busy summer season its residents get on with normal life . . . which is probably what happens all the time anyway!

I wondered why it was called Fort Augustus and it turns out the name dates back nearly 300 years. After the defeat of the Jacobite uprising of 1715, when the Old Pretender James Stuart attempted to gain the thrones of England, Ireland and Scotland, a defensive fort was built there and the village, originally Cille Chuimein in Gaelic, was renamed after King George ll's younger son, William Augustus.

Back in Bessie we continued our journey, with a quick photo stop at the picturesque

Loch Tarff . . .

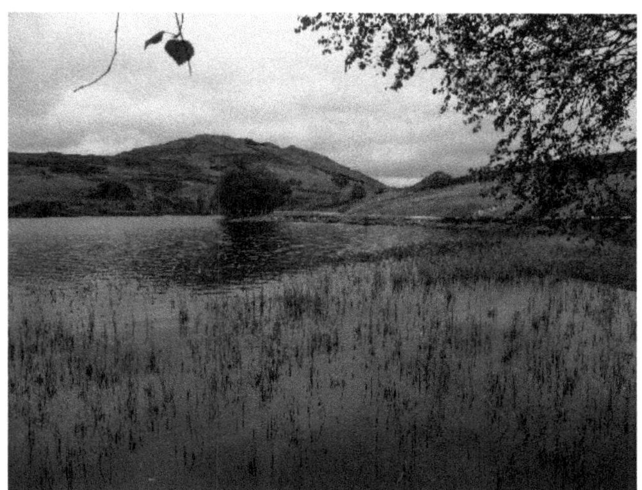

Loch Tarff

. . . and then a longer break at Loch nan Eun, where we followed a well-marked path up the hillside to a viewpoint 400 metres above sea level. From here, on a clear day, you can see seven lochs. We were lucky with the weather and we counted six. This picture can only hint at what it was like up there.

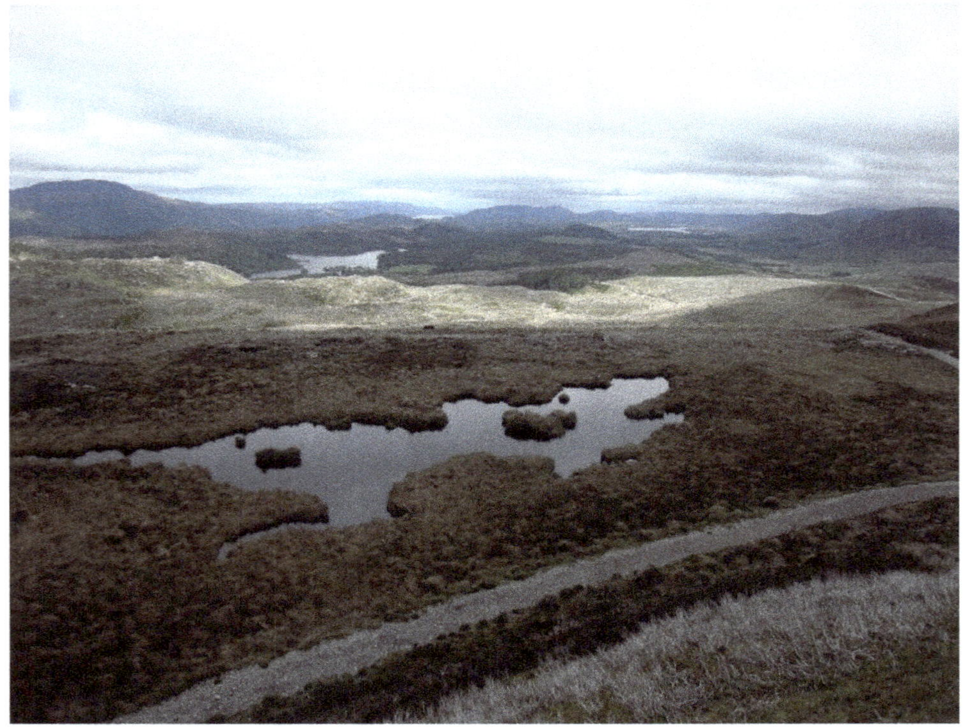

View from the top

Next came the Falls of Foyers – neither of us had ever heard of this place but it was marked on our road atlas so we stopped to investigate. We were glad we did. The waterfall is in an area of woodland where bluebells were still flowering and where, if you are lucky, you can see Scottish crossbills and red squirrels. We weren't lucky. But we followed the trail to the first lookout point and then descended much steeper to a second viewing platform. With a direct drop of 140 feet there is nothing to obstruct the slender cascade as it crashes over and onto the rocks into a circular pool below. Flying droplets, captured for milliseconds by the sun, shimmered in an iridescent rainbow and the noise of the torrent drowned all other sounds. Enclosed by dense forest greenery and vertical banks, this is a breathtakingly beautiful and almost secret place.

The force and intensity of the falls used to help drive British Aluminium's nearby smelting plant but the factory closed in 1967; now the site is part of a power storage station and the electricity from it helps supply Scottish towns and cities.

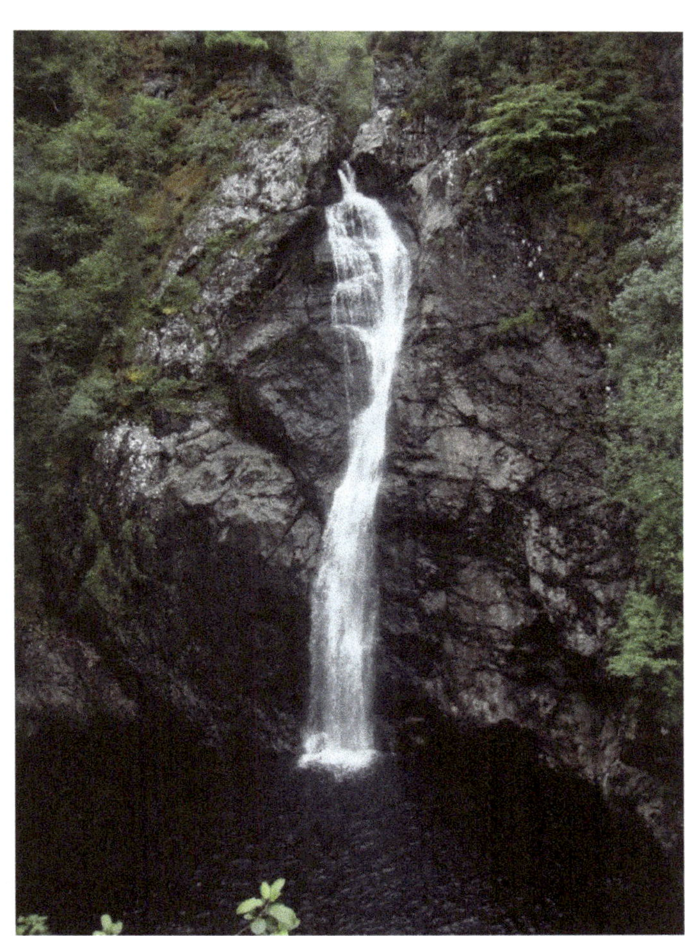

It's difficult to capture the full power of the falls in a still photograph

From the pool at the bottom of the trail Mike counted 320 steps back up to the top so even today it's not for the faint-hearted, the arthritic or the vertiginous. We could only begin to imagine how it was for early visitors, who had to slip and slide their way down, hanging onto roots and branches as best they could.

Along the pathway are stone slabs engraved with quotations from the works of Robert Burns, who visited the falls in 1787 and was so impressed he wrote a short poem about them while he was there.

Lines on the Fall of Foyers Near Loch Ness ends with: *And still, below, the horrid cauldron boils.*

According to an information board, one early aristocratic visitor 'was so scared by his descent that he gave £5 to start a fund to create a path.' His companion that day was a civil engineer, Joseph Mitchell, who raised the rest of the £45 needed to build the 'first safe access' in the 1830s.

The famous English writer Dr Samuel Johnson, together with James Boswell, the Scottish writer who wrote Johnson's biography, were other early visitors of note. After their visit in 1733 they wrote: *We saw a channel torn, as it seems, through black piles of stone, by which the stream is obstructed and broken, till it comes to a very steep descent of such dreadful depth, that we were naturally inclined to turn aside our eyes'.*

Mike and I weren't the only people there today who also found it awe-inspiring. It's amazing what a difference a path can make!

After a sandwich lunch back in the van we dove up the eastern side of Loch Ness until, early in the afternoon, we found a peaceful lay-by opposite Urquhart Bay for our overnight stop. The water was grey and calm, with little to disturb the silken reflections from the bank. That is, until a cruise liner steamed into our line of vision, followed close and low by a small red and white helicopter. This naturally aroused our curiosity but we never did find out why it was there! Later, as the sun went down behind the hills on the far side of the loch, reflecting a wide silver path on its surface, we were yet again struck by the timeless majesty of the Scottish

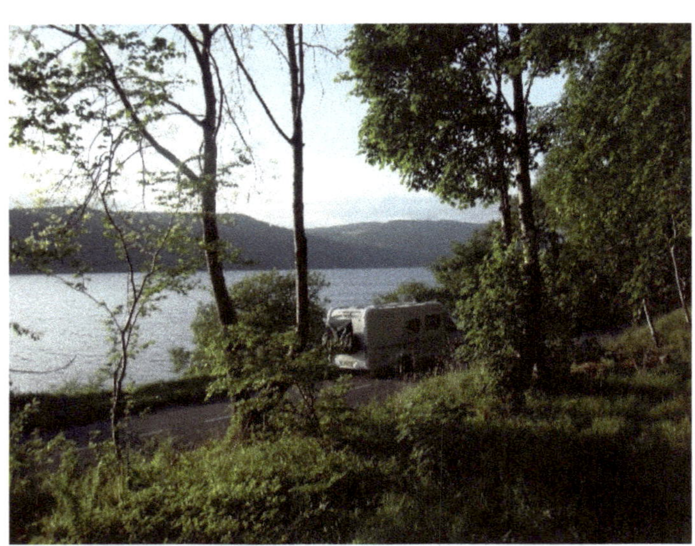

Bessie's car park for the night

landscape. Once more, we were the only visitors and the road was traffic free all night.

We ate dinner and were all set to spend the evening watching a movie. We had a brief discussion about which one to select from our small library of DVDs, before the penny dropped. We were wild camping. No electricity!

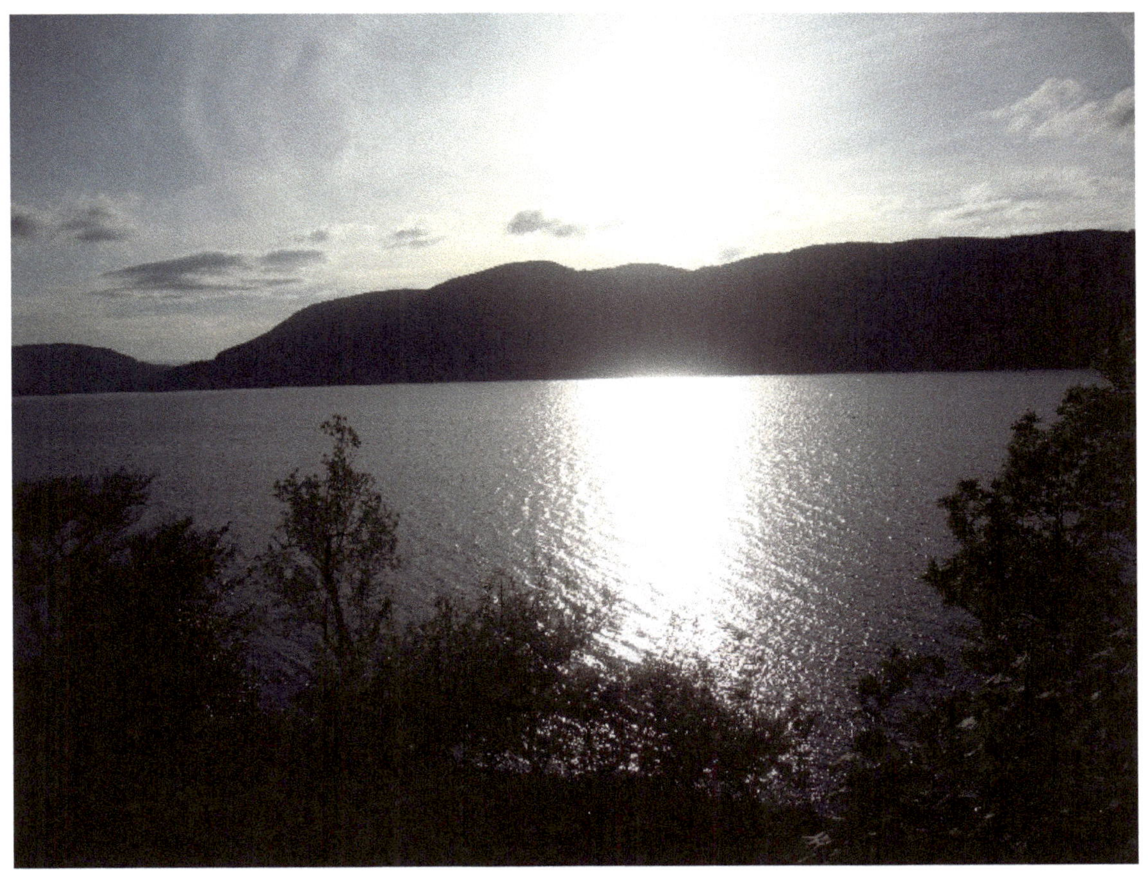

Loch Ness

Today's mileage: 38

Culloden Moor and Inverness

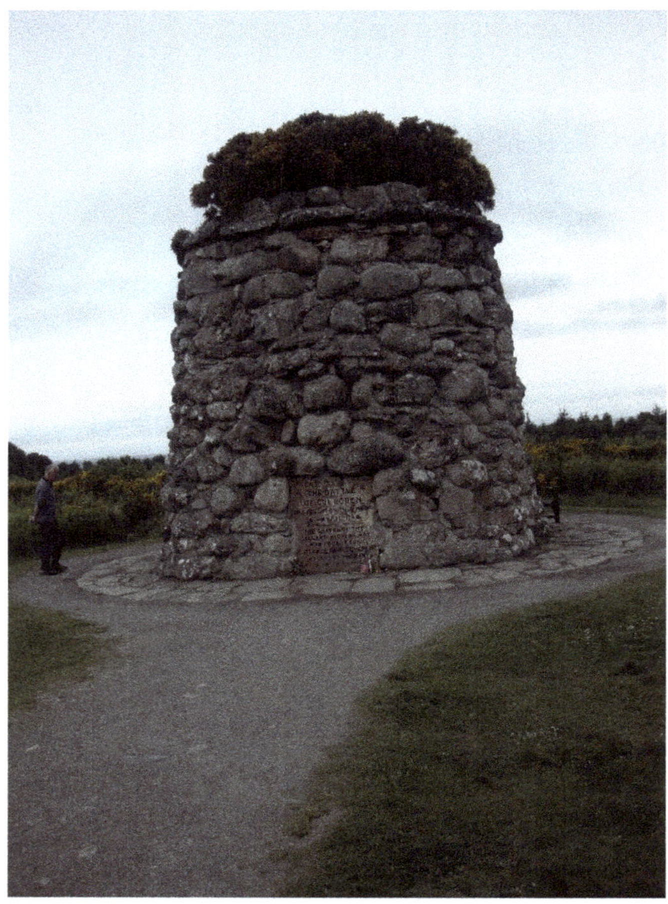

Culloden Memorial

Spring Bank Holiday, Monday 29th May

No lochs or mountains at Culloden Moor Caravan and Motorhome Club site, but a beautiful pine forest instead. Walking through the forest tracks this afternoon, and trying not to trip over roots that had come up through years-worth of trodden leaf mould, we met a fellow motorhomer with two dogs – one a miniature Portuguese podengo, the other a collie cross. We chatted about our travel plans and she warned us that Skye was getting busier and busier, year on year, and especially with people in motorhomes. Last year it was so bad, she said, that Police Scotland had officers manning the Skye Bridge and advising campers and motorhomers to turn back unless they had a firm booking for somewhere to stay.

She is here at Culloden for two nights with her husband, who has cancer. Every month they have to make the three-hour journey from their home on Skye to the hospital in Inverness, for him to be seen by the consultant before he can be issued with a prescription. The trip costs them at least £100 a month in fuel and campsite charges. This is undoubtedly a beautiful part of the world in which to live, but clearly not great if you need ongoing medical treatment.

We have enjoyed nearly a month of almost undiluted sunshine but today is cooler and cloudier, with odd spatters of rain. After a dark and silent night in our lovely exclusive lay-by, we made an early start today in the hope of getting parked in Inverness so we could top up our food supplies. The later you leave it the more difficult it becomes to find what we call a double: that is, parking bays one in front of the other, and preferably with spaces on each side as well. Perhaps it would be more accurate to call it a sixer! Doubles are most likely to be found at supermarkets and today Morrisons was the one we graced with our presence.

From there it was a short drive to Culloden Moor, site of the ferocious battle of 1746 that claimed hundreds of lives and ended the Jacobean claim to the Crown. The last pitched battle to be fought on British soil, it saw the defeat of the Jacobite army of the 26-year-old Young Pretender, Charles Edward Stuart. The Government's army was led by the Duke of Cumberland, who ordered his troops not only to bayonet the injured and dying Jacobites as they lay on the ground after the battle, but also to hunt them down and kill them on sight. This command resulted in his notorious nickname,

Butcher Cumberland.

It's difficult to be precise but it is likely that 1500-2000 Jacobites died in the battle or its immediate bloody aftermath. On the Government side, records show there were 50 deaths and 239 wounded.

After the battle on 16th April 1746 Charles, immortalised in popular lore as Bonnie Prince Charlie, was assisted by a young woman called Flora MacDonald and managed to escape, in the words of the Skye Boat Song, 'over the sea to Skye'. In fear of his life, he set sail for France and then on to Rome, where he spent the rest of his life. He died there from a stroke in 1788, aged 67. Although Charles got away, his supporters were not so lucky: many were captured and some were executed.

I was disgusted at the £11 per head admission charge at Culloden Moor. As far as I'm concerned this is an important place in our national history and should be open to all. After I'd ranted a bit about it I jumped off my high horse when I realised it costs nothing to walk around the battlefield, which was what I wanted to do all along. So that's what we did.

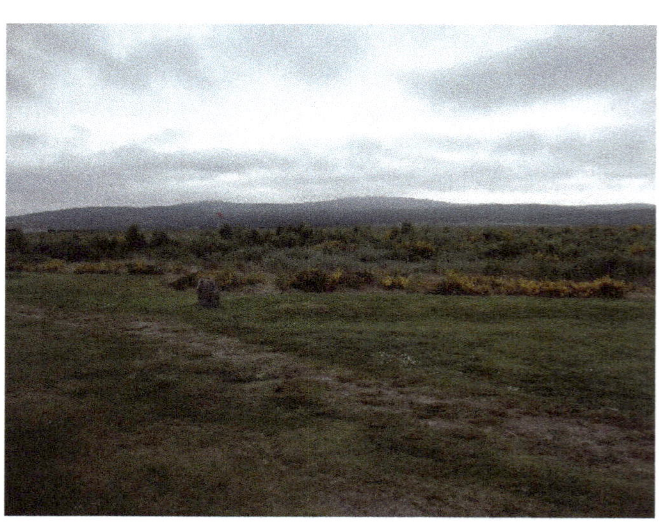

The Battlefield – a bleak reminder of a terrible battle

The adjacent National Trust for Scotland Visitor Centre is a bit touristy, and it's their exhibition and film show for which you pay the fee. A granite wall bounding the centre has a stone jutting out to represent every soldier that died in the battle, while signs around the field, quite rightly in my opinion, remind visitors the battlefield is a war grave and should be treated with respect. Stones mark the place where members of the various clans – as well as the Government forces – fell and I couldn't help thinking that under the grass, the scrub and the heather were the bodies of all those who had lost their lives.

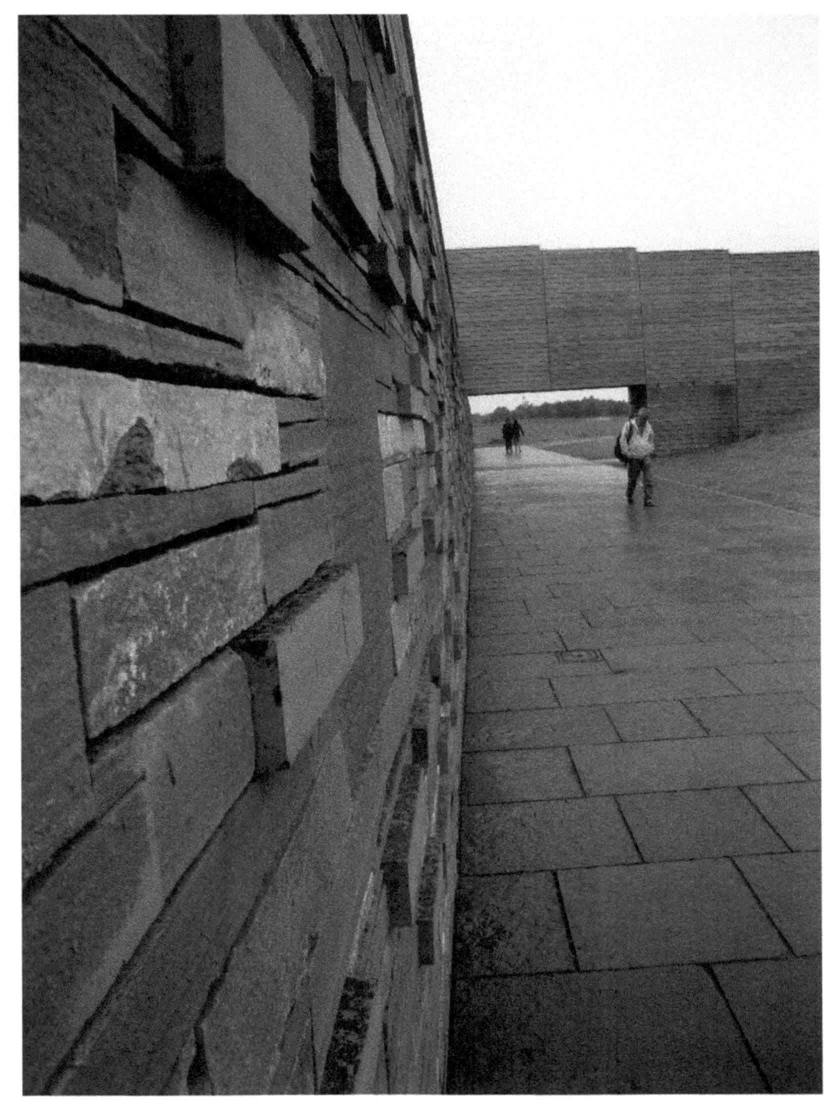

Every stone in the wall represents a fallen soldier

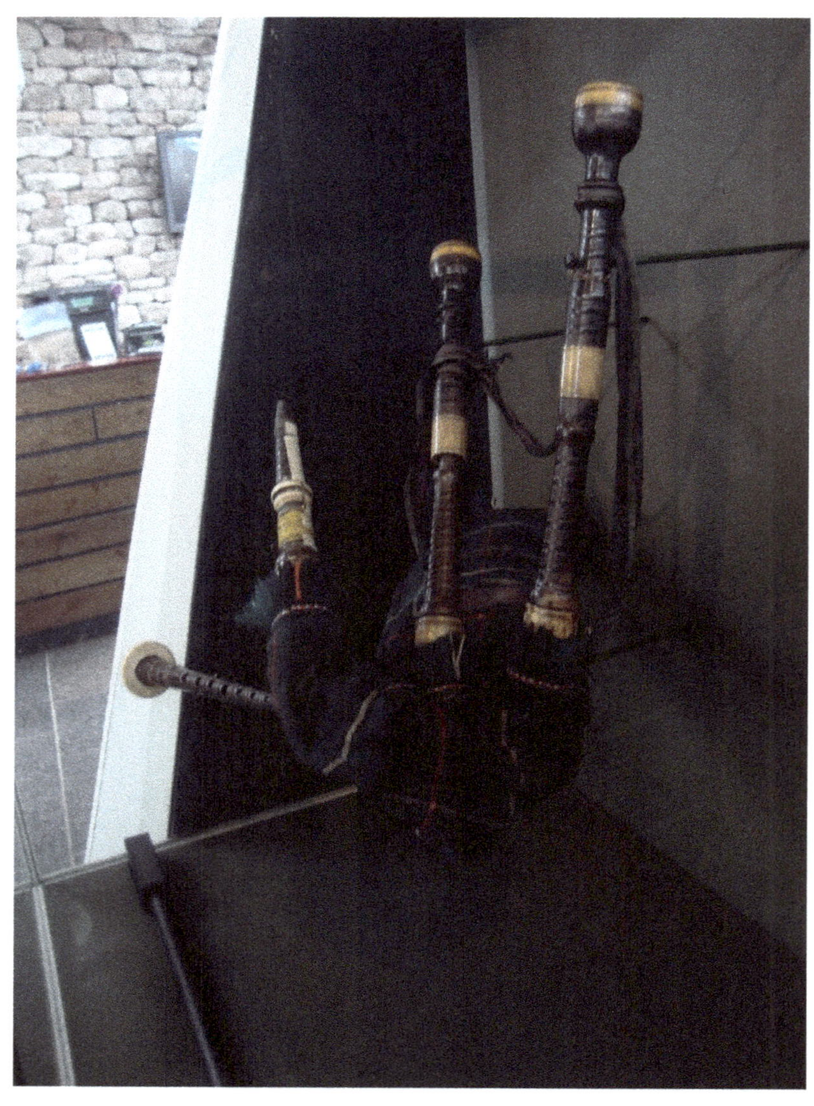

These Highland pipes are believed to have been carried into battle by a piper on the Government, rather than the Jacobean side.

'This is so moving and interesting,' I said to Mike. 'Being here brings the past to life so well, and helps you to understand it all better.'

'Yeah,' said Mike. 'Can we get back to Bessie now before it rains, and have a cup of tea?' He clearly doesn't share my sense of drama and history!

We've been away from home three weeks today, have bought one newspaper and, although Mike had fitted the little TV from the kitchen at home into Bessie, we haven't watched it once. I have already mentioned we brought DVDs to keep us amused on rainy days. This was one of them.

'Let's watch a DVD,' said Mike, after dinner. He selected *Argo*, a gift to him from son Alex. He got the DVD thingy on the TV working, we sat through all the ads and trailers and then looked at the time. Far too late – we'd never stay awake long enough to see the credits. So it's back on the shelf for the next rainy day, by which time we'll have worked out how to fast forward and will begin watching a *wee* bit earlier (note the Scottish vernacular).

Today's mileage: 27

Cromarty and Tain Hill

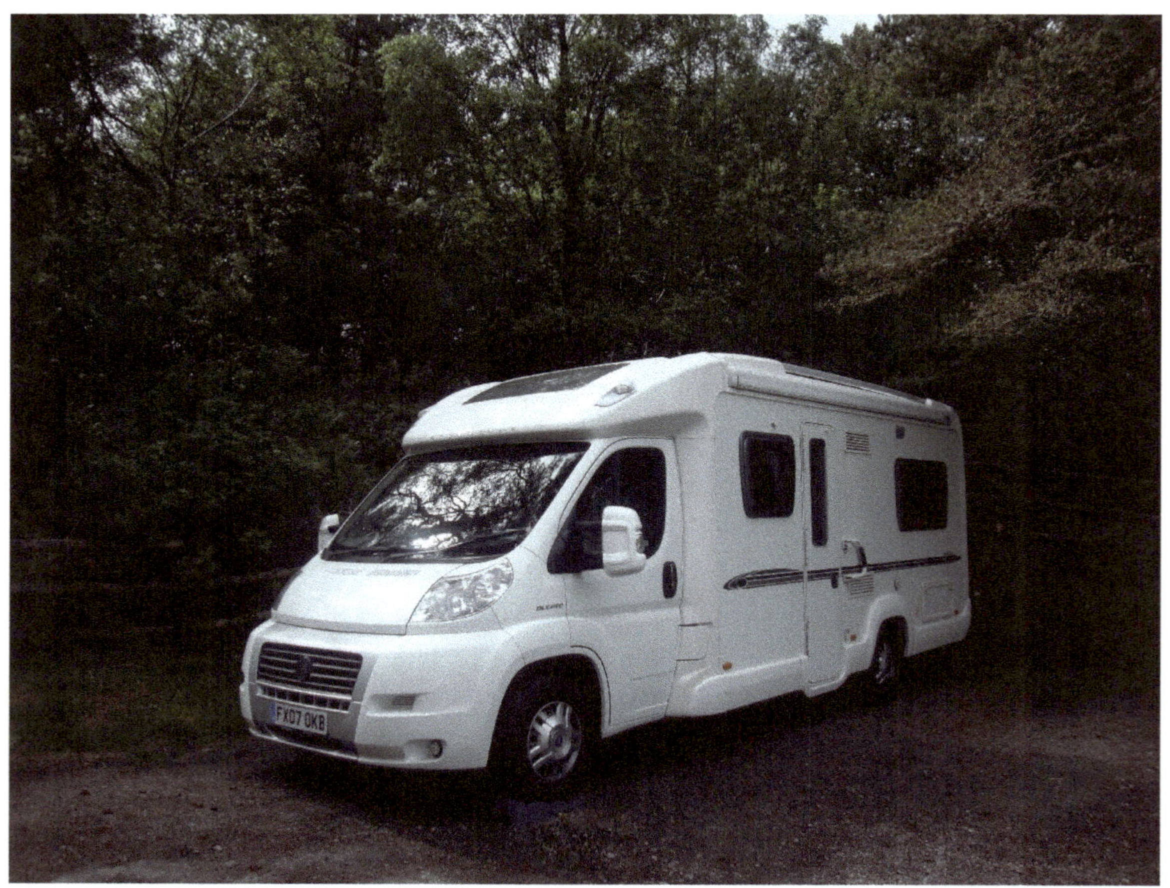

Bessie at Tain Hill in the Morangie Forest

Tuesday, 30th May

We're still, broadly, following the North Coast 500 route but we took another detour today to circle the Black Isle, from where, so we've been told, there's a chance of seeing whales. Whilst there we are visiting Cromarty, the scene of one of our sailing adventures. It was Monday, 9th June 2008 and we were sailing round Scotland in our Westerly Tempest *Jacqueline* (yes, I know, height of vanity). My notes for the day make interesting reading all these years later.

It is one of those days that I just wish was over. The wind is roaring through the rigging, the sea is coming at us like a steam train on all sides and Mike's face is set in grim lines as he battles to hold us on course. We're trying to sail down the Moray Firth into Inverness and the Caledonian Canal but it's tough going. We've been sailing into the wind since leaving Findochty at six o'clock this morning. It's now three in the afternoon, the wind's getting stronger all the time and we still have another 15 miles to go. I peer at the instruments from under the peaked hood of my oilies. The wind is gusting at 44 knots. Oh my God. That's a Force 9. Strong gale. My stomach lurches. I feel . . . what? Fear? Panic? Adrenalin? All of them. Then I think, smaller boats than this have got through worse conditions than these. I have faith in Mike, my skipper, my husband. I trust the boat will see us through. I know we'll be okay. We zip our oilies even tighter over our chins, check our life jackets are properly fastened and life lines secure. We increase the engine to maximum revs and reduce the big foresail to a tiny corner. The main is fully reefed. We're steaming along – speed over the ground is well over six knots. We discuss man-overboard procedures. Just in case.

We debate our options at length. Battle on to Inverness? Or run for shelter into Cromarty? We decide on Cromarty. The harbour is full and the entrance blocked by a ferry. We drop anchor in the bay and eat a scratch dinner of corned beef hash and baked beans – the best I can do in these conditions. The tide falls and we're bouncing hard as the yacht's keels hit the hard-packed sand. Safer to keep going. The anchor is fouled on a cable and we struggle on a still falling tide for nearly an hour before, with a super-human heave, Mike manages to get us clear. The skies are dark with blood-rimmed pewter clouds, bringing an early dusk as we motor-sail out of Cromarty. The wind has lessened. It's only 28-30 knots now. Only! We tuck ourselves in as close under the cliffs as we dare, and soldier on. We reach a deserted basin on the Inverness side of the Kessock bridge and drop anchor at one thirty in the morning. Fifty-four miles in nineteen hours. Calm waters at last.

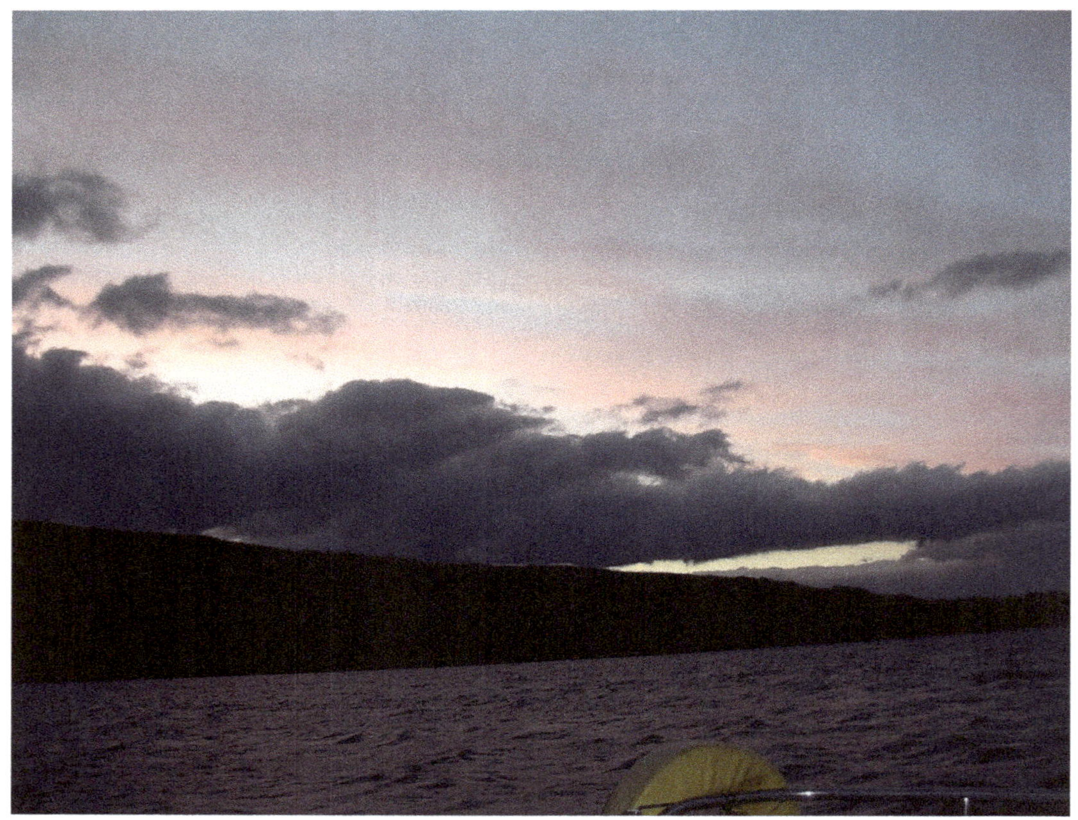

After the storm

Today the ferry was again tucked just inside the entrance to the harbour, this time waiting to start its summer trips – four cars at a time – across the firth to Nigg Ferry, but the sea couldn't have been calmer.

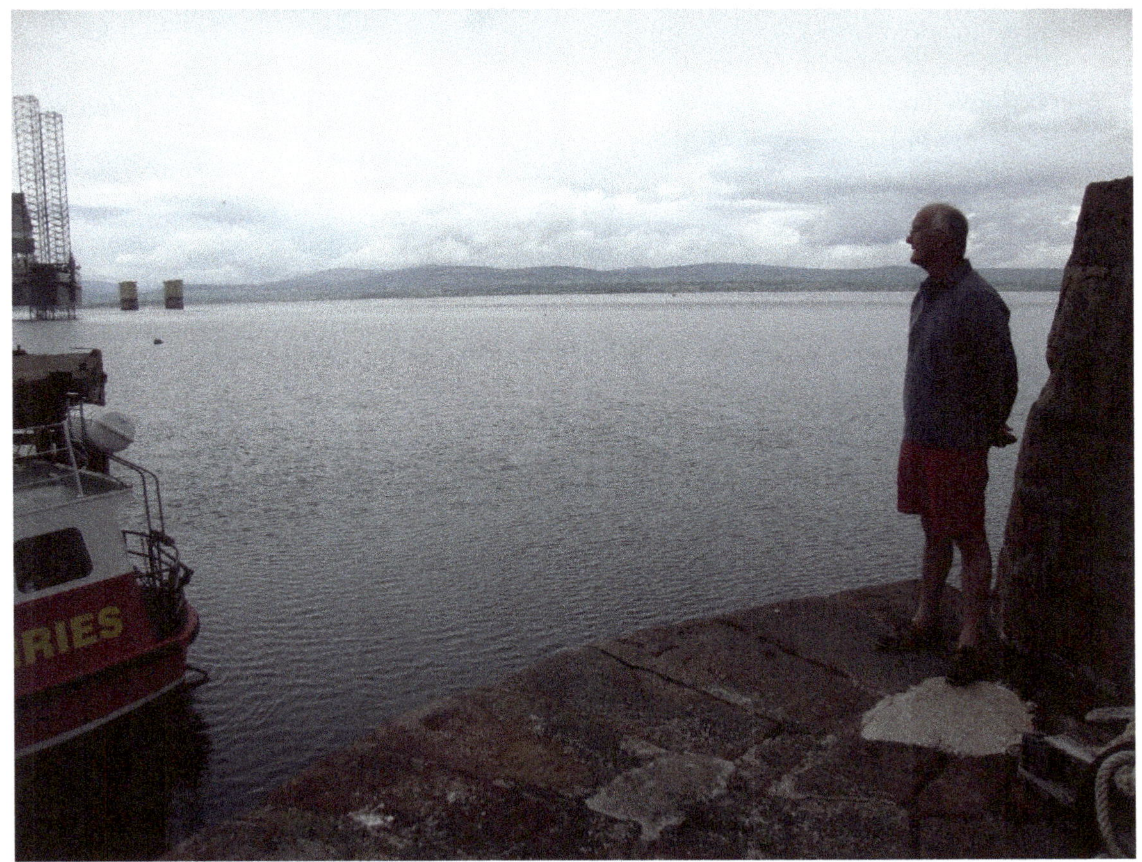

Mike remembers the narrow entrance to Cromarty Harbour

We had a wander around Cromarty, a peaceful, cared-for and welcoming little town with a proud maritime history but, as with most sea-going communities, not without its tragedies.

One disaster to strike these shores took place on 30th December 1915, when HMS Natal exploded during an end-of-year shipboard party, to which many local people had been invited. The ship sank within five minutes of the explosion and more than 400 perished, including the captain, Eric Percy Coventry Black. Strangely, the number of women and children who died were never included in the official death toll. I can only think there must have been some kind of official cover-up, to conceal the true figures.

The Firth of Cromarty is crowded these days not with the ships of the Royal Navy but with rigs from the North Sea, brought in over the past few years as a result of a decline in the oil and gas industries.

We didn't see any whales!

The Conan Bridge took us across the firth and we were back on the NC 500 route, heading for Tain, home of the Glenmorangie Distillery and the location for tonight's wild camping stop-over: Tain Hill in the Morangie Forest.

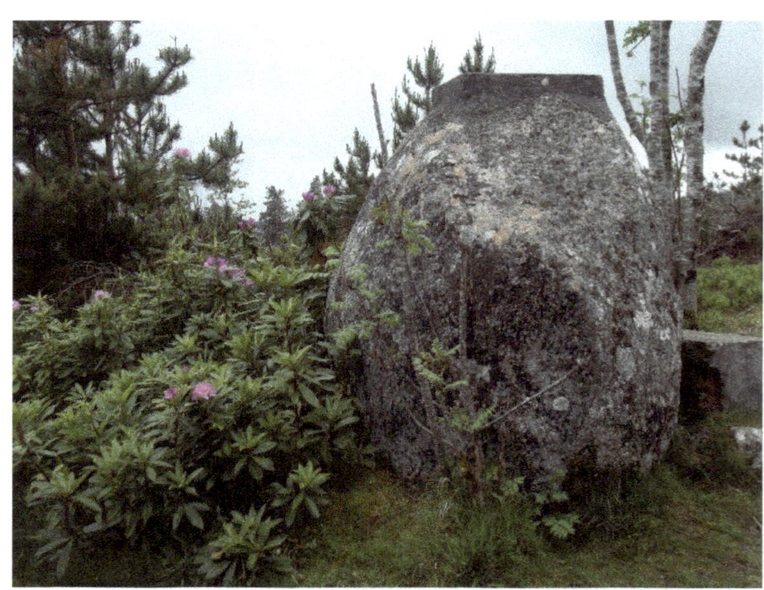

Pulpit Rock, Tain Hill

We parked in a clearing near the edge of the forest and went for a walk in the woods. Once the few early evening joggers and dog walkers had departed we were alone. We're beginning to get used to this solitude, and we love it.

Today's mileage: 74

Helmsdale and Dunbeath

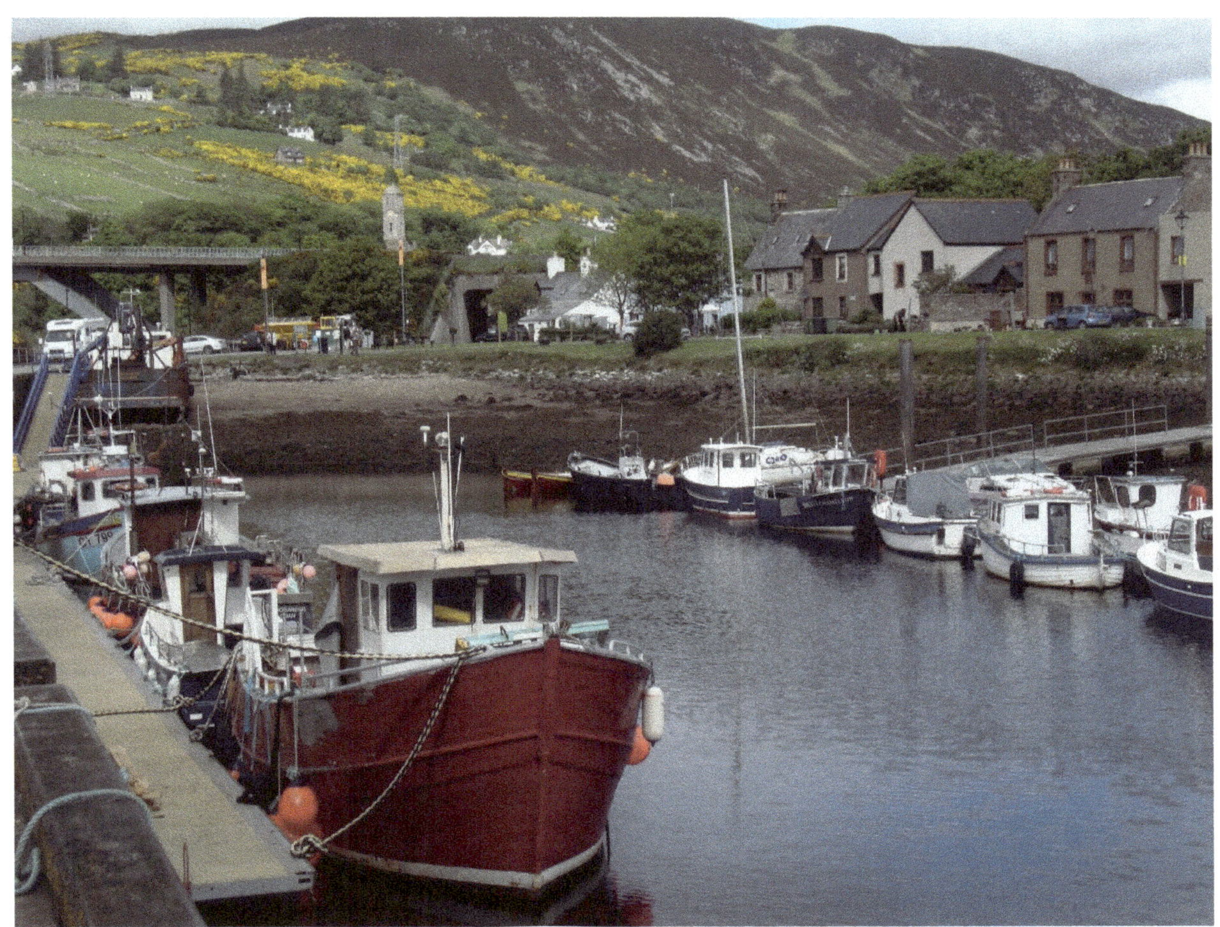

River moorings at Helmsdale

Wednesday, 31st May

Mike is a brilliant map reader and navigator. I am not. This holiday, because I am still getting pain and 'electric shocks' in my right shoulder and arm as a result of the boring old broken collar bone, he's been doing all the driving. He also does all the route planning. All I have to do is sit with the road atlas on my lap and tell him when we need to turn off. This morning, not for the first time, I got it wrong and, en route to Helmsdale, we went the wrong way. We ended up on a narrow, unclassified road out of Donnach. We do have a satnav but they aren't much use up here – either you can't get a satellite or the suggested roads are unsuitable and we find it's better to do it the old fashioned way. As it turned out, it was a good move on my part as it was a lovely drive through open countryside and along Loch Fleet.

We topped up with Autogas this morning. Mike was confident we still had plenty but as our route took us past a filling station he thought it might be an idea to get some while we could. Bessie's gas bottle took 5.2 litres of gas, at a cost of £3.75. This isn't bad when you consider the fridge runs on gas when we are stationary and off-grid, and we have been cooking with it every day.

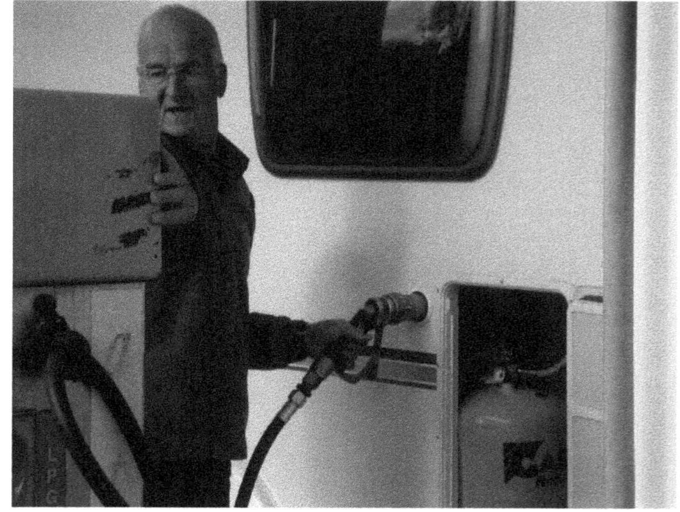

Autogas top-up

Driving on through heather and gorse clad mountains, we could see in the distance the chilly waters of the North Sea with its wind turbines, oil and gas rigs. We were heading for Helmsdale which, for some reason, I wasn't particularly interested in visiting and had no high expectation of the place. Once there, I was pleasantly surprised by how interesting it is and how much I like it.

It is a small town at the mouth of the Helmsdale, a salmon river that brought a degree of prosperity to the town after it was built by the future Duke of Sutherland in 1813, although it was originally intended as a herring port. For me, its three most prominent features, after the river, are Thomas Telford's two-arched bridge, the war memorial in memory of the 56 local men who lost their lives in the two world wars, and the ice house that was built during the salmon boom.

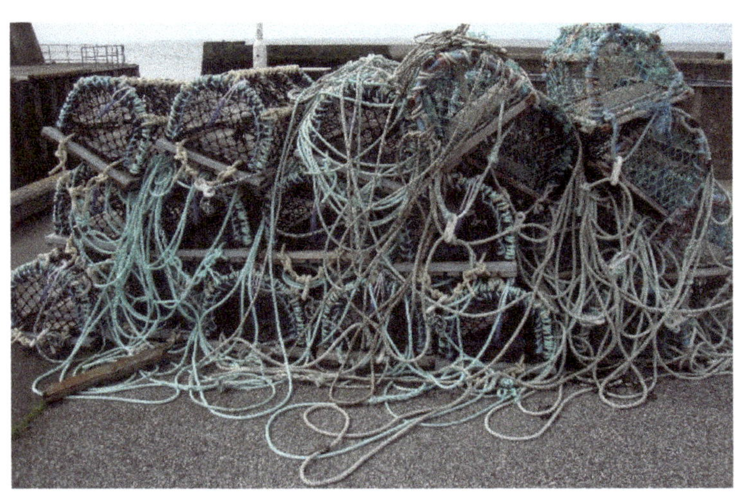

Crab and lobster creels on the harbour wall

The other boom to hit Helmsdale was the 1869 gold rush, when 600 prospectors set up camp in a bid to make their fortune. They paid the Duke of Sutherland for the right to pan for gold in the Helmsdale and its streams. It wasn't long before local sheep farmers and sportsmen complained about the invasion and the duke withdrew the prospectors' licences. The 'gold rush' lasted less than a year and I have no idea whether any gold was ever found there.

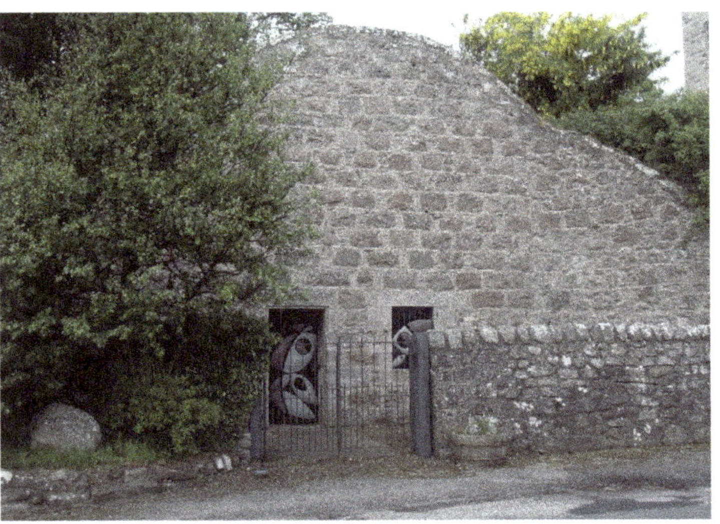

Ice house

Today Helmsdale was also the port of call for Boris, a big old 1954 Austin A40 Devon estate. My friend Tim Murray tells me this is 'a rare model, even by the standards of the day, and is certainly very rare today'. Lovingly restored and cared for by his present owners, Boris is currently serving as a mobile home for them during their tour of Scotland. He's certainly big enough!

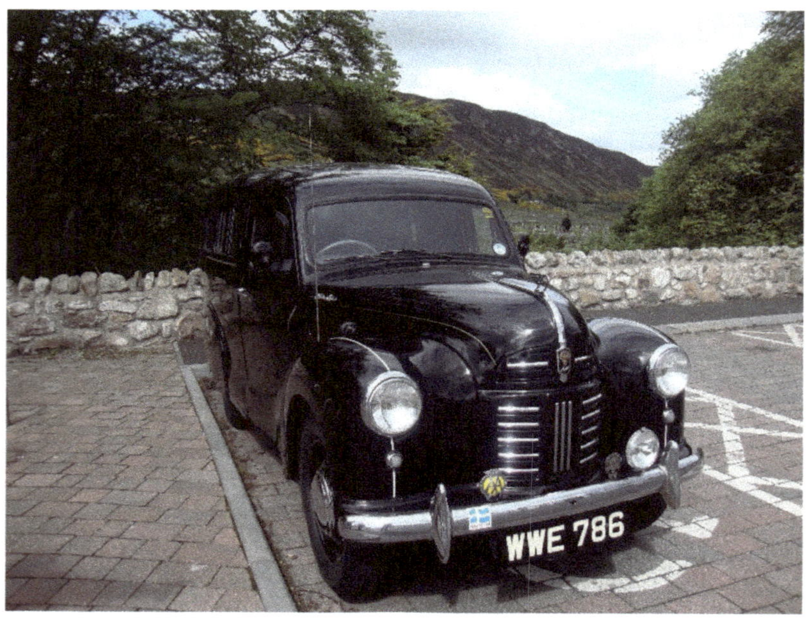

Boris

We ended the day at Inver Caravan Park, Dunbeath. This is a small, quiet site with excellent facilities, where we took advantage of the washing machine for £3 and made use of the fresh breeze and warm evening sunshine to dry our laundry on the line provided.

Today's mileage: 55

Dunbeath to Bighouse

Thursday, 1st June

I remember when my dad was in the RAF he was stationed in Scotland and did some research into our Williamson family tree,' said Mike this morning. 'It seems that way back we were members of Clan Gunn.'

And guess what? Just up the road from Dunbeath we spotted the Clan Gunn Heritage Centre! It was an unmissable opportunity for Mike to dig for his roots.

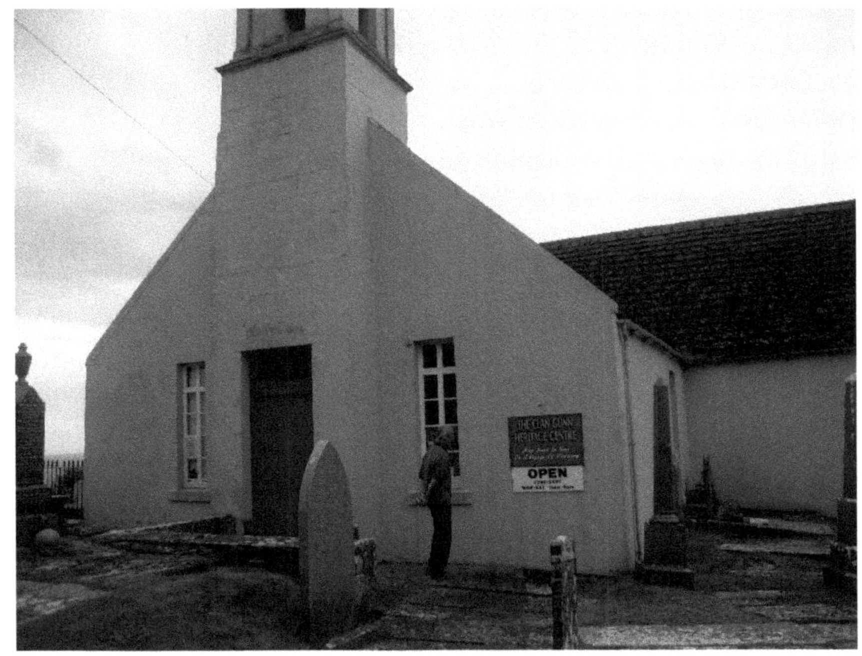

Clan Gunn Heritage Centre

It's based in a little old church surrounded by 200 year-old lichen-covered tombstones and run by volunteers. The centre had a sign on the wall proclaiming the museum is open from June to September, 11am to 5pm. We'd made an early start this morning and it was just after nine thirty when we arrived. Of course, it was all locked up. We peered through the dusty windows to see what we could see, which wasn't much, other than pictures on the walls, displays of old sepia postcards and cardboard boxes full of small brown paper carrier bags. We didn't want to hang around for another hour and a half, in the hope of someone arriving, so we took a few photos for posterity and went on our way.

The road to Wick took us past scores of derelict crofts and bothies, some with grass growing on the roofs and others that are little more than piles of stones in the barren landscape. It is easy to imagine how bleak this area must be in the winter, and I thought about the hard life of the shepherds who had only these small draughty buildings for shelter. I suppose these days they all whizz around on their quad bikes and can go home after they've checked their flocks. The little stone refuges look appealing at this time of year, but I'd hate to be forced to hole up in one during ferocious winter gales and snowstorms.

Wick is another of the places we'd visited on our sailing tour around Scotland in 2008 and was much as we remembered it, other than that the harbour-side hair salon, where I'd had my hair cut from long to short for £7, was no longer there. We paid a quick visit to the thriving and busy harbour and bought pasties for lunch. Although the town centre isn't especially attractive, there is a pretty riverside walk and lots of interesting places to visit, including castles, a distillery and heritage museum.

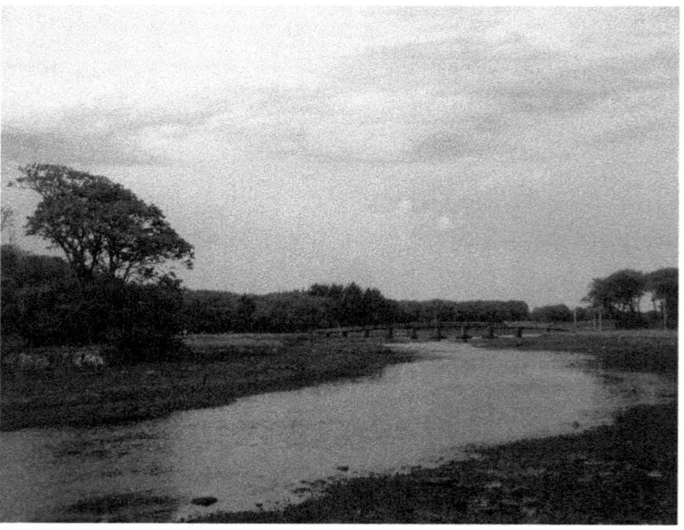

Riverside walk at Wick

The coast road from Wick is pleasant rather than spectacular so we carried on to Thurso via John o' Groats and Dunnet Head. We posed for photos at the iconic finger post, where Mike remembered being taken during a family holiday as a child, and admired the old hotel, now known as The Inn at John o' Groats. With its tower at one end and brightly painted buildings at the other, it has views of the sea and is surrounded by the wild Caithness landscape.

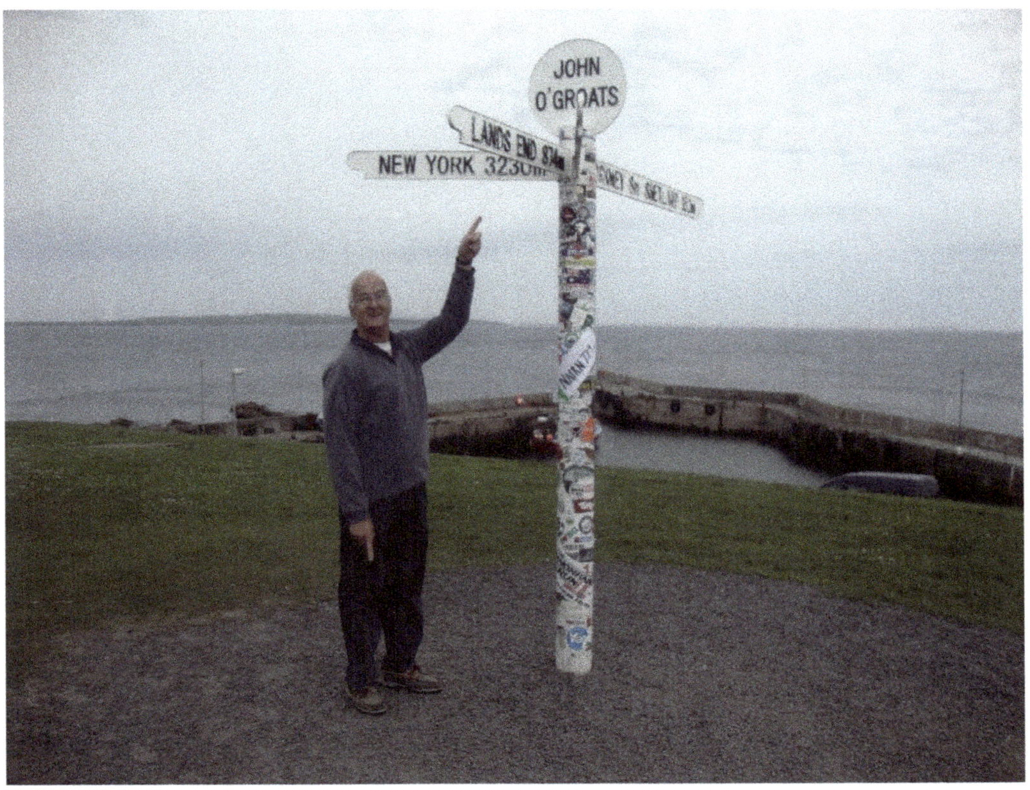

The famous John o'Groats fingerpost: only 3230 miles to New York!

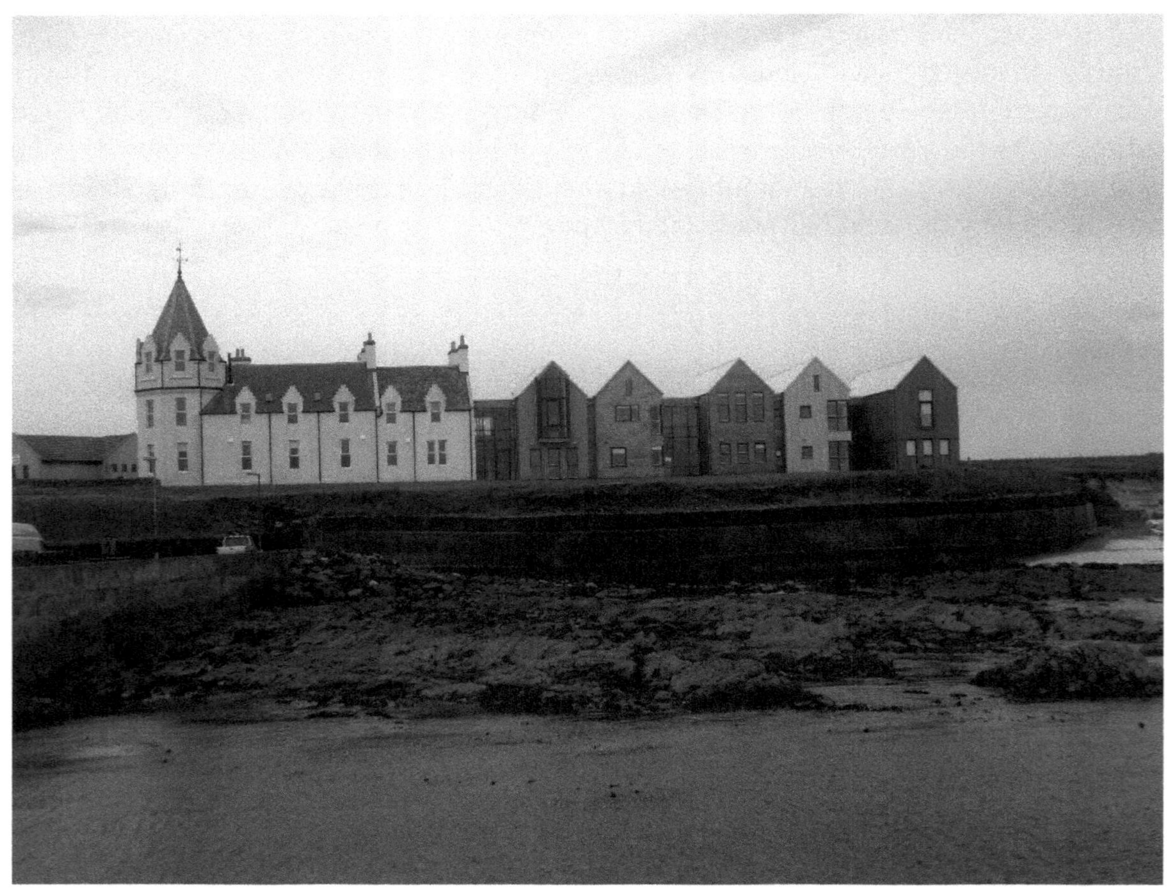

Hotel with a view: you might even be able to see the Orkney Islands on a clear day

It's a funny old name, John o' Groats. Legend has it that it's named after a Dutchman called Jan de Groot who, back in the mists of time, used to ferry people over the Pentland Firth between the mainland and Orkney: a perilous crossing of nearly 40 miles.

Being there and posing for photos under the famous signpost to New York, Land's End, Orkney and Shetland, reminded me of the day three years earlier when I joined a group of fellow supporters of Beagle Welfare at Land's End, to welcome back the magnificent Tour de Beagle cyclists who had pedalled the 1,000 miles from John O'Groats in ten gruelling days and raised more than £20,000 to buy Beagle Welfare a fully kitted out van. They crossed the finishing line exhausted and emotional, to be met by a welcome party of family, friends and beagles. We devoured hot Cornish pasties and toasted the doughty cyclists in cold champagne; everyone was deeply impressed by their enormous achievement.

After a few miles we stopped for another photo call at the Queen Mother's much-loved Castle of Mey, and although we didn't actually go inside the house or gardens, we did have a quick look in the shop and restaurant before backing hastily out, eyes watering at the high prices. Ironic, when you remember the Queen Mother reportedly paid the less-than-queenly sum of £100 for the decaying old fortification on the weather-beaten headland.

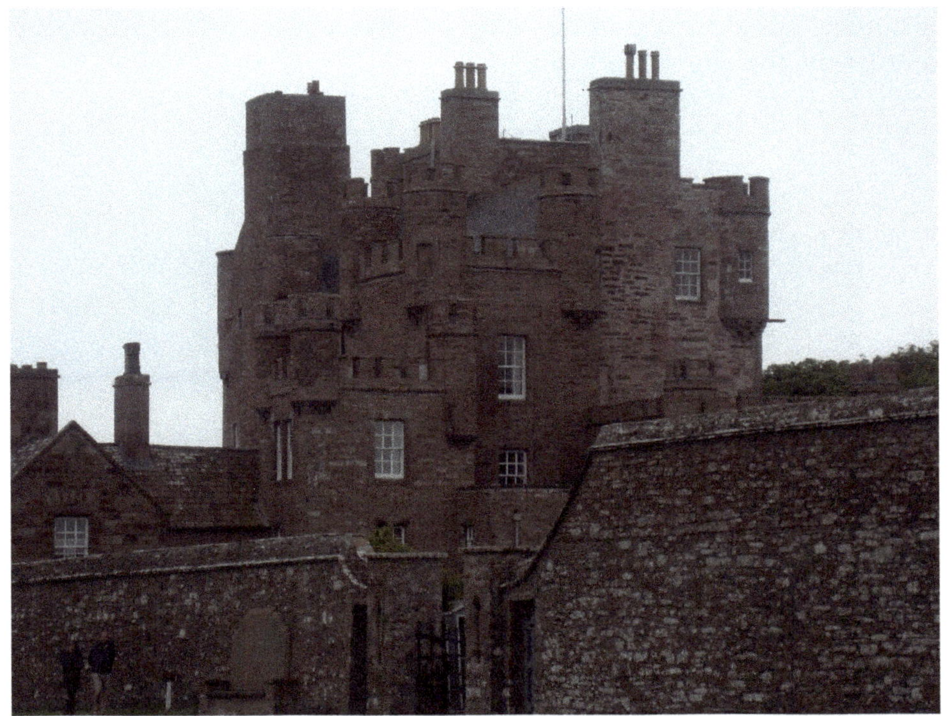

Castle of Mey

This was in 1952, a few months after the death of her husband, King George VI. She was visiting her friends Commander Clare George Vyner and Lady Doris Vyner, the owners, and the deal was struck. The Queen Mother then set about restoring the castle and its grounds, and for the rest of her long life she holidayed at the castle for several weeks each year during August and October.

Also known as Barrogill Castle, it dates back to 1566 and was built by the 4th Earl of Caithness for his second son, William Sinclair. But it wasn't to be William's home for long: in 1573 he was murdered by his older brother John, who was himself then murdered, and the castle eventually went to the third son, George. What was that I was saying about the Scots and their bloody history?

In the castle's car park we spotted a couple of classic Triumph TR4s, bedecked with brollies to protect their pristine paintwork from the weather. Our friends, the aforementioned Tim Murray and his wife, are classic car enthusiasts and collectors so, Tim and Jenny, this picture is for you.

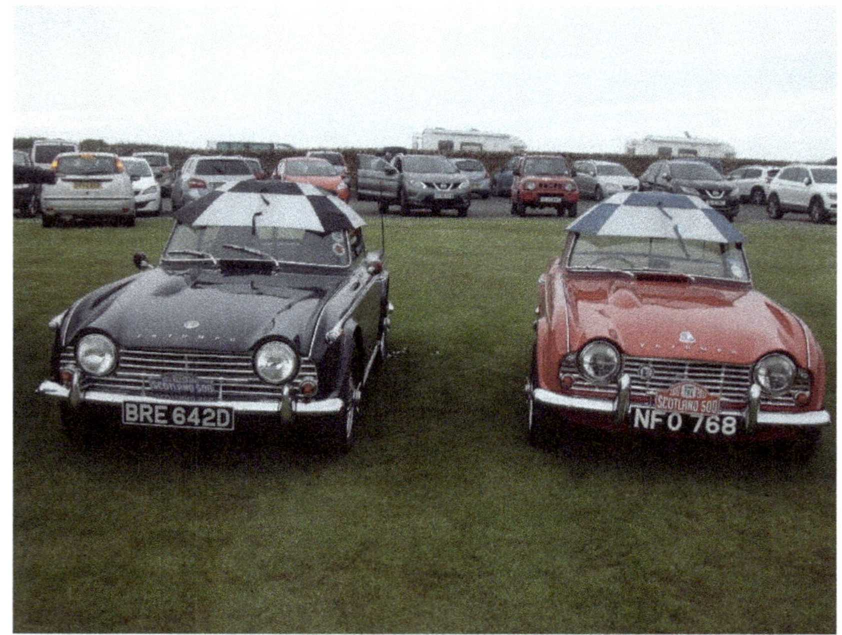

Too cool to get wet!

As well as all the ruined crofts and cottages, you can't help but notice the number of graveyards along this route. Every village, every hamlet, every settlement has a cemetery. And they are all packed. 'Considering there are so few houses in this area,' I said, 'where do all the bodies come from?' We didn't stop to look at the headstones, so I can only assume they date back to before the Clearances, when many more people inhabited this area.

A few miles further on we turned off the NC500, now the A836, onto the B855 for the short detour to Dunnet Head. I think most people, me included until today, think of Britain's most northerly point as John o' Groats, but it's actually quite a bit further south than Dunnet. With towering sea stacks, dizzying sandstone cliffs and its exposure to the wild tides and fearsome currents of the Pentland Firth, it is a rugged, untamed landscape.

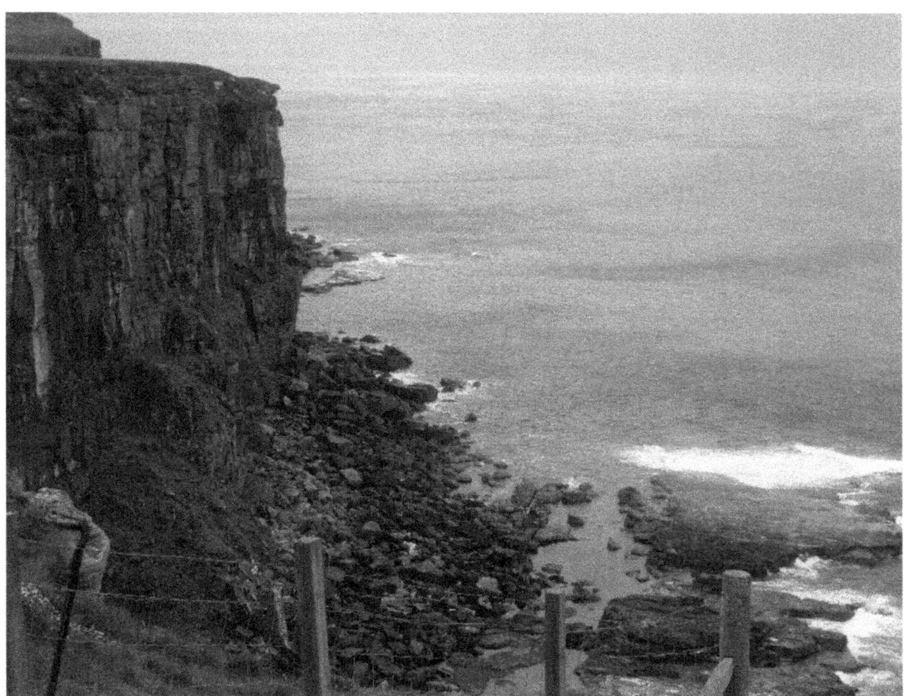

Old Red Sandstone Rocks, Dunnet Head

Dunnet Head is also an RSPB reserve and is home to kittiwakes, fulmars, razorbills, puffins and guillemots, including the now protected black guillemot. Their black plumage, white wing streak and red feet make it easy to distinguish these striking looking auks from their more frequently seen cousins, who have much whiter plumage.

In our sailing days Mike and I made up our own name for these appealing little auks: flappalots. Because that's what they do. I remember sitting on the deck of the yacht one day watching them, their wings beating furiously as they skimmed only just clear of the wave crests, and being inspired to come up with this daft little ditty:

It's easy to spot a guillemot, because they flap their wings a lot.

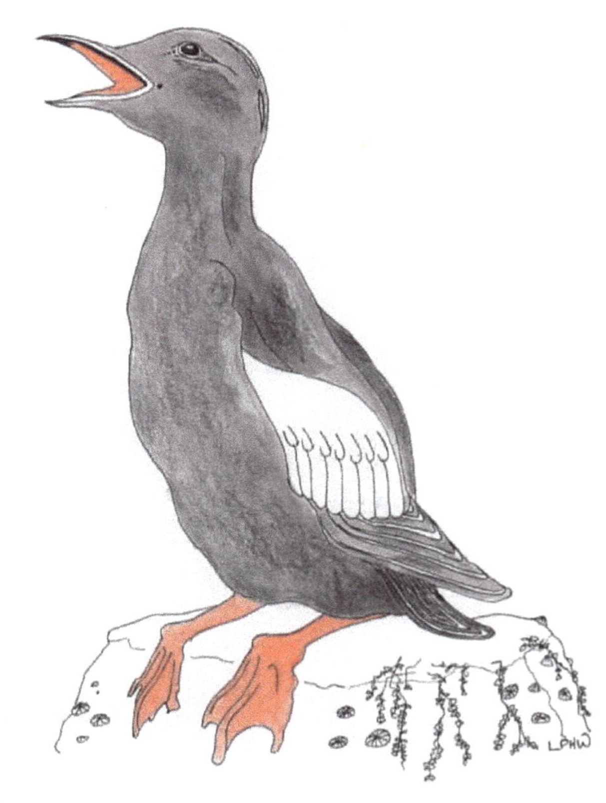

Black guillemot

The most noticeable man-made feature here is Robert Stephenson's lighthouse. Built in 1831 at a latitude of 58º40' 29" it marks the most northerly point of the Scottish mainland.

The tower stands only 20 metres high but at an elevation of 105 metres above sea level it lights the way for vessels as far offshore as 23 nautical miles – the equivalent of around 26 land miles. Not to be confused with the Scottish Robert Louis Stevenson, author of *Treasure Island,* this Stephenson was an early civil and railway engineer who was born nearly half a century before his namesake. He was respected, along with Isambard Kingdom

Brunel and fellow Scot Thomas Telford as being among the great engineers of the 19th century.

Not far from the lighthouse are the remains of some World War ll fortifications that were built to protect Scapa Flow, which was Britain's main naval base during both World Wars. A sheltered body of water in the Orkney Islands, it was chosen for that role because of its remoteness from Germany. A thousand years before that, its waters also provided safe anchorages for Viking longboats. Nowadays, it is arguably the northern hemisphere's most popular scuba location for deep wreck divers who travel from all over the world to explore more than 50 relics of the German fleet.

From Dunnet Head it was a short drive to Thurso, birthplace of the founder of the Boys Brigade, Sir William Alexander Smith, and then on to Bighouse, where we parked for the night on an elevated lay-by overlooking the River Halladale. A renowned salmon river, it attracts anglers to the traditional lodge at the settlement of Bighouse, a mile and a half down the lane from our lay-by.

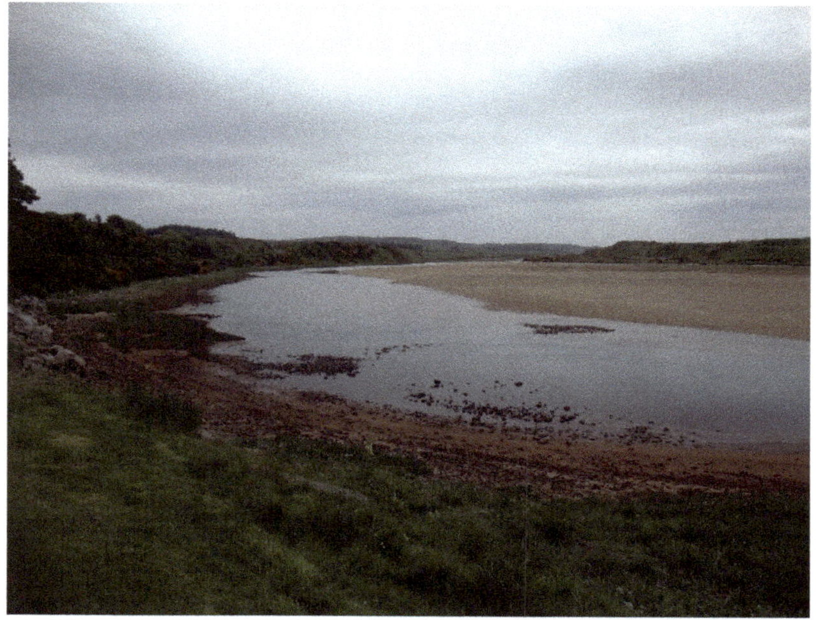

The River Halladale

Built in 1765 the eponymous mansion is the former home of the Bighouse and Sandwood chieftains of Clan Mackay. These days the house and estate provide the perfect setting for fishing, stalking, shooting and other country pursuits, bounded on one side by the sea at Melvich Beach and on the other the distant hills of the Northwest Highlands.

It's a quiet and serene spot that attracts a variety of wild birds. We had a walk down the lane and strolled along the riverbank, where we saw curlew, grey heron, common tern, stonechat, oyster catchers and lapwings.

Later, the trill of the curlews and the call of a cuckoo was the last thing we heard as we dropped off to sleep in broad daylight – night comes late in the Scottish Highlands, and dawn comes early.

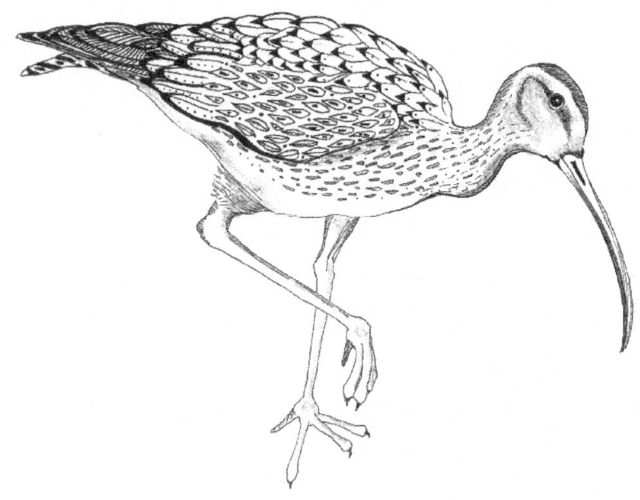

Today's mileage: 88

Ceannabienne

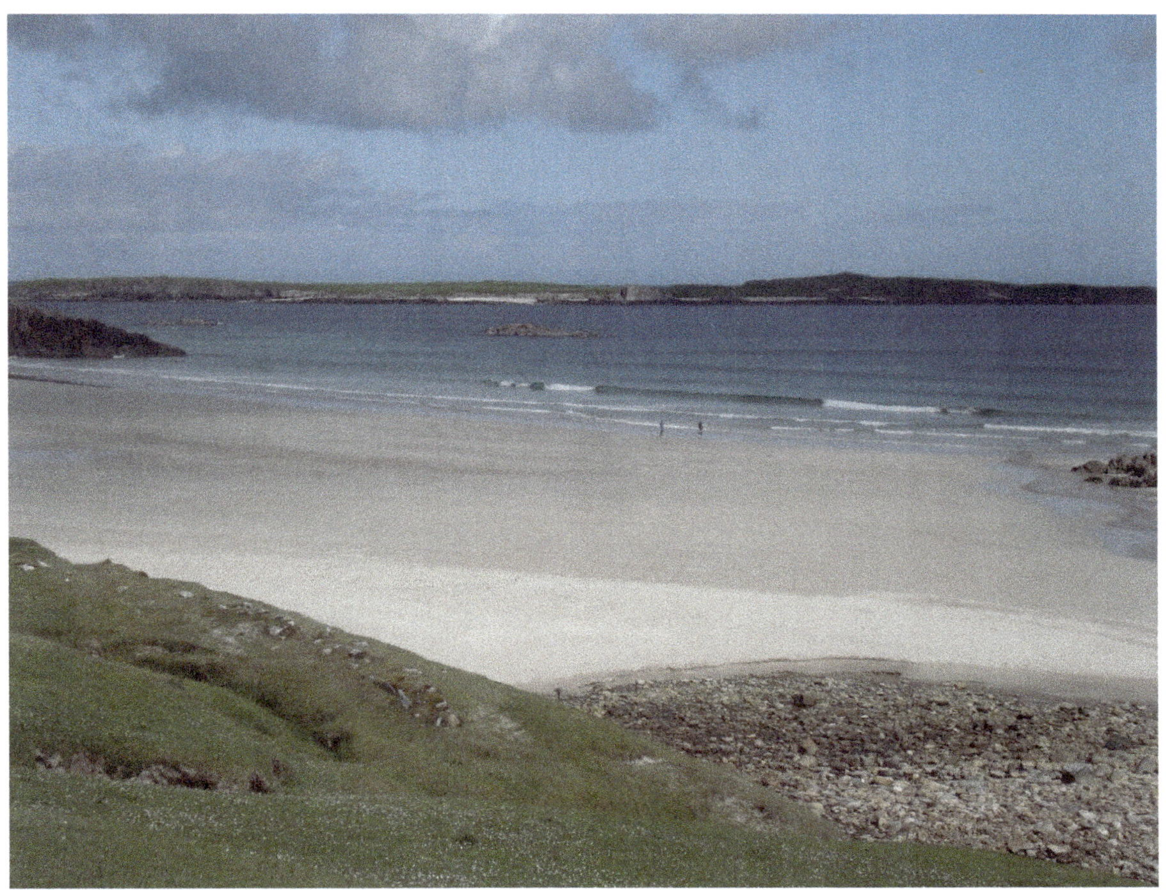

Friday, 2nd June

At a guess, where would you say the picture on the previous page was taken? Seychelles? Caribbean? Mediterranean? Wrong! It's Ceannabienne (no, I don't know how to pronounce it either), on Scotland's most northerly coastline and where we are wild camping for the night.

Woken by cuckoos at 5am, we made an early start from Bighouse and continued on the NC500 route. It rained during the night but the clouds were clearing as we left, with blue skies and sunshine beginning to break through.

Our route took us past the dunes and sandy beaches that are typical of Scotland's east coast but are also prevalent up here in the north, through peaty moorland and down into the green pasture land of Armadale. This is a tiny village with a shrinking human population and grazing sheep on the verges.

Then it was back into the rock-strewn moorland, with the hills becoming higher and craggier and every bend opening up a never-ending vista of cloud-topped mountains fading into the distance.

After a while the A836 narrowed into a single-track road with well-marked passing places just about wide enough for everyone to squeeze through. It makes for interesting driving, especially when a lorry, coach or convoy of motorhomes approaches. We have never before been on an A-class road this narrow – it's just the width of a bus, with a few inches to spare on each side.

At the quaintly named village of Bettyhill we got a glimpse of a heavenly 'tropical' beach and at Borgie, a hamlet named for the river on whose estuary it stands, the road took us through a wooded valley and on to the Kyle of Tongue, another place we'd visited on our round-Scotland sailing trip. Unfortunately, appealing as it was from the road, we were unable to find places to stop to catch it all on camera.

The road took us down one side of Loch Eriboll and up the other. Had there been a bridge we'd have been across in no time but as there isn't it took 40 minutes. But we have no complaints as the scenery was stunning. I must admit to feeling a bit guilty at Mike having to do all the driving while I just sat there and soaked it all up.

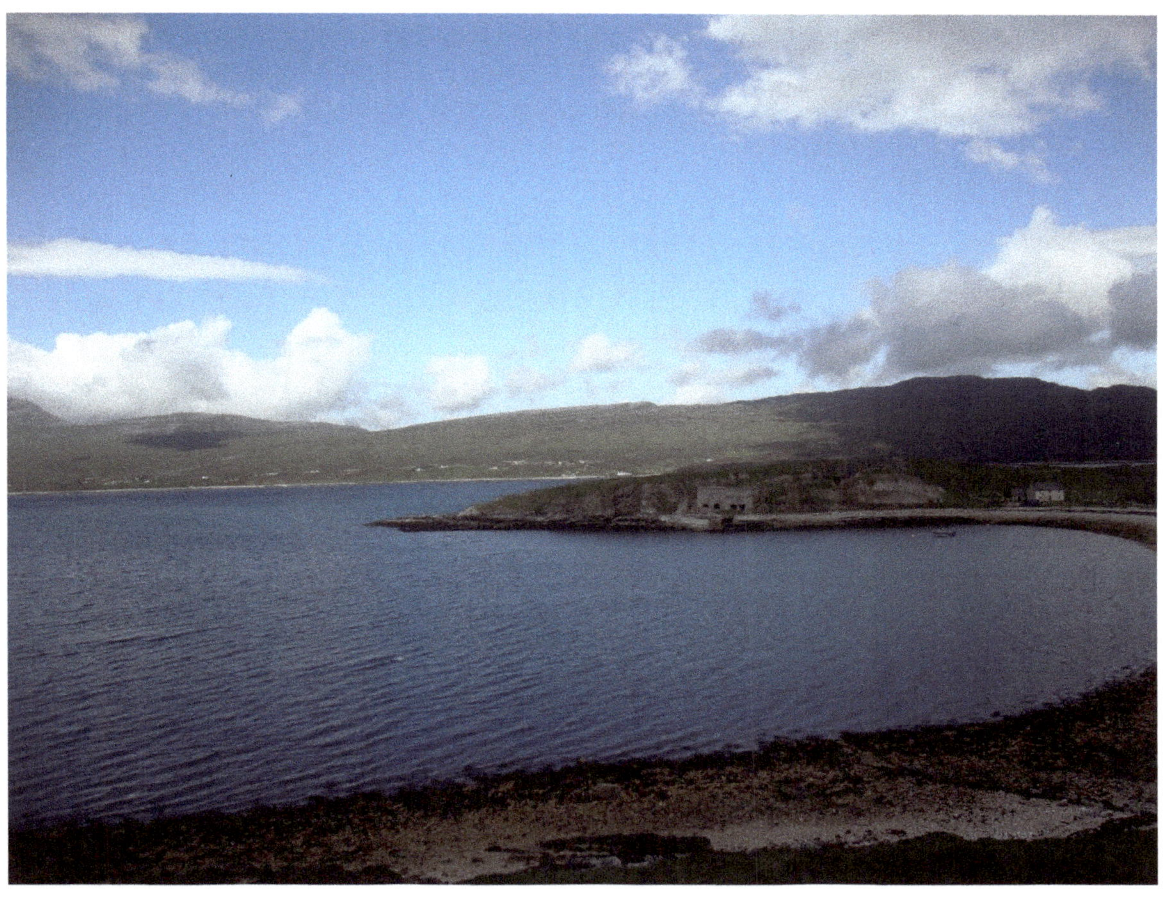

Loch Eriboll

We were also stunned when we rounded the crest of a hill at Rispond and were faced with Ceannabienne beach below us. This was definitely the place to stop for the night. I say night, but at this time of year, this far north, it doesn't get completely dark at all. We find we are still reading, with the sun still shining on the hills, at 10.30 in the evening. By midnight there's a sort of velvety twilight and by 3am it's daylight again.

A fascinating but tragic history lies behind the tranquil beauty of the Ceannabienne we see today. There is a hint in the old schoolhouse, perched high above the village, and in the traces of a long-forgotten settlement, still visible through the undulating grassland on the clifftops.

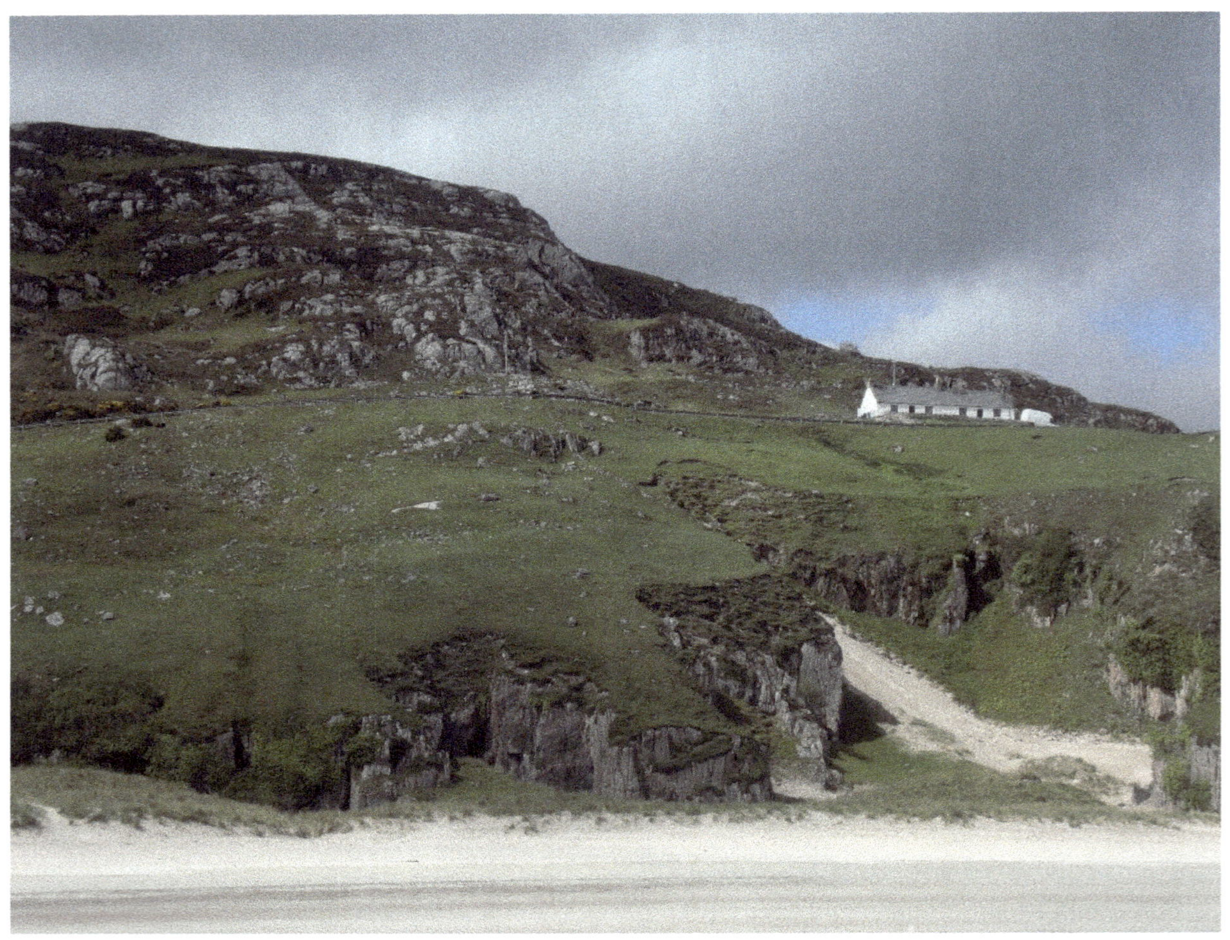

You can just make out the old schoolhouse on the hillside.

During the hundred years or so up to the middle of the 19th century, the crofters of the Highlands were forced out of their homes by wealthy landowners, who wanted to claim the land for sheep grazing. These actions, known as the Highland Clearances, not only caused great distress and hardship, but also laid the foundations for the destruction of the traditional Scottish clan system. The populations of entire villages were compelled to move out of the countryside and forsake a way of life that they had enjoyed for generations. Many, faced with homelessness and starvation, had no alternative but to migrate out of Scotland altogether to start new lives in Canada, the United States and New Zealand.

In the 1820s-40s, the old township of Ceannabienne fell victim to the scheme. Crofts were left to the mercy of the elements and the old schoolhouse on the hillside is the only complete building still standing.

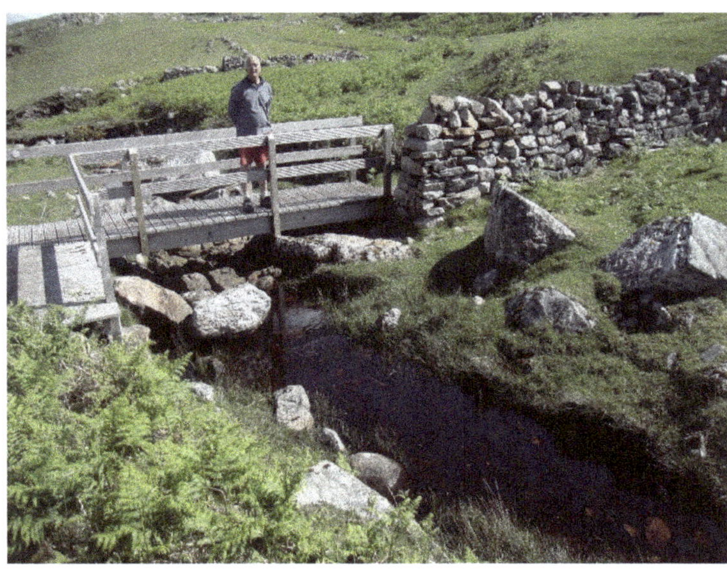

We had a walk around the remains of the crofts

These days the village enjoys Geopark status – a UNESCO project in which local people manage their landscapes, making them accessible and attractive to visitors. At Ceannabienne a grassy trail winds through what's left of the foundations of the old buildings, while well-presented information boards tell the story of the villagers' everyday lives before they had to leave.

We have visited so many wonderful places during this trip but wherever else we go I know that Ceannabienne will remain in my heart as the favourite.

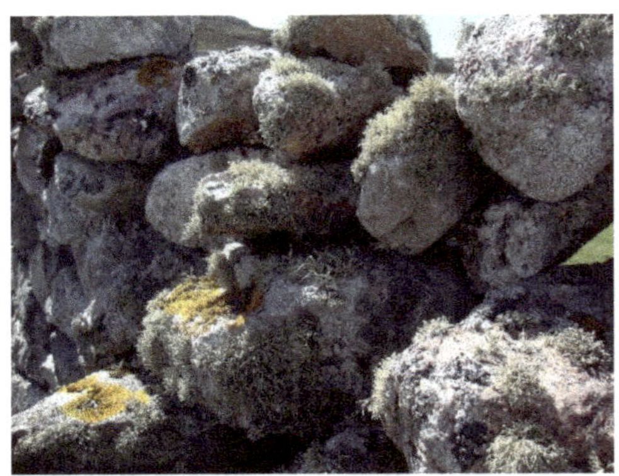

The crofters used lichen from the rocks to dye the wool from their sheep.

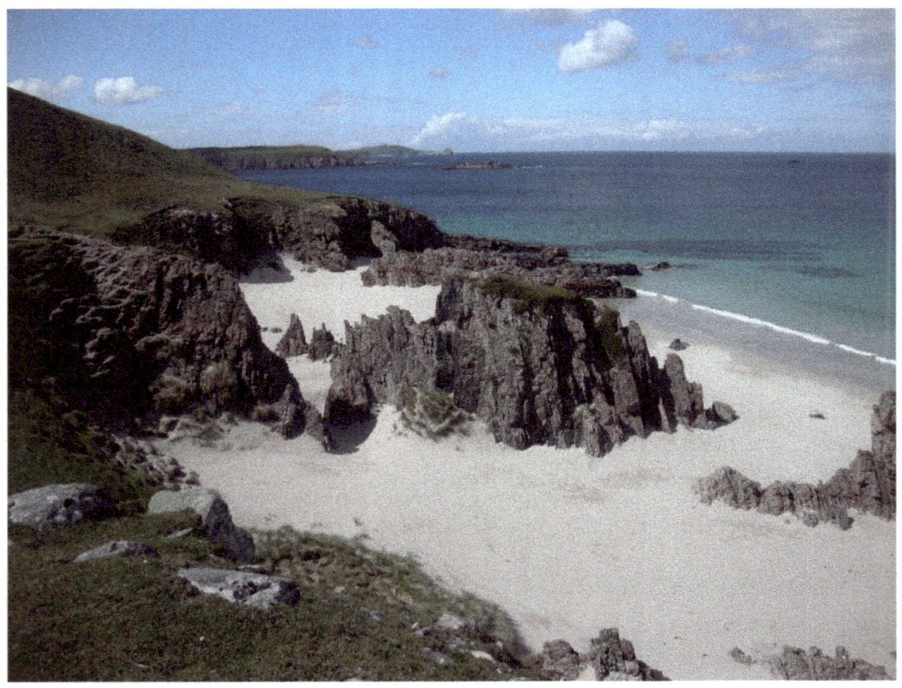

Another view of the Beach

Today's mileage: 55

Kinlochbervie and Scourie

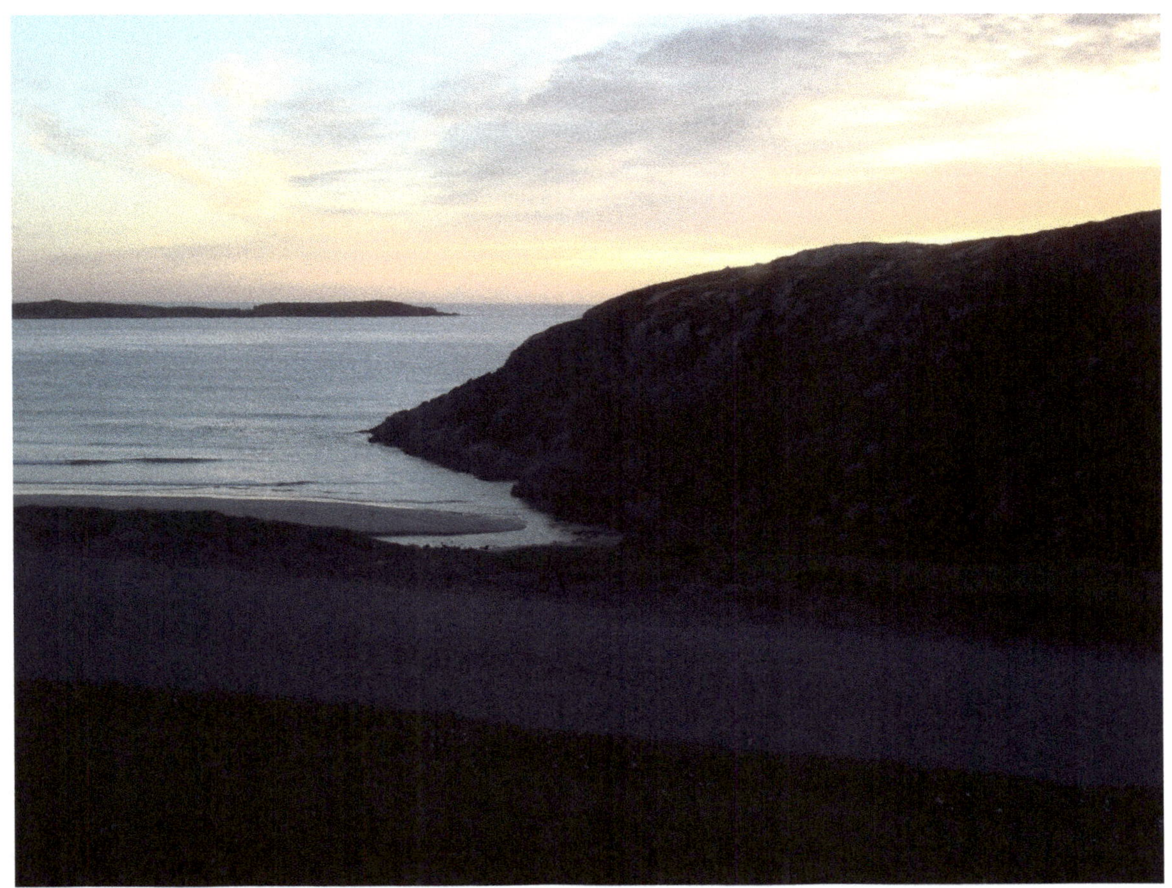

Sunrise

Saturday, 3rd June

I'm not writing much about today's trip. It's all about the natural surroundings and I think that, although my limited mastery of photography can never show the true glory of this part of Scotland, these pictures will still do a better job of it than I can with the words.

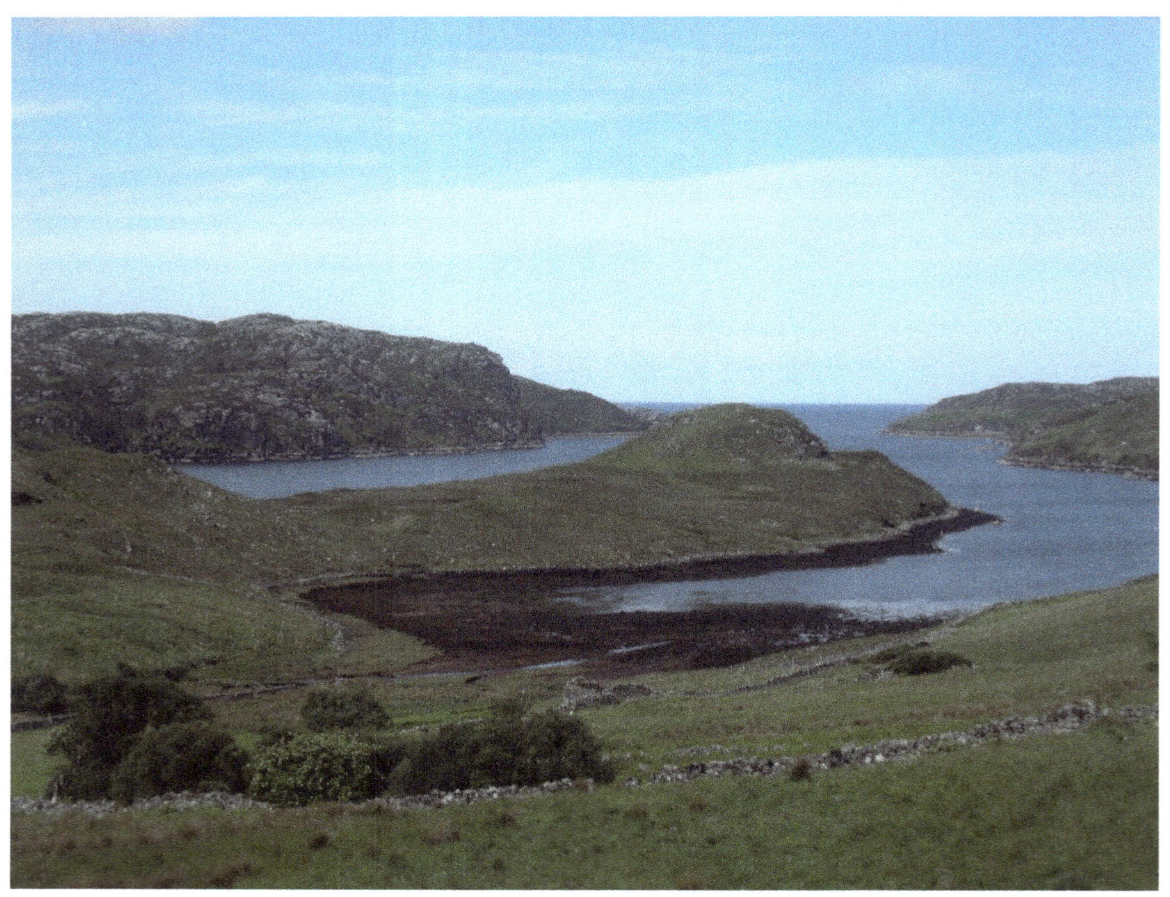

Loch Inchard

Our travels today took us from the lay-by in Ceannabienne and past the John Lennon Memorial Garden at Durness. You may wonder why John Lennon is so special to this isolated community – after all, it's a long way from Liverpool – but it turns out that as a child he used to holiday here with his cousins and later, in 1969, he made a return visit with his son Julian, his wife Yoko Ono and her daughter Kyoko.

From Durness we soon rounded the southern side of Cape Wrath, ending the day at Scourie Camping and Caravan Site. We debated whether to make a short detour to visit the Cape, mainland Britain's most north-westerly point, but access is only by foot-ferry and then mini-bus. The advertised cost for the two of us was £38 for just 50 minutes exploring time before making the return trip. So we opted against it. We did think about driving to the bus stop and then setting off on our bikes but . . . 20 miles each way on mountain roads with no real preparation? No way!

Our single-track A-class road stretched and wound its way far into the distance – at one point what we thought was a sheep track curling around the hillside was actually the A838! This is a wild and remote part of Scotland and Mike summed it up perfectly: 'It's a great wilderness of nothing'.

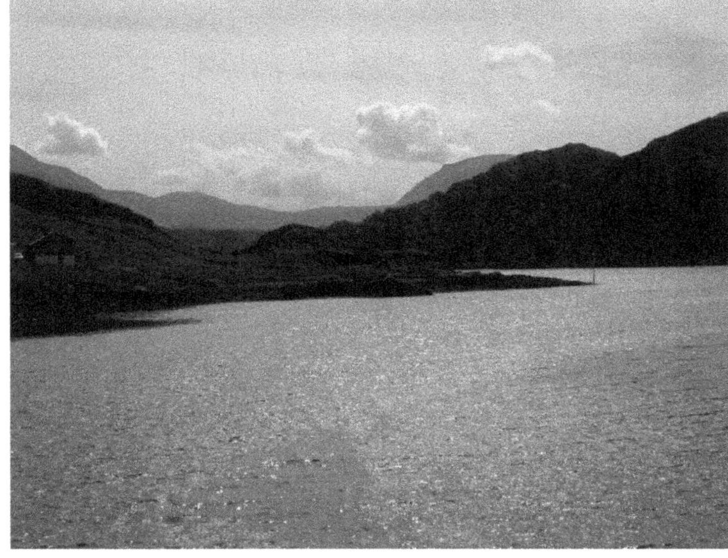

Kinlochbervie

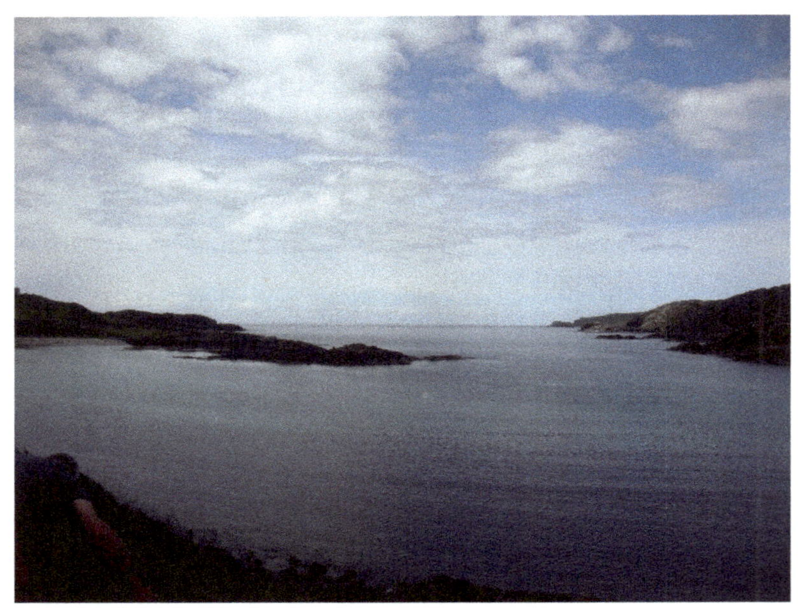

The view from our pitch for the night at Scourie

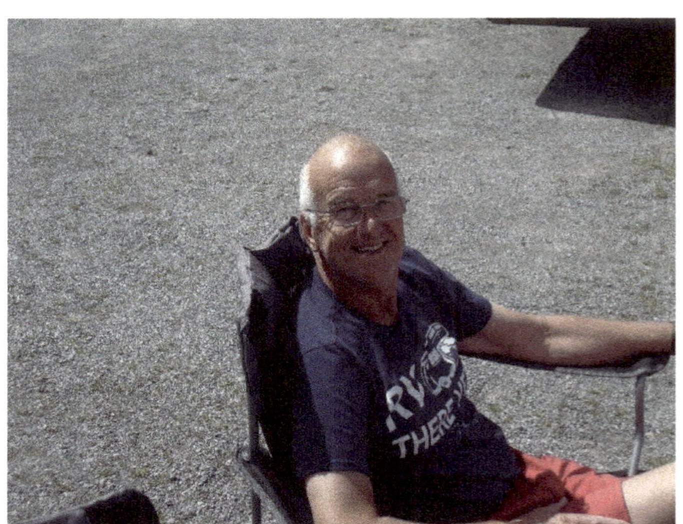

Time to relax

Today's mileage: 39

Sutherland

Scourie to Ardvreck Castle

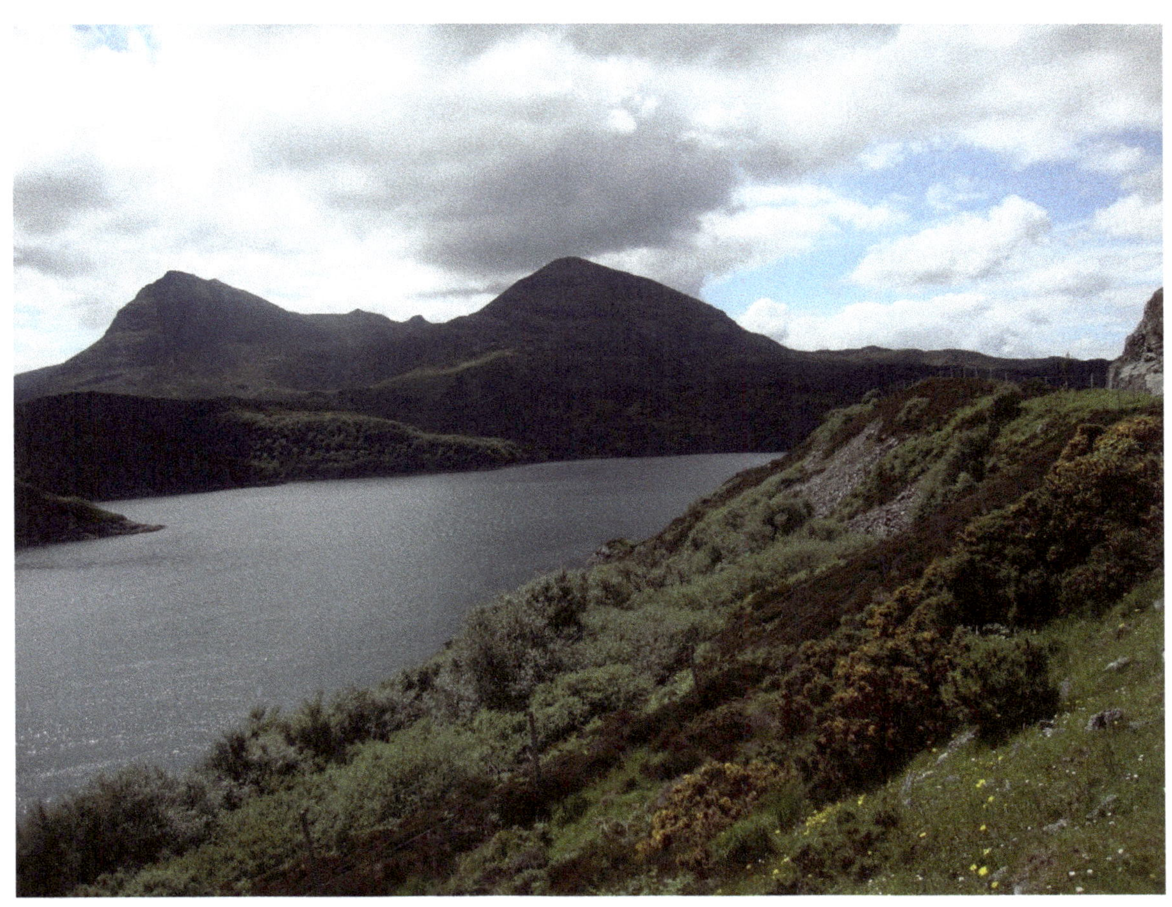

Loch a' Chairn Bhain

Sunday, 4th June

Today we tackled part of the Wester Ross Coastal Trail. I say 'we' but actually it was Mike that tackled it. I just sat there enjoying the ride and snapping away with the camera while he coped with the twists, turns, steep hills, hidden dips, blind bends and oncoming traffic on a narrow, single track through the mountains. But he's a good, courteous and highly qualified driver (thank you Thames Valley Police for the brilliant advanced driver training you gave him) and he coped admirably.

We'd left Scourie around midday and joined the trail on the B869 half an hour later, after crossing the elegantly curved and award winning Kylesku bridge over Loch a' Chairn Bhain (Gaelic for White Cairn Rock). The loch is a sea inlet that reaches a depth of more than a hundred metres in places and was the site of a submarine training base during World War ll.

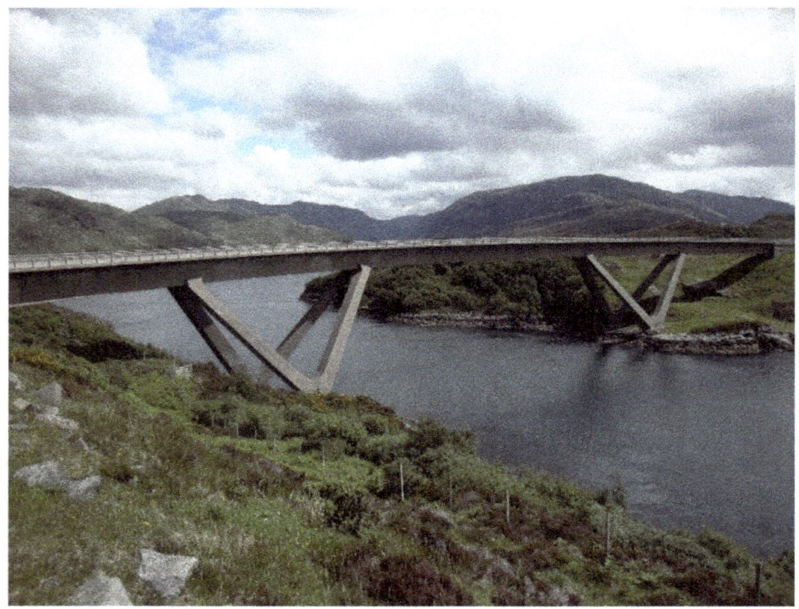

The bridge over Loch a'Chairn Bhain

At the point where you join the B-road there is a sign warning it is not suitable for coaches and caravans. This was a little daunting, but as it doesn't say anything about motorhomes we reckoned we'd probably be fine.

It's a fabulous drive through towering mountains and although the road is only just wide enough for one vehicle there are frequent and well-signed passing places. We were impressed with the good standard of driving and level of courtesy from everyone on the route, which includes inclines of 1:25 and 1:17, plus a sign warning of 'pigs, piglets, lambs and sheep on road'. We didn't see any pigs but we did see what we are fairly sure was a golden eagle soaring above the hillside in the distance. And we loved having to stop at one point when a red deer stag and two hinds skipped off a rocky overhang and danced into the road to get to the other side.

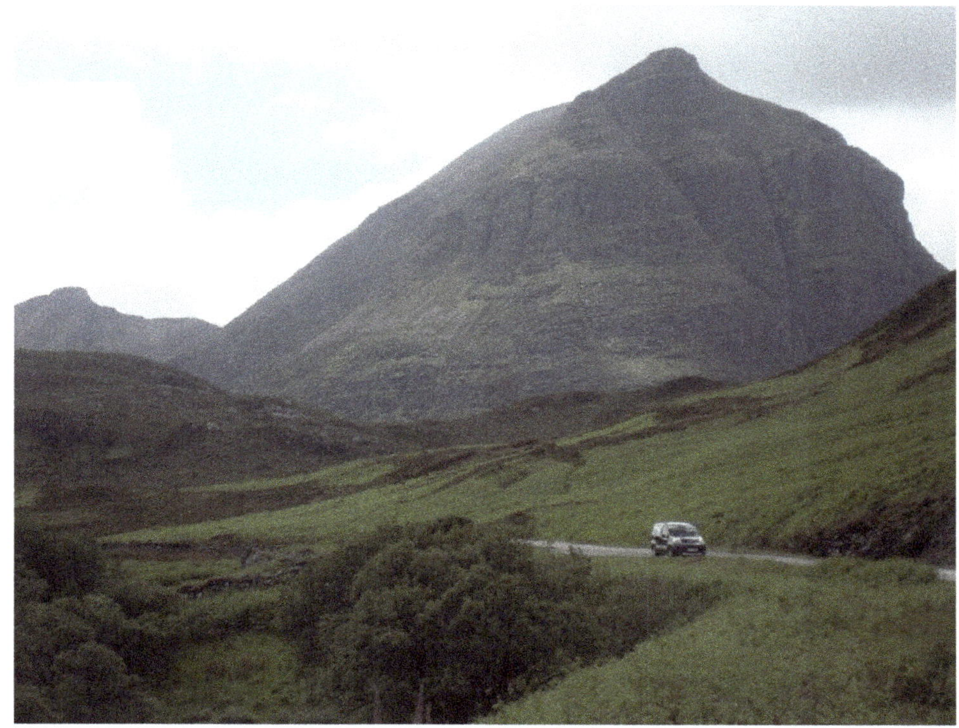

Mountain scenery

By one forty-five we were both ready for lunch. Mike needed a break after what had been a tough drive – and we were still only half way round the trail. Conveniently for us, the village of Drumbeg had a big layby looking over Edrachillis Bay, as well as *The Best Village Shop in Scotland* and a welcome committee of enthusiastic midges.

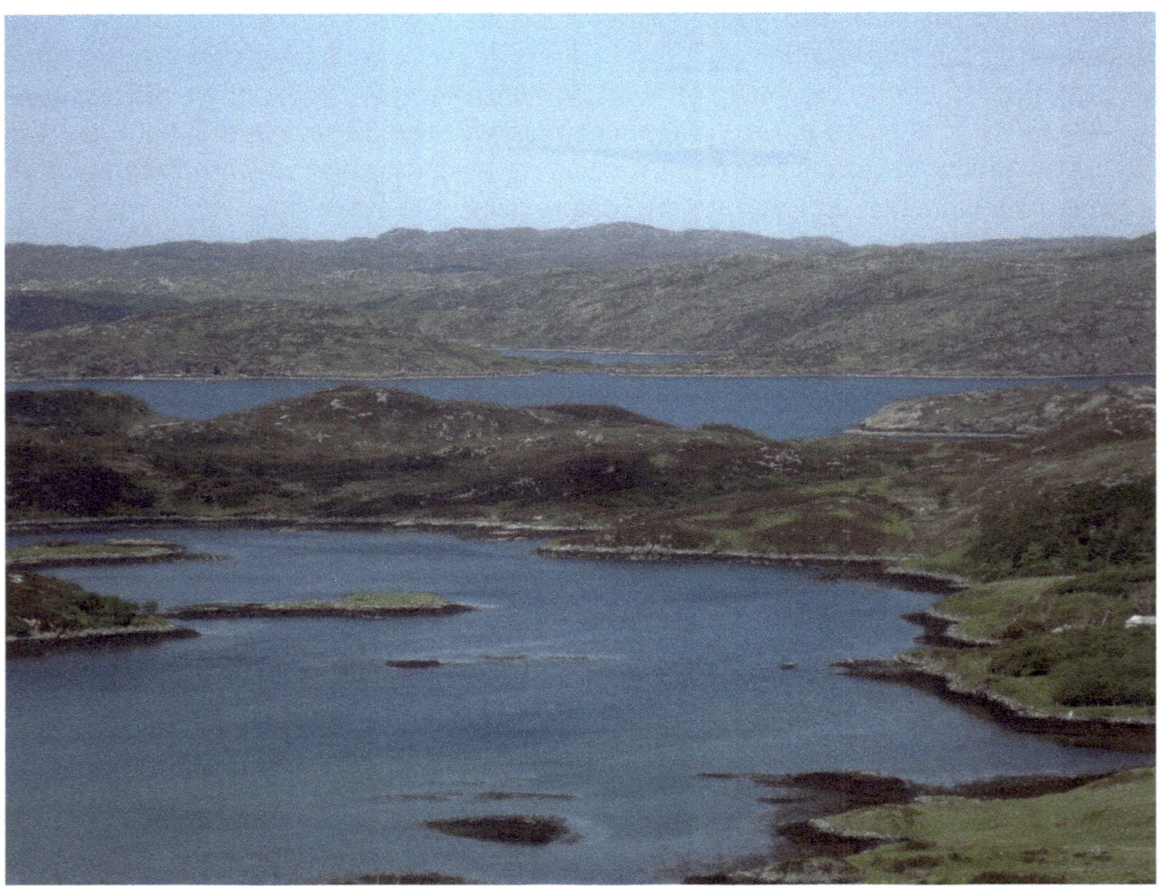

Edrachillis Bay and some of its 35 islands, seen from Drumbeg

On our way again we came to a sharp narrow corner in a gorge of sheer rock at the top of a steep hill, with no view of the road ahead and no way of telling if anything was coming towards us. 'I could get out and walk ahead waving a red flag,' I offered helpfully. But instead, Mike leaned on Bessie's hooter – and it's just as well he did. There was another car coming around the corner towards us!

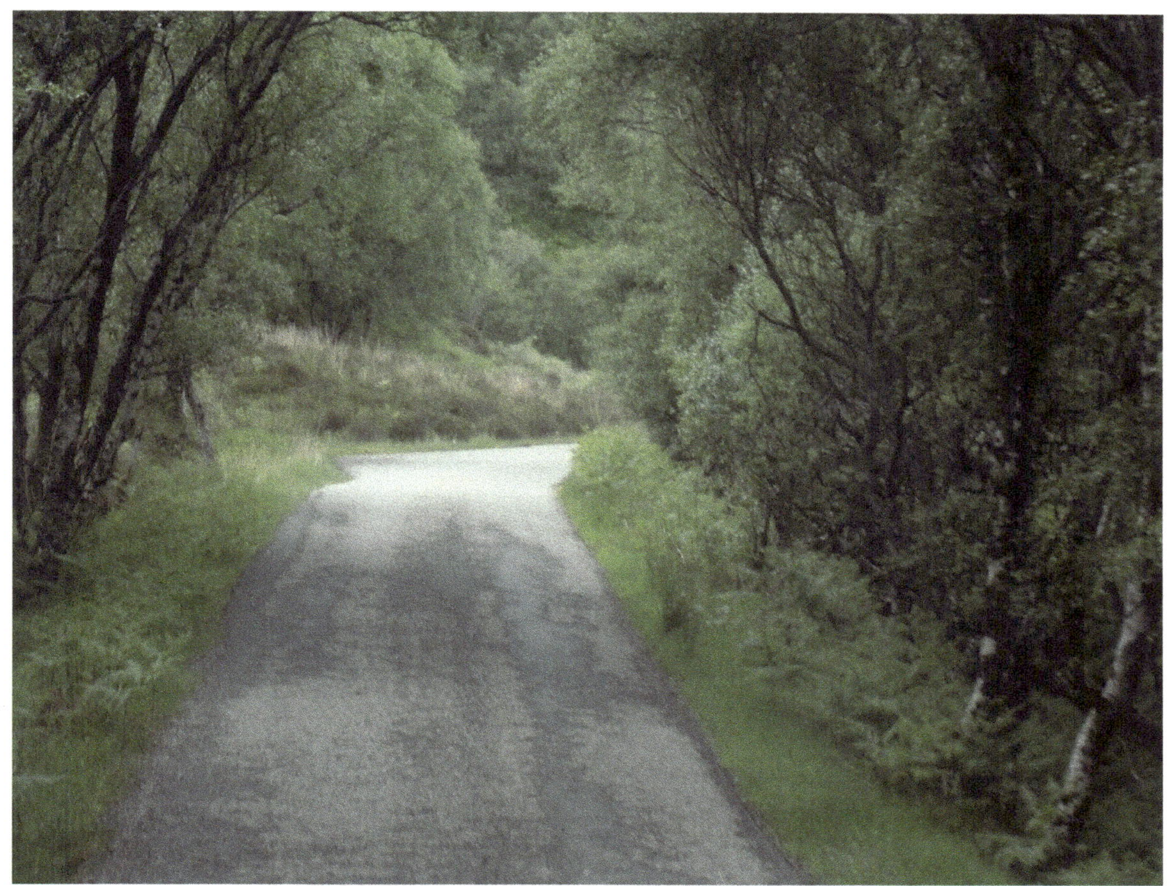

Narrow road

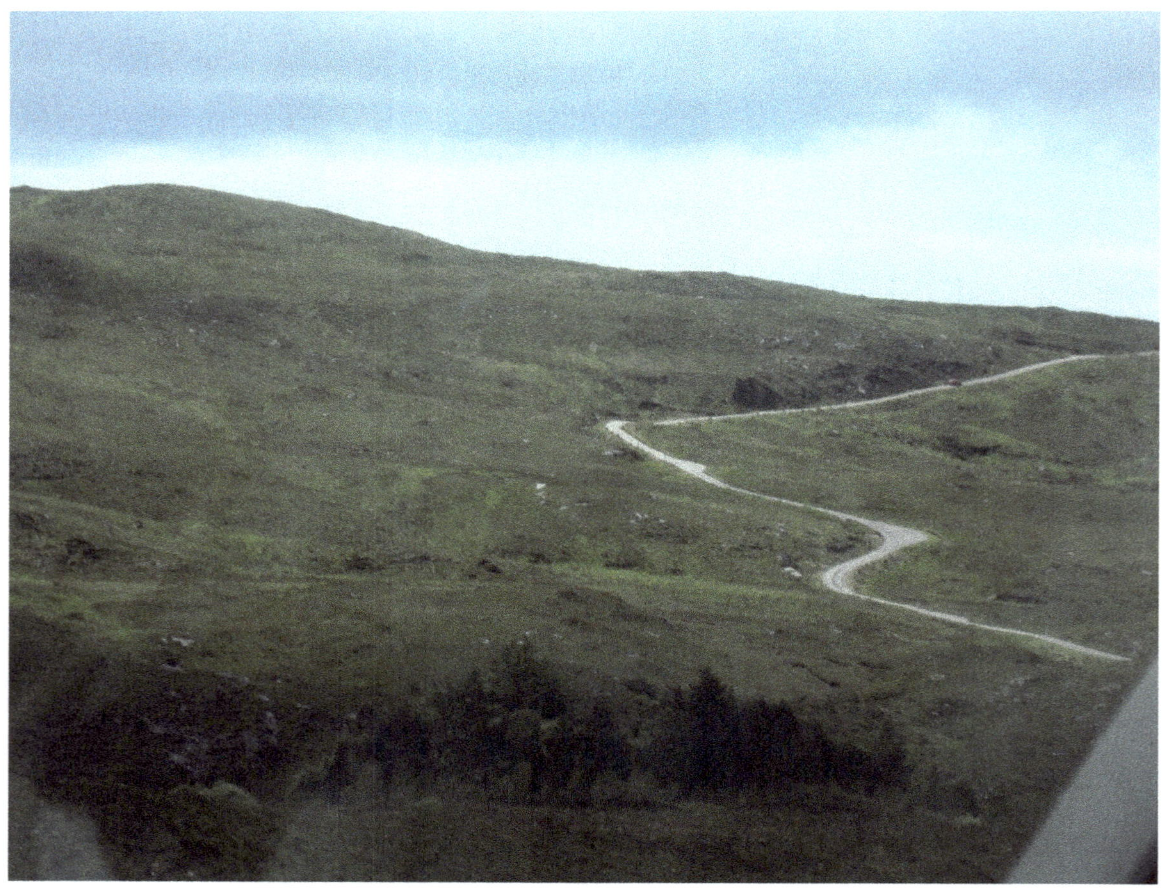

The road ahead

By the time we reached the end of the 23-mile route Mike had sore eyes and was exhausted.

'How was it for you,' I asked in in my best journalistic interviewing mode. He thought about it for a minute. 'It was good but mentally tiring because of having to concentrate all the time, and stressful because of all the blind bends and blind hill crests. I'm pleased to have done it because it was a challenge and we saw lovely scenery and red deer but I don't know that I'd want to do it again.'

It was mid-afternoon when we pulled into a lay-by on the edge of Loch Assynt for our overnight stop. We used the spirit level in the van to check how much of a slope we were on and to see if we needed to put the wheels on ramps to even things up. Here the ground was perfectly level (always a bonus) and a great vantage point for both the loch and the ruined Ardvreck Castle. Even if you aren't particularly interested in the past, you can't help but absorb Scotland's history and I continue to find the vast, bleak mountainsides make it so easy to picture the Highlanders, the way they lived and the battles they fought, both among the warring clans and with the enemy from over the border.

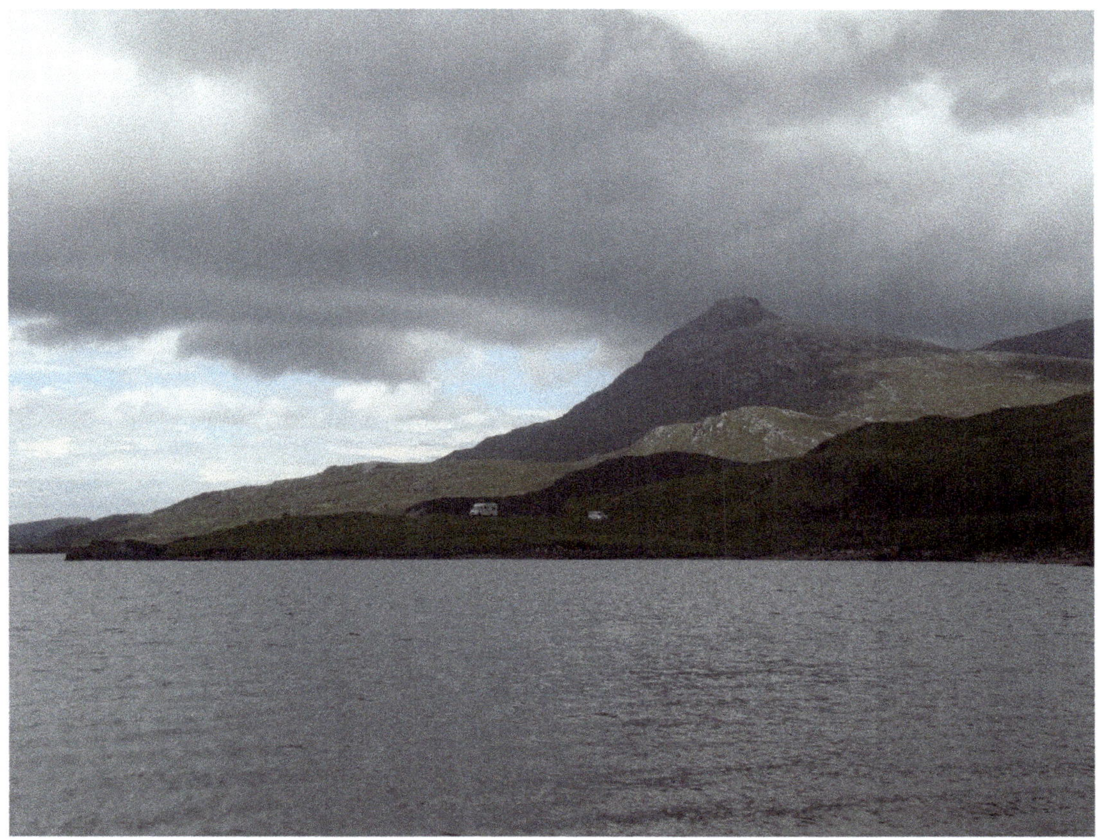

Our layby. Bessie is the white dot, centre left.

The surface of the loch was grey and still, reflecting the sky, the clouds and the mountains but we were given a stark reminder that these lochs are not always as amenable as this one looked today. Down by the water's edge we came across a wooden bench. It is a memorial to a young man who drowned in Loch Assynt on a July evening in 1985. Craig Hutchison, who was only 20, had been enjoying a camping and fishing trip with friends. He went for a swim but got into difficulties as he tried to get back to shore. He never made it. This is such a quiet and isolated place yet the bench still looks as good as new. I wondered if the seat had been installed only a couple of years ago, to mark the 30th anniversary of the drowning, or whether it has been lovingly maintained over the years. In either case, it's a moving tribute to a young life lost.

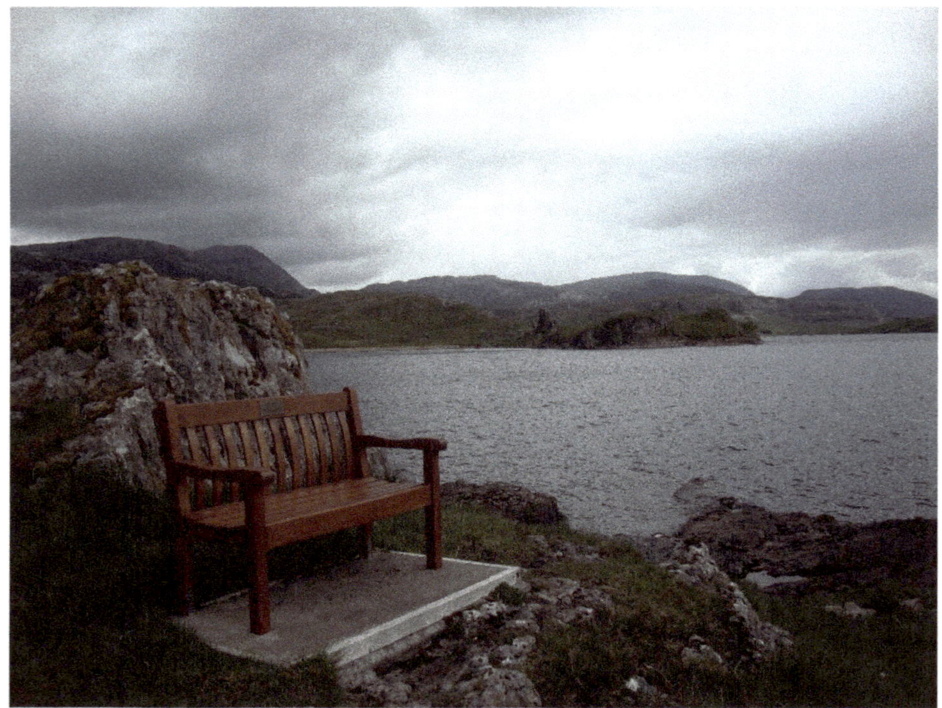

Memorial seat erected by the family of Craig Hutchison

The Castle was an easy walk from our lay-by but when the waters of the loch rise, they form a natural moat and cut the castle off from the mainland. Dating from the 15th century, the once imposing structure is now little more than a fragile and crumbling ruin. Despite, or maybe because of that, it is still eye-catching and atmospheric, regardless of the notices warning visitors of falling masonry. The remaining tower and vaulted basements are pretty much all that is left of the castle today, although it must have been an imposing structure in its day, with a defensive wall, a walled garden and formal courtyard. You can still see remains of the foundations poking up through the grass.

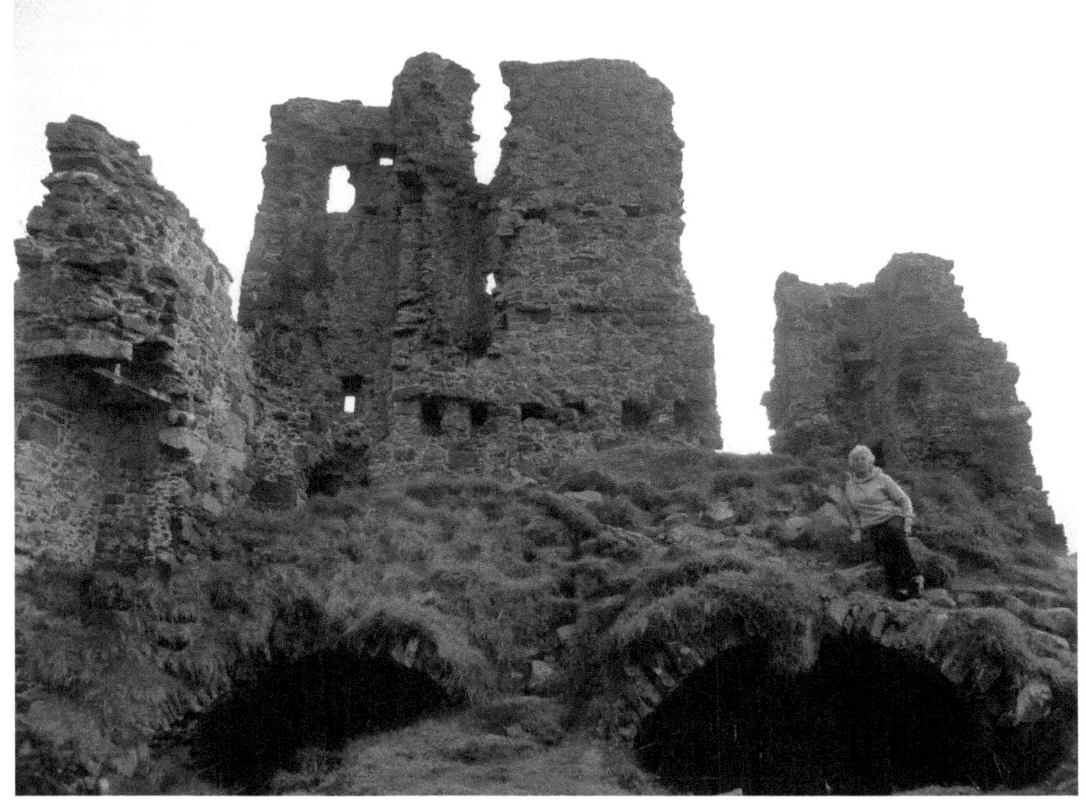

Ardvreck Castle tower, vaults . . . and visitor

Ardvreck has a fascinating, if turbulent and bloody, history. It was built by the Clan MacLeod, who had already owned Assynt and huge stretches of the surrounding area since the 13th century. In 1650 the Laird of Assynt captured the royalist Marquis of Montrose and held him at Ardvreck. A favourite of King Charles l of Great Britain, Montrose was regarded as an enemy and traitor in the eyes of his staunchly Presbyterian and anti-royalist fellow-countrymen. In 1637 Montrose had signed a covenant promising to defend the Scottish religion against Charles's attempts to impose Anglicanism. Despite this, he led his army to a series of victories for the king, against the anti-royalists, during the English Civil War.

After his capture he was sent off to Edinburgh, where he was hung, drawn and quartered at the age of 38.

Years ago, I read an historical novel by Nigel Tranter entitled *The Young Montrose,* about the life of this youthful and charismatic nobleman who ultimately gave his life in service to his king. I intend to reread it once I get home.

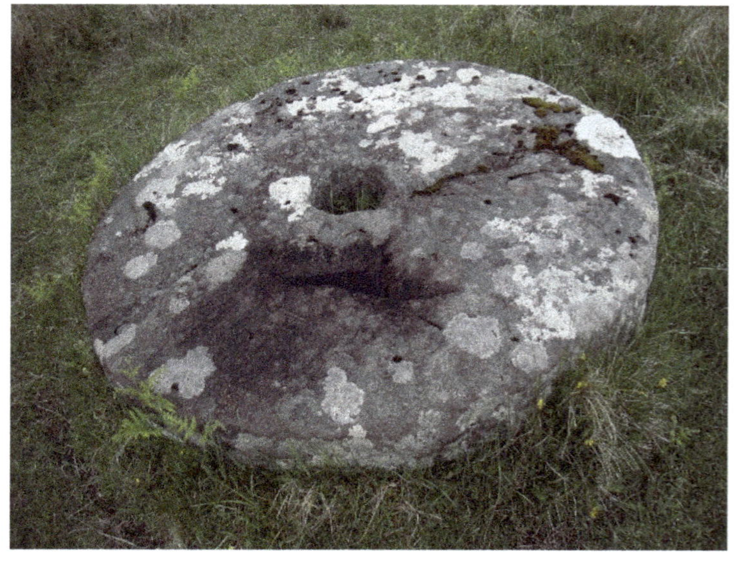

Millstone

Across the road from the castle is a waterfall and as we walked over for a closer look we came across this old millstone lying in the grass. We can only guess that the waterfall and river must have once powered a mill here, although there appears to be nothing remaining of a mill house now.

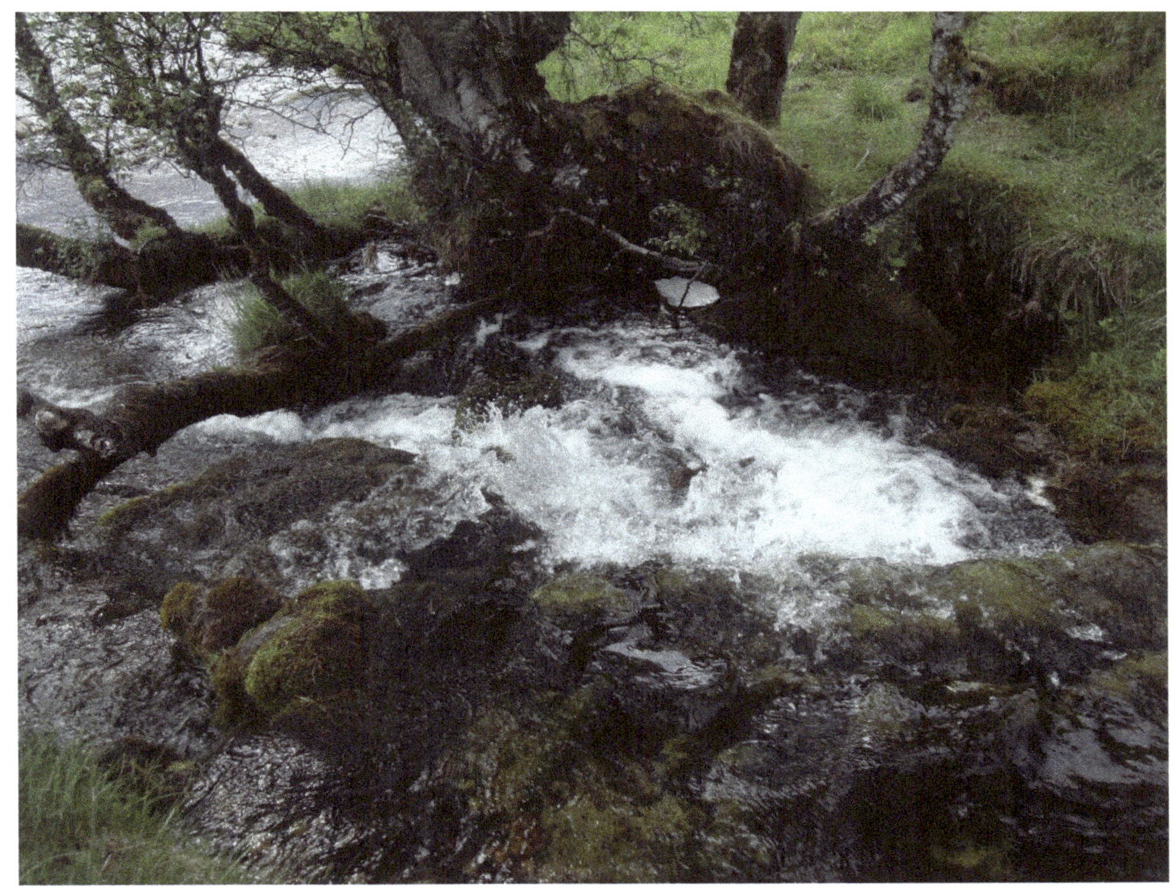

Millstream

Today's mileage: 45

Highland

Ardvrek Castle to Gairloch

Monday, 5th June

It's 4am. Mike has just woken up. 'Jack,' he whispers to me. Urgently. I panic.

'What is it? What's up?'

'Shhh. Look out of the window. Deer.'

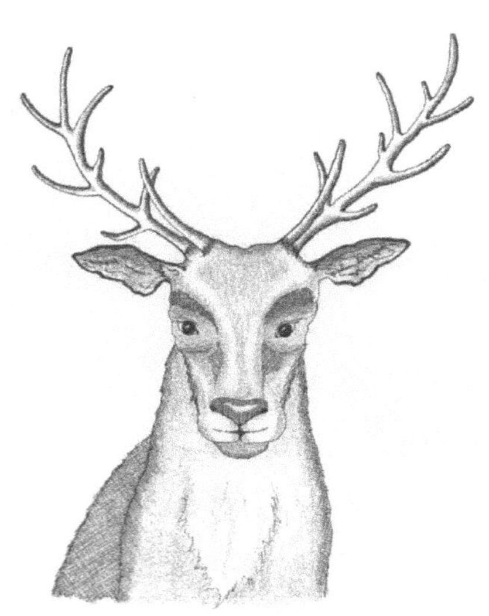

Only a few yards from Bessie's window is a magnificent red deer stag, with an impressive set of antlers. I grope for my camera, but my movements startle him and he trots off, followed by his harem of hinds. I creep out of Bessie as quietly as I can, camera in hand, but the deer have grown twitchy and they move off up the hill. I return the camera to its case and go back inside.

Back to bed for deer watching, listening to cuckoos, car counting and tea. I have said before you have to be a certain type of person to enjoy this sort of holiday, and our pleasures are simple. We sit up in bed watching the deer make their nimble-footed way up the mountainside, and we count cars. Cars are very few and far between on this road this early in the morning. Mike says when he gets to ten, he will make the tea. This doesn't happen until 7.30, by which time we can see 16 deer on the hillside and a meadow pipit hopping around in the grass beside our lay-by.

We were away by 9.15 and back on the North Coast 500, heading for Ullapool, a favourite holiday haunt of the celebrated Scottish crime writer, Val McDermid. This was another place we visited on our sailing holiday, and the scene of yet another potential disaster when we tied up overnight to a pot marker buoy in Loch Broom, in the mistaken belief it was a mooring buoy. Good job it was a calm night! It was calm in Ullapool today too, but raining so we only stayed long enough to top up Bessie with diesel and to take a couple of photos, before setting off again.

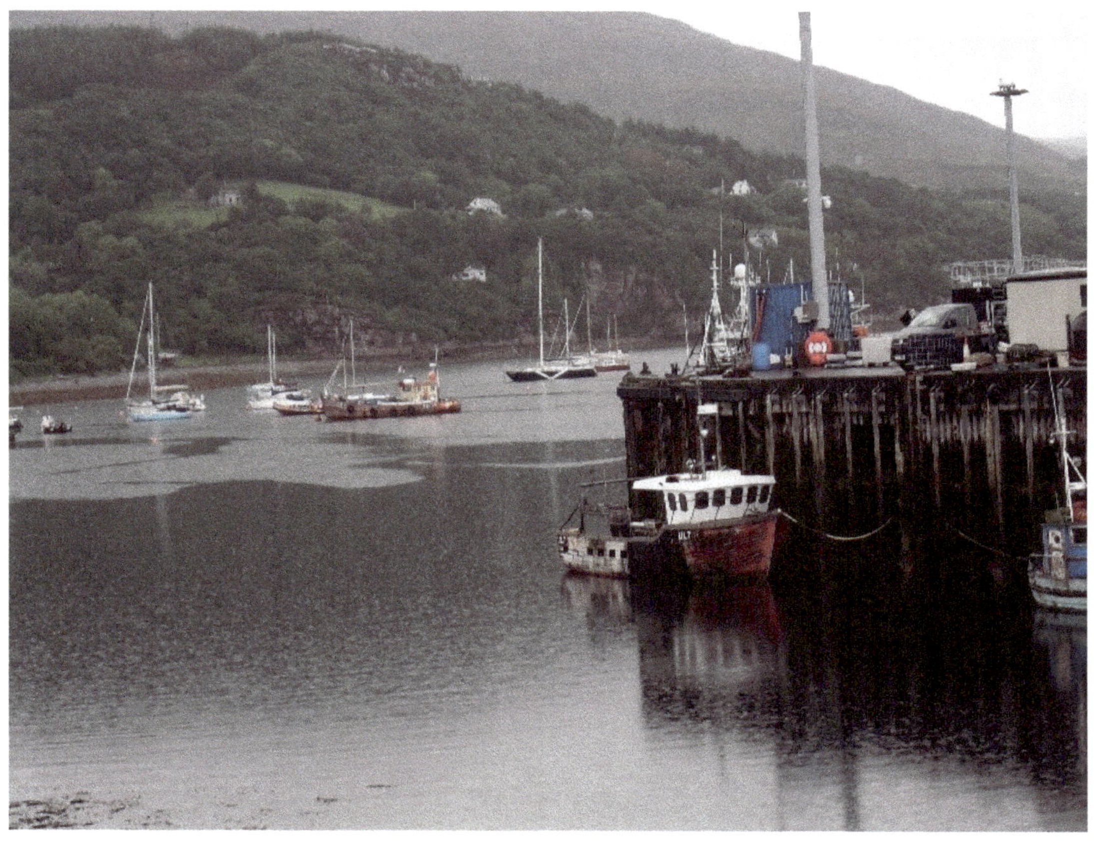

Ullapool quayside

We drove along the eastern side of Loch Broom and were delighted to see a sign warning of red squirrels for the next three and a quarter miles. We didn't see any!

Next stop was Corrieshalloch Gorge. It was a short walk down to the gorge and the 45 metre drop of the Falls of Measach, where the only word I could come up with was 'wow!' It was sensational. We crossed a suspension bridge over the gorge and continued along the rough path to a viewing platform. If you're thinking of going it's well worth a visit. But not if you suffer from vertigo!

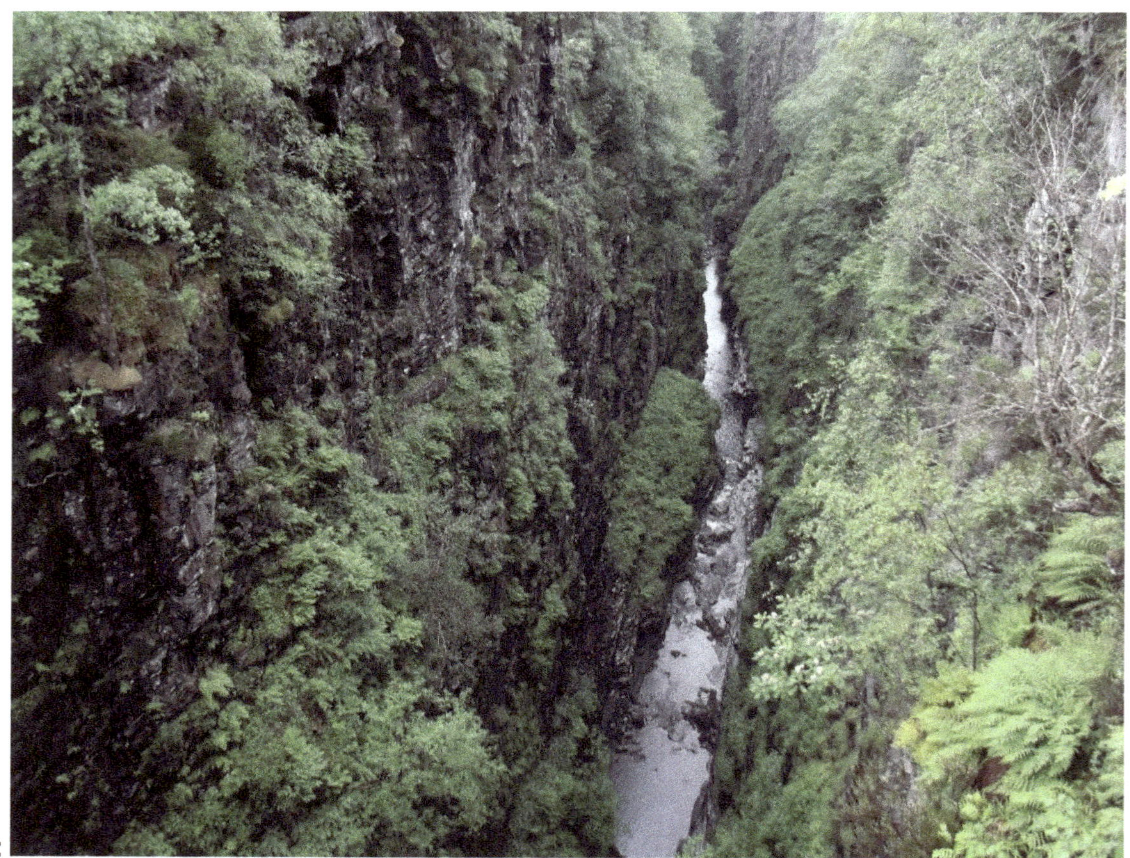

Corrieshalloch Gorge

After that the road ran more or less parallel with the western side of Little Loch Broom. We had a lunch stop at Gruinard Bay and continued round Loch Ewe to Poolewe. It's been raining all day, which is a shame because I'm sure if the sun had been shining I would be raving about the views, as usual. But it's not the same when everywhere is veiled in rain.

We ended up spending the night at Gairloch Holiday Park, with Loch Gairloch and the Isle of Skye just visible through the mist.

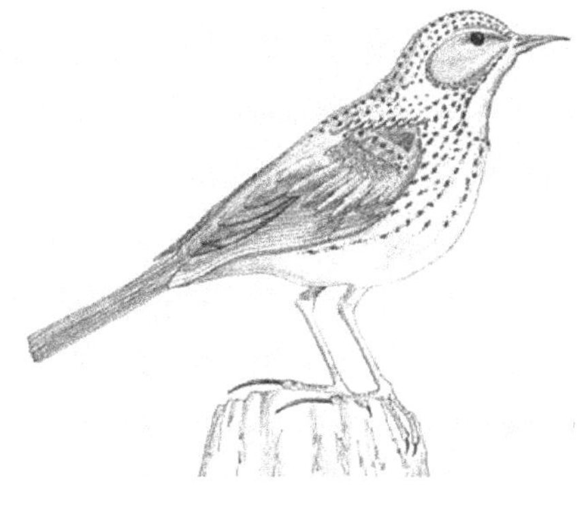

Meadow pipit

Today's mileage: 84

Gairloch to Applecross, Morvich and Kyle of Lochalsh

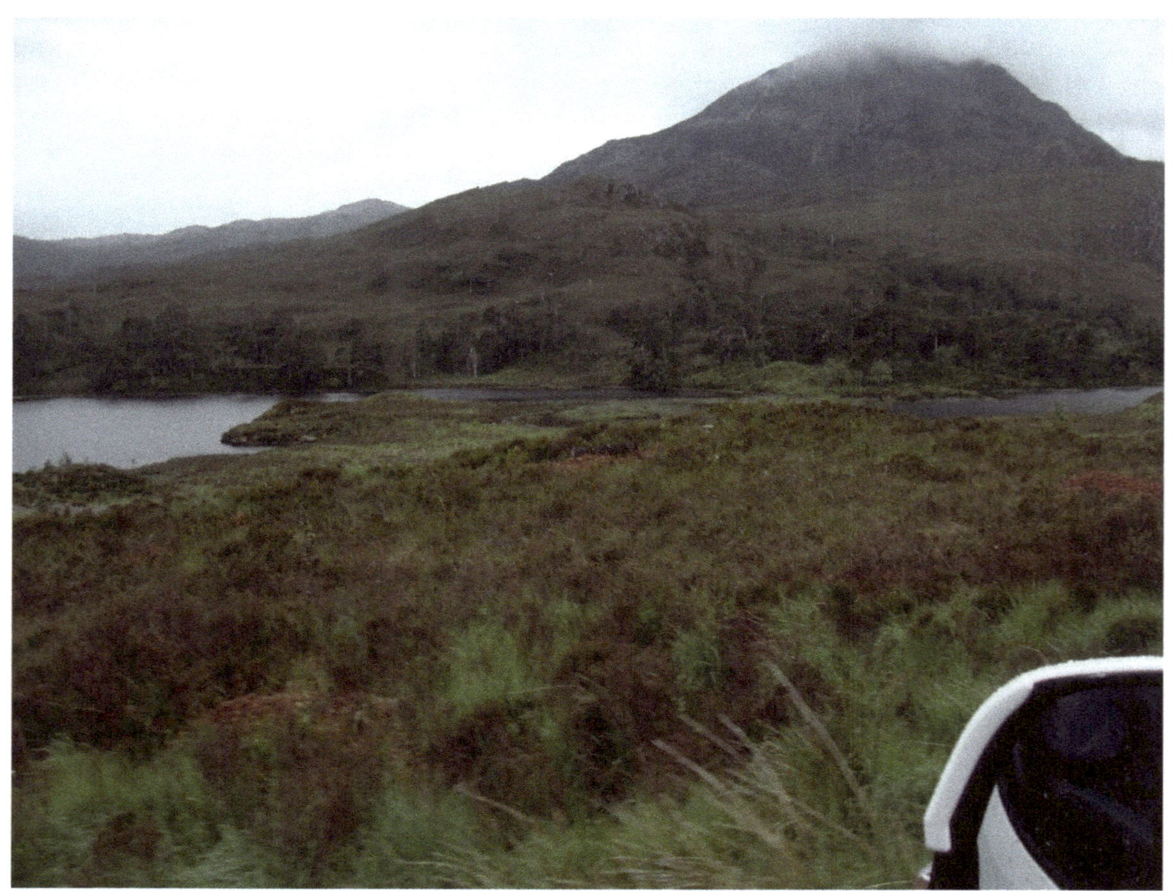

Cloud covered mountains at Loch Maree

Tuesday, 6th June

From Gairloch it's just a short drive through striking scenery on the A382, to Loch Maree. At 12 miles long and two and a half miles at its widest, this is the fourth largest freshwater loch in Scotland. It's a scenic drive round the loch, with few houses but interesting rock formations above its shores. It's as though the mountains are built from big individual stones that are stacked upon each other by a builder – like giant Lego blocks.

Next we drove through Glen Torridon (in the rain) and stopped for coffee and cake at a viewpoint overlooking Upper Loch Torridon, in Ob Gorm Mor – the Big Blue Bay. Again, it was a shame about the weather as it would have been spectacular in the sun, but as this is pretty much the first real rain we've encountered since leaving home four weeks ago, we don't have much to complain about. The peaks of Beinn Eighe mountains on our right were lost in cloud but they are pretty big at over 3,000 feet and they make an impressive sight, whatever the weather.

At 145 metres, parts of Loch Torridon are so deep that it provides a habitat for creatures such as sea pens that are usually only found out at sea. It is also home to Scottish langoustines and the site of a number of mussel farms. The mussels grow in thick clusters on submerged ropes, to keep them safe from the predatory star fish that live on the loch floor.

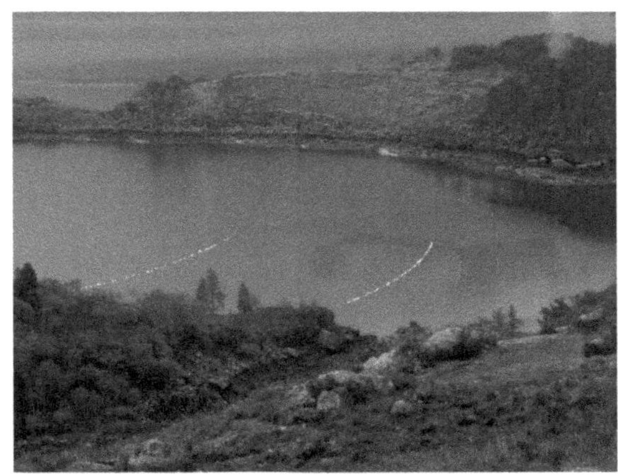

Mussel farm in Loch Torridon.

Once round the southern edge of the loch we aimed for Sheildaig and, would you believe, the start of the next leg of the Wester Ross Coastal Trail. What was that Mike said about wiggly winding roads and never again?

To begin with it was comparatively easy driving, despite the narrow single-track road and the non-stop rain. The route took us anti-clockwise on an unclassified road round the Applecross peninsular and down its west coast to Applecross village.

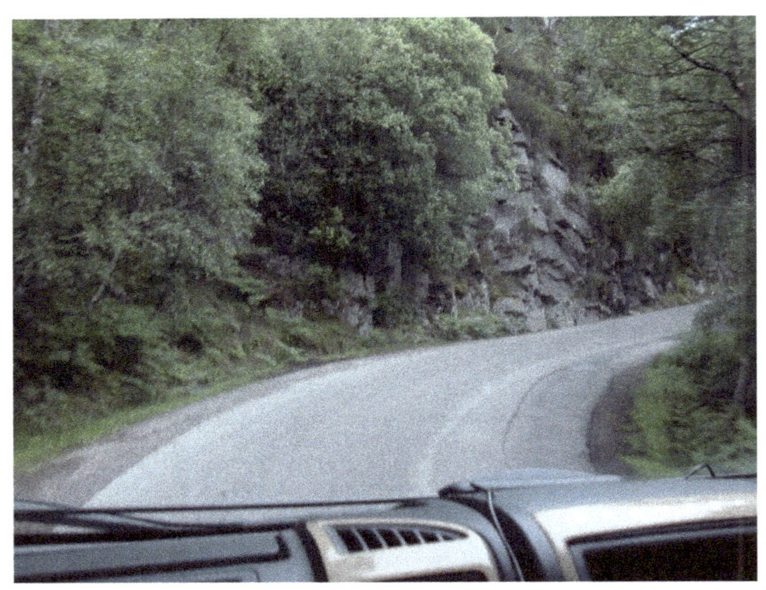

Narrow road, sharp bend

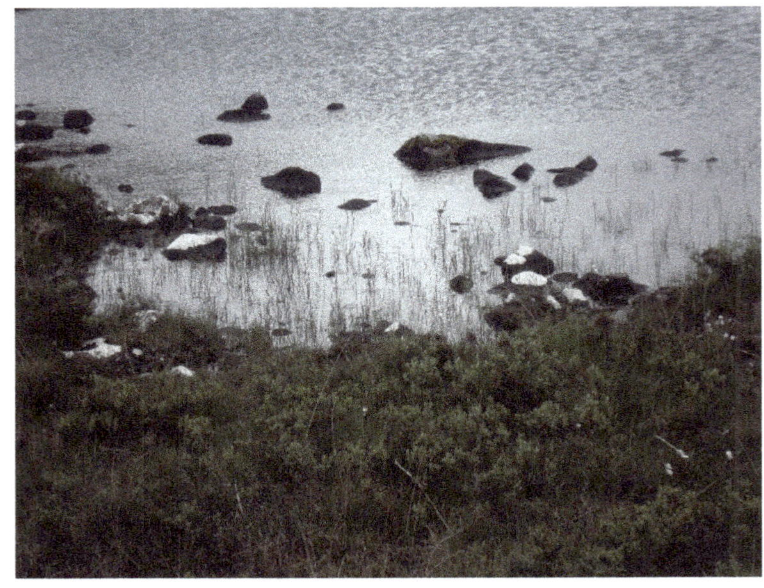

Not icing, but pure white lichen on the stones in this lochan

This is a small, remote and close-knit community looking out over the Inner Sound and the Isle of Raasay. It has one pub, a shop and lots of visitors. When we arrived, it was packed with holidaymakers, meaning that manoeuvring Bessie was more than a little tricky: the village was crowded with cars and we were unable to find a parking space. For a few minutes we watched a gaff-rigged yacht sailing in frisky conditions in the bay, but we were concerned we were causing an obstruction and didn't linger.

There are only two roads to the settlement: the way we got there and the way we left – the Bealach na Bà. Gaelic for The Pass of the Cattle, this is yet another winding, single track, this time over the mountains. Full of tight hairpin bends that form a switchback up and down the mountainside, and gradients of up to 20%, it is the steepest road in the UK.

As you leave the village there are signs warning the road is impassable in winter. We should have taken heed. On this early summer's day, it was well-nigh impassable too! To start with, as we were going up a near-vertical incline, we saw a lorry heading towards us. The driver went straight past a passing place on his side and forced Mike to reverse back down the hill until it could squeeze by.

Undaunted, we continued. We had no choice! In places the road has fallen away, leaving not much space between the carriageway and a vertical drop to the valley floor a very long way below. The terrain is bleak, it was raining heavily by this this time and as we gained height on what is one of the highest roads in Scotland at more than 2,000 feet, we entered the clouds, reducing visibility to about 50 yards.

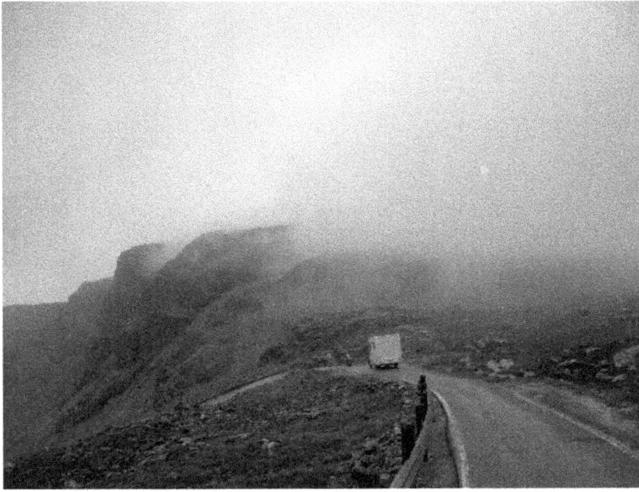

Entering the clouds - visibility got a lot worse than this ...

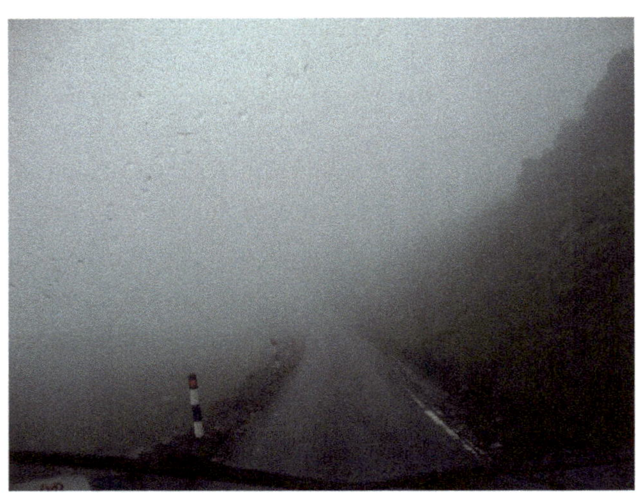

. . . but surely couldn't get any worse than this. The fallen-away verge and the sheer drop to the valley below simply added an extra frisson of anxiety!

After half an hour we started the descent, emerged from the clouds and entered a series of steep hairpin bends with towering cliffs on both sides of the road. By now we were behind another motorhome (from Switzerland, so perhaps they were used to such roads) and behind us were two Porsches. Coming up the hill in front of us was a cyclist, followed by a lorry.

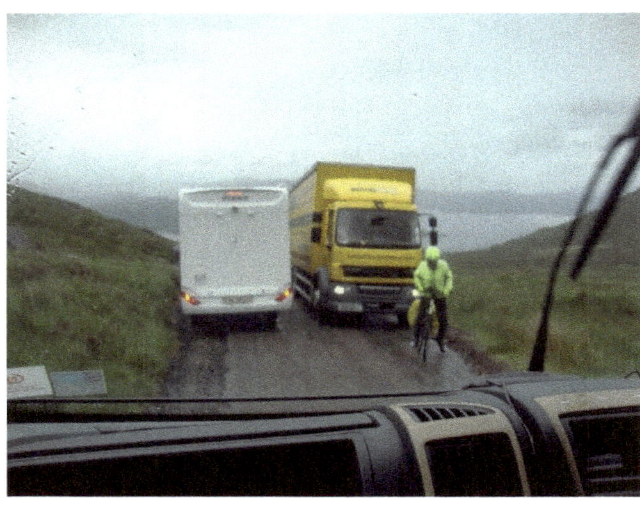

Traffic jam

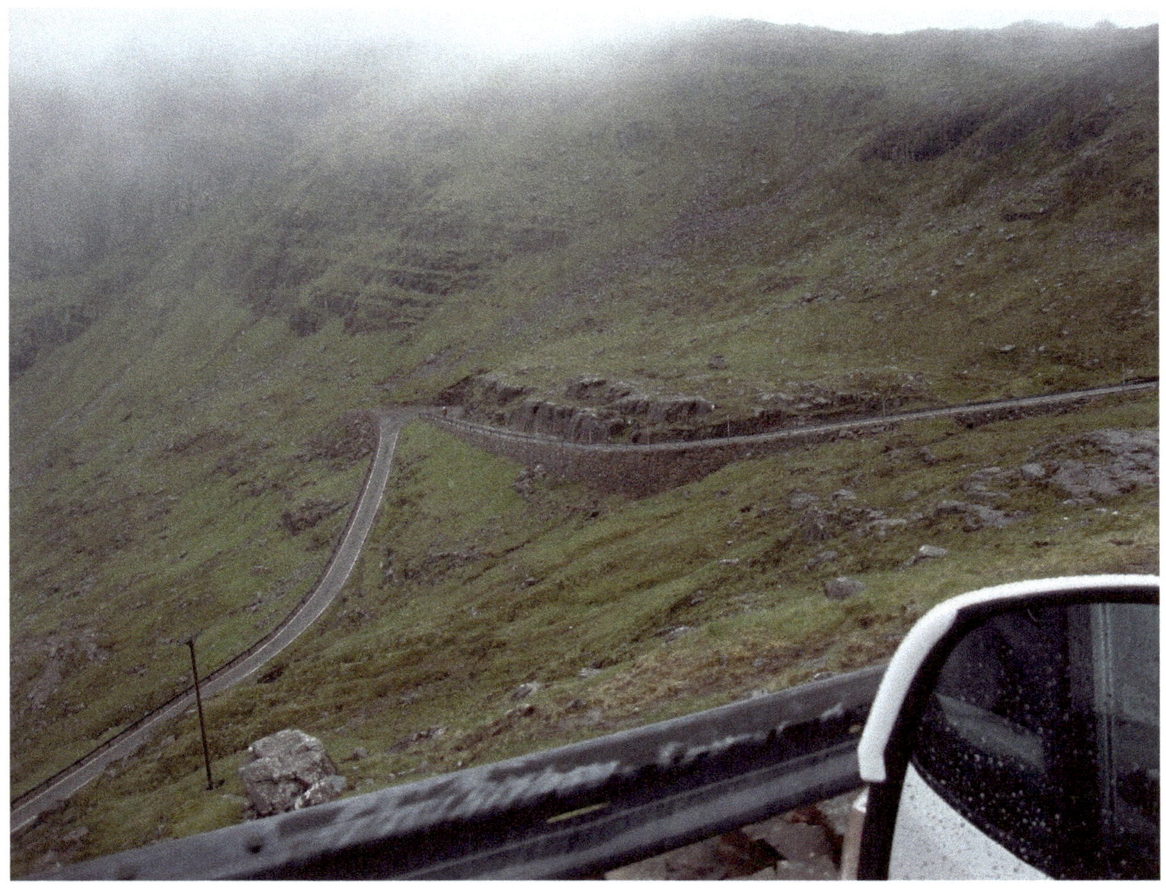

The long and winding road!

We finally made it safely to the bottom, at the junction with the A896, where Mike had to stop for a stress-wee and where we noticed a barrier that is used to close the road when conditions are bad in winter. Not for nothing is Applecross reputed to be the most isolated community in Britain.

From there we skirted Loch Kishorn, passed Stromeferry and headed down Loch Duich. Because of the horrible weather we settled on a Caravan and Motorhome Club site at Morvich tonight and tomorrow night. We agreed yesterday to stay here at Morvich Caravan Park for two nights. Mike needs a break from driving and I just want a lazy day, with time to go walking or cycling and to catch up with writing my blog.

Close to the biscuit-tin pretty Eilean Donan Castle in the Kyle of Lochalsh, this is another great place to stay, with all the usual club amenities and attractive pitches.

Today's mileage: 109

Rest day in Morvich

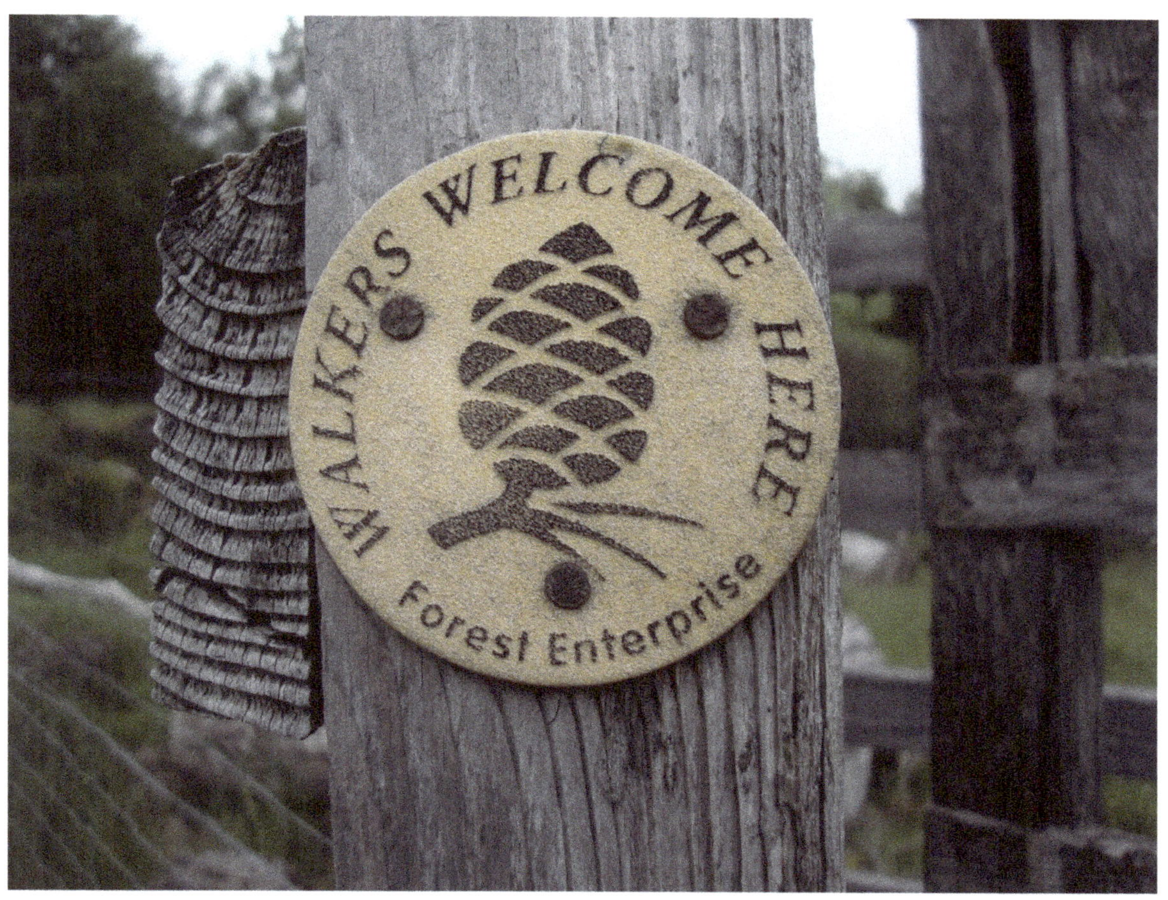

Scotland gives a warm welcome to tourists

Wednesday, 7th June

I said a few days ago that Mike is brilliant at planning and navigation. The downside is his fixation with maps. Everywhere we plan to go, or everywhere we actually DO go, he has this almost obsessive need to know exactly where he is at all times. This drives me potty.

I, on the other hand, am perfectly happy just going where the mood or the road or the trail takes me and maps could be in Japanese for all the sense they make to me. This drives Mike potty. So all things being equal, we balance each other out and remain on a fairly even keel most of the time.

On the subject of 'even keels', because of our many years of sailing together we are used to living for extended periods in a confined space, but it has to be said a 24 foot motorhome provides considerably more living space and luxury than our 30 foot yacht ever did. To start with, you can stand upright throughout the entire length of Bessie, which we couldn't do in the boat. And secondly, if we feel like pulling into a lay-by for a cup of tea or an overnight stop, we can. You can't do that on a boat either: when you're halfway across the Irish Sea there are no convenient harbours, marinas or beaches – you just have to keep going.

Back to maps.

It hammered down with rain all night and most of this morning, which gave us a reason to have a lazy start, a bacon-and-egg breakfast and time to get the laundry done. But by midday the sun was breaking through and we set off on a circular walk, Mike with map in hand, that took us through mountains, woods and river-side paths. This is the Kintail region – a fabulous part of Scotland for serious walking and hill climbing, that includes the famous Five Sisters peaks. But we weren't tempted to clamber up the hill trails: our walk was relatively level most of the way, with a bit of scrambling over slightly steeper, rougher ground in places.

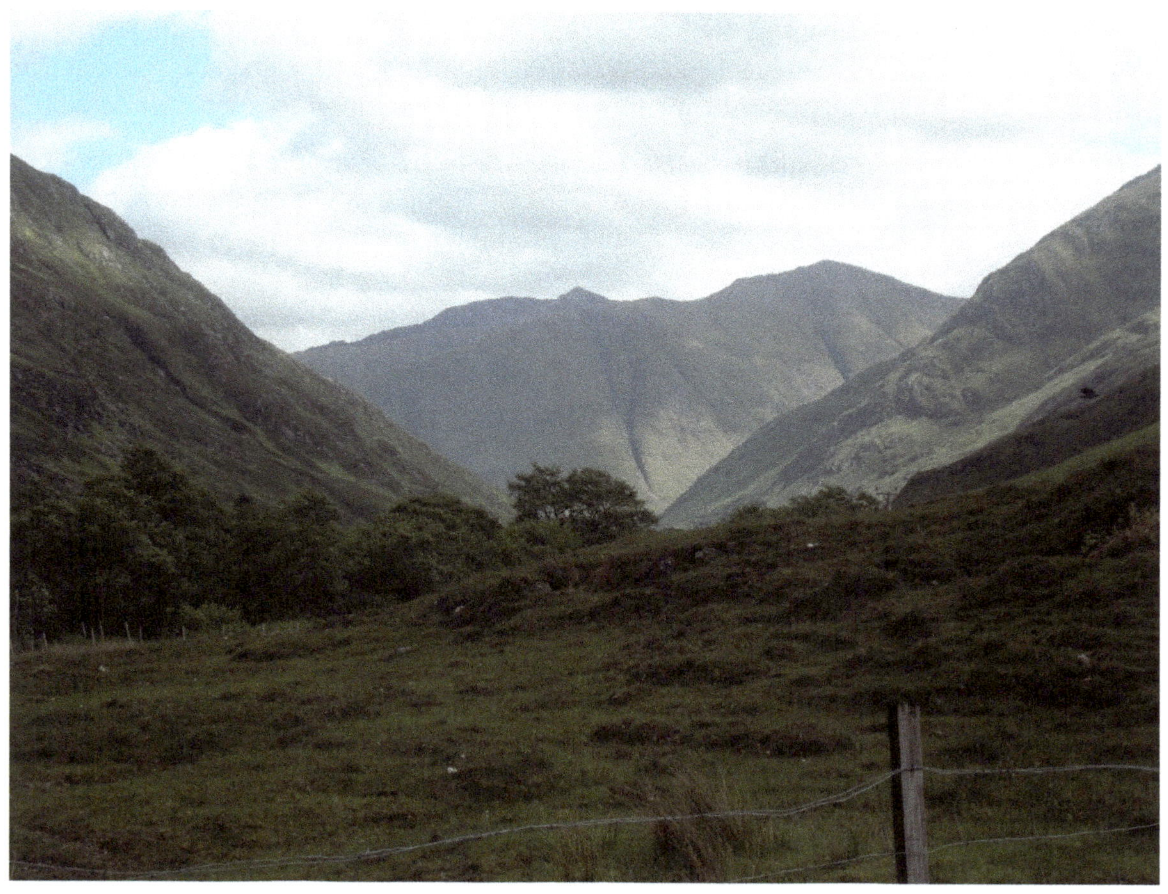

Kintail mountains

We still haven't had a confirmed sighting of a golden eagle but we did spot a wheatear and we lost count of the red deer grazing on the hillsides. They were too far away to photograph, and they blend in well with the rugged, boulder-strewn hillsides, although their white scuts are a bit of a giveaway. Every so often one would raise its head and be sufficiently clear for us to see his antlers, which enhanced the privilege of being among them. They were upwind of our path, so they were fully aware of our presence, but seemed unperturbed by us.

We got talking to a farmer who had just released some sheep on the hill. He told us that although the deer were wild and free to roam, the herds were still managed to the extent that food was put out for them and they came down to the valley to be fed.

Our five-mile walk took us two and a quarter hours, so I suppose it was more of an amble than a route march, but we had to keep stopping to soak up the surroundings. Here are a few photos to give you a small idea of what we enjoyed.

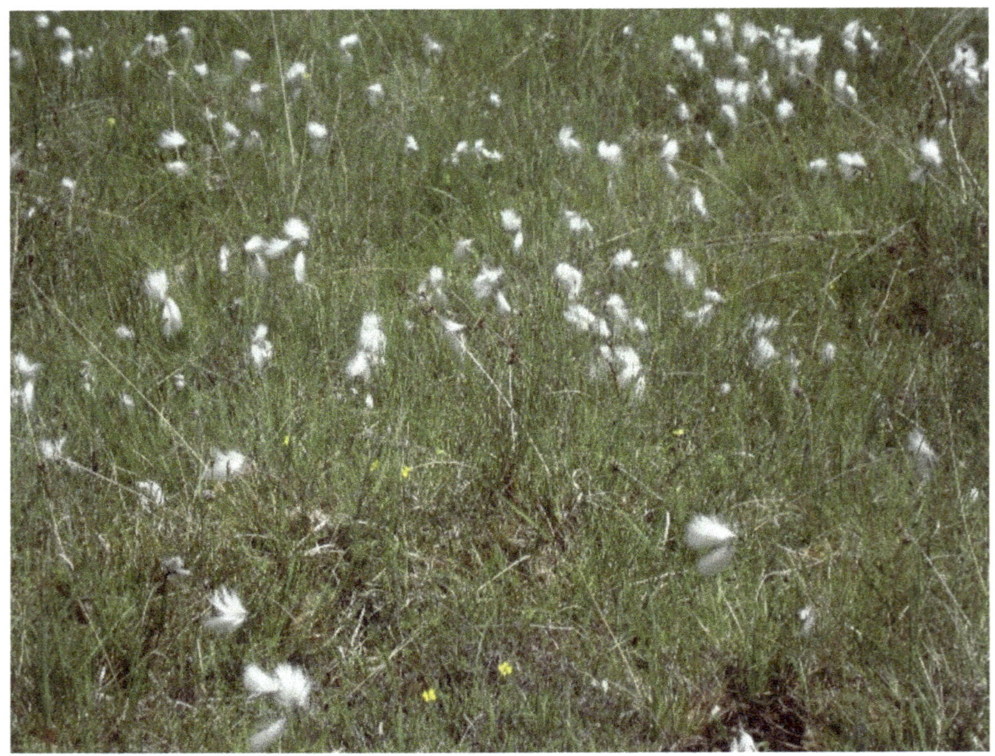

Cotton grass thrives in damp areas all over the Highland region

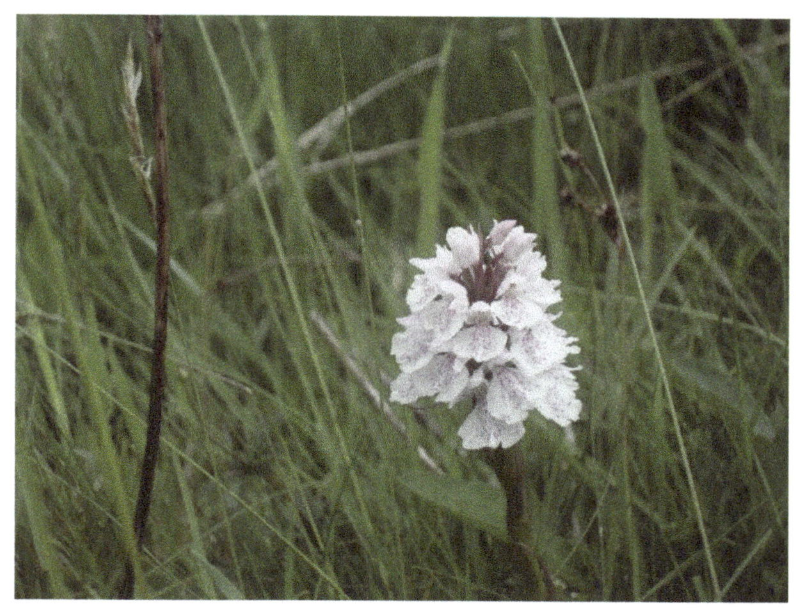

Lucky to find this heath spotted orchid Dactylorhiza maculate (thank you Dave and Faye for checking that out)

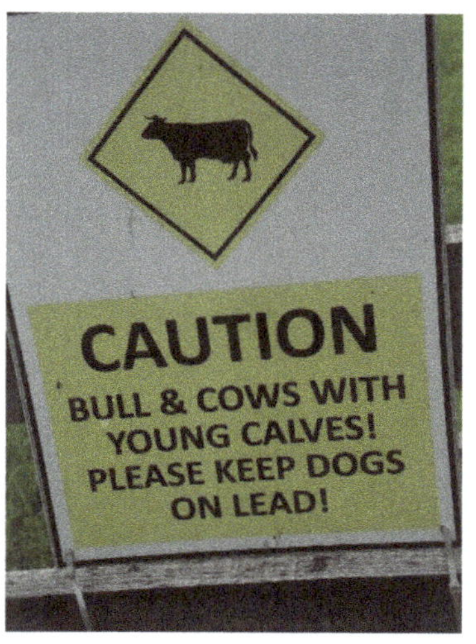

We saw no bull, no cows, no calves!

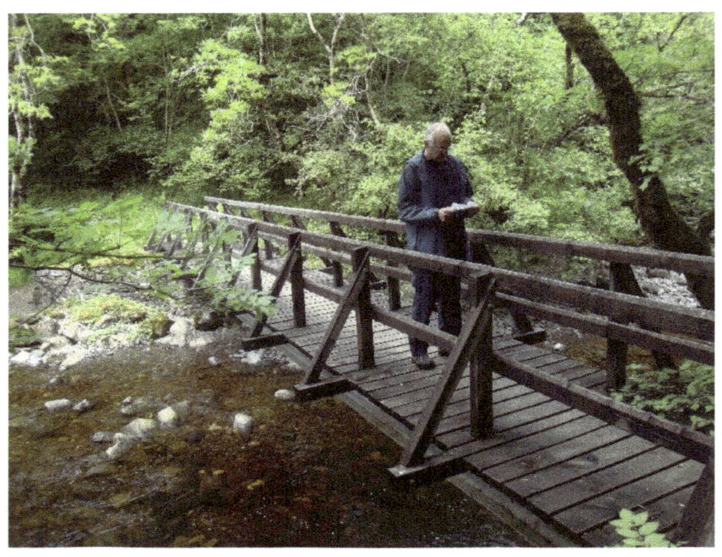

Mike consults his map as he crosses the River Croa.
The bridge was constructed in June 1991 by 590 Squadron of the Royal Engineers

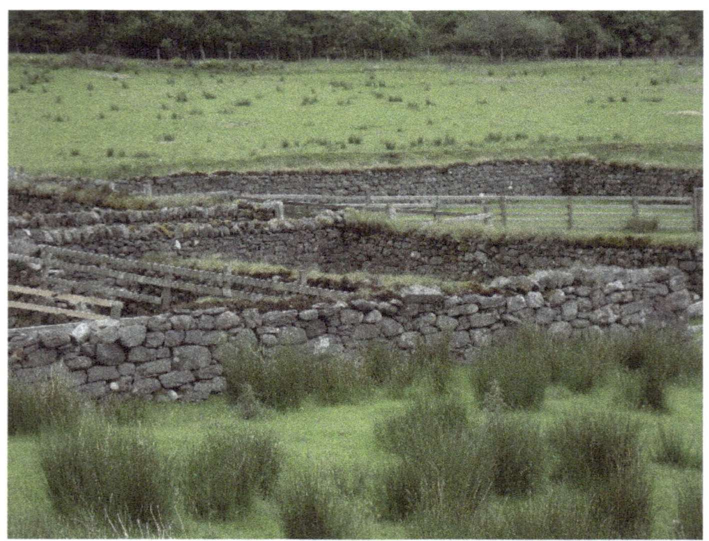

Some of these dry stone wall collecting pens had an overhead shower for drenching the sheep, a process that rids them of parasites.

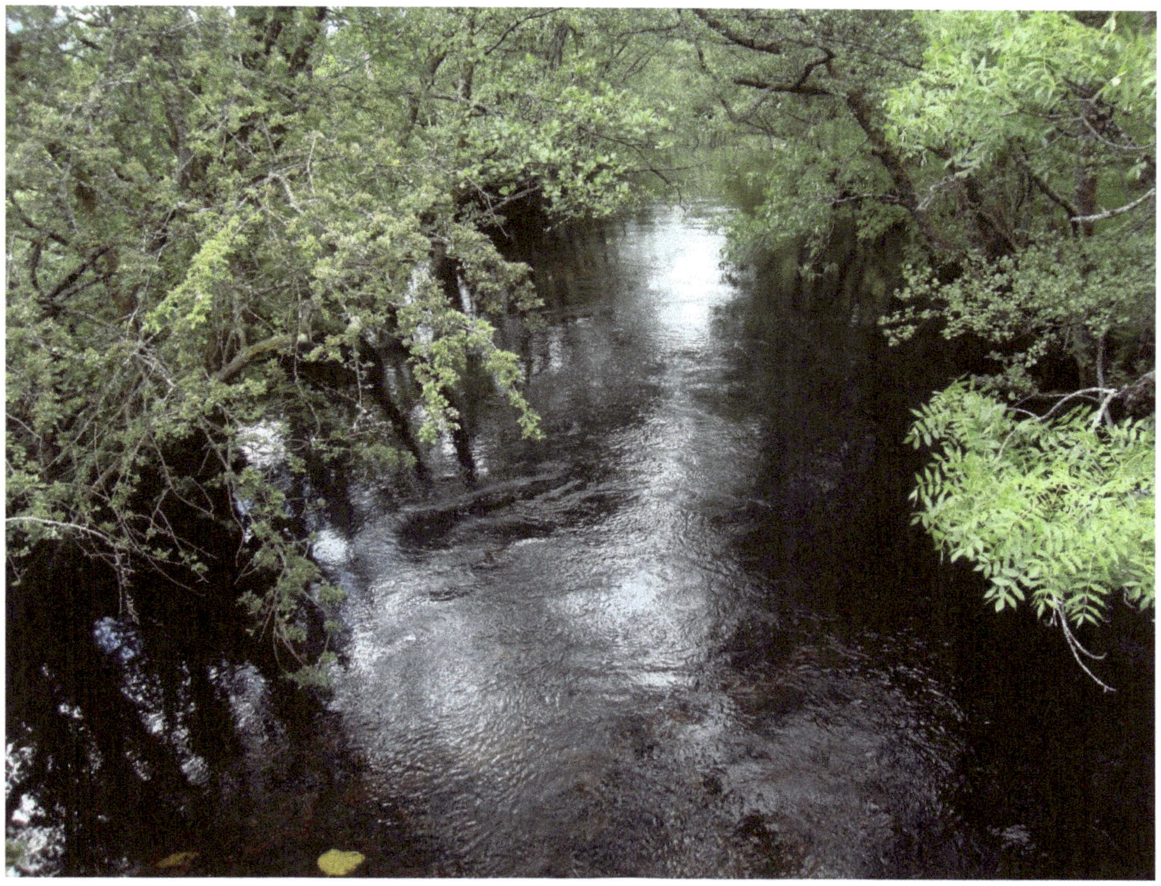

River Croa

Great excitement as we were cooking dinner this evening. The peace of the valley was shattered when four RAF fighter jets screamed between the mountains over our heads at low level, most likely on low-flying exercises. Thrilling for us to see and hear. Not so thrilling for those people in war zones for whom their appearance is the real thing.

Morvich to Eilean Donan Castle and the Isle of Skye

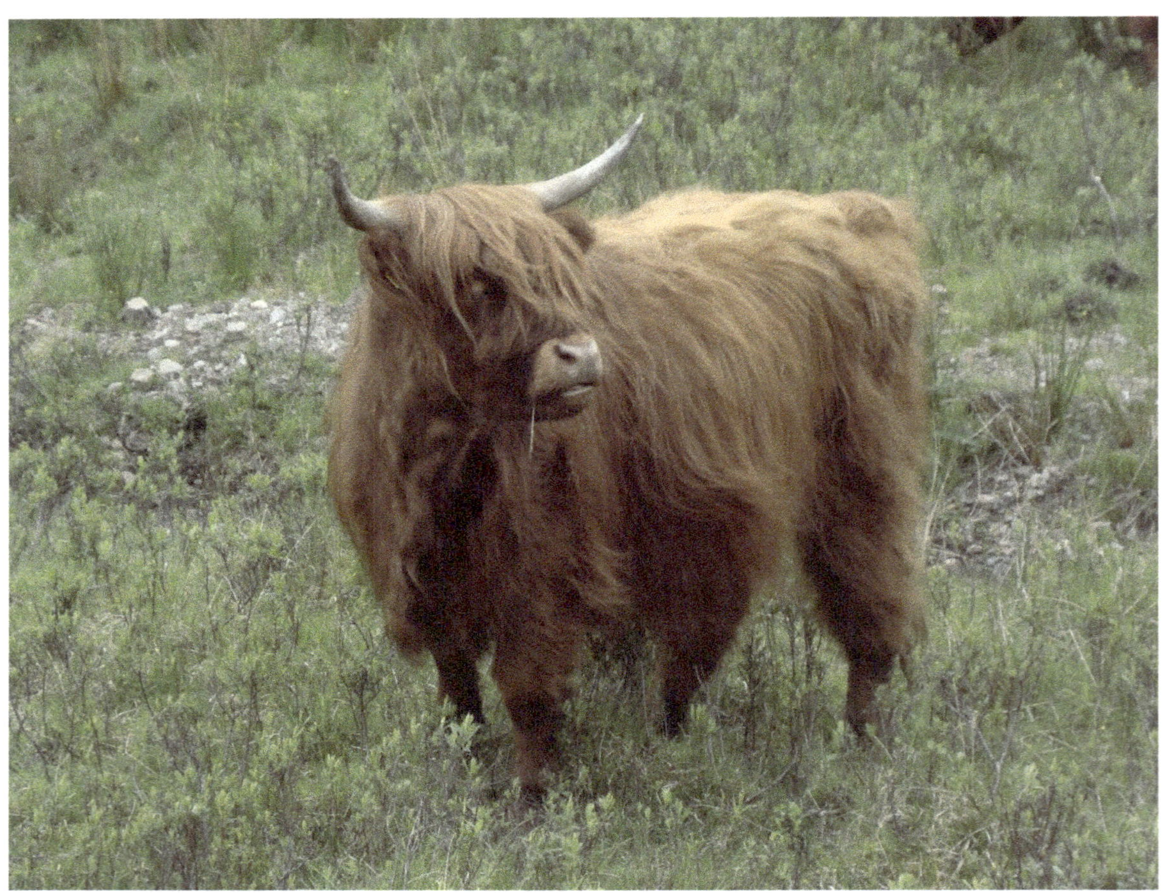

Highland calf – they always look sad and grumpy.

Thursday, 8th June

When I was about ten years old, I went on a family holiday to Cornwall. It was the best childhood holiday I ever had. I never forgot the seaweed curtained cave I found on the beach at Carlyon Bay, and I promised myself that when I grew up I would return. About 40 years later Mike and I went and I was so disappointed. There was nothing there to match the picture in my mind and I wished we hadn't gone.

Today we visited the iconic Eilean Donan Castle at Dornie – the one whose image appears on postcards, tourist leaflets and tins of Scottish shortbread. The first time I saw it I was 17 and it was the most romantic and atmospheric place imaginable. As with Carlyon Bay, I longed to go back. As with Carlyon Bay, I wish I hadn't. It isn't the peaceful, isolated castle of my memory but an enormous visitor attraction with a vast coach and car park, a shop, a restaurant and hundreds of visitors. And this was only half past nine in the morning.

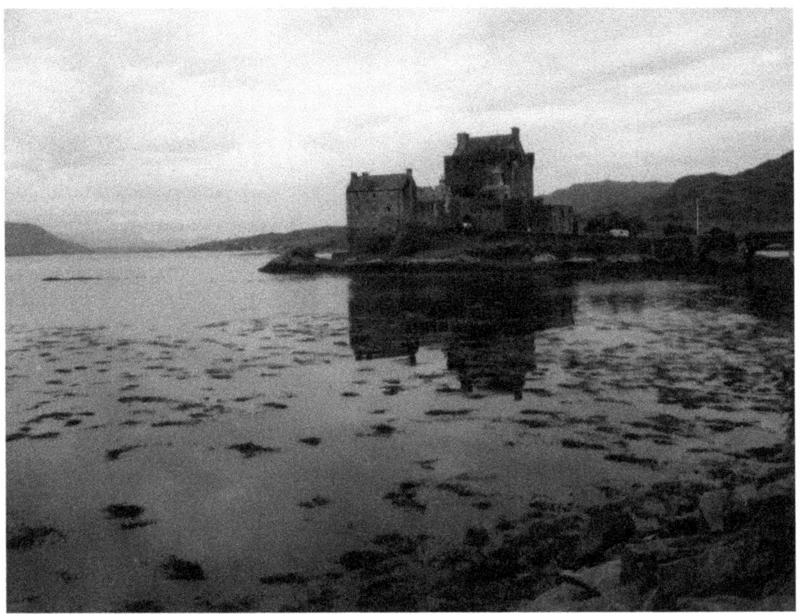

Low water at Eilean Donan Castle, Dornie

The main car park was already too full for Bessie so we followed the sign to *'extra car parking and parking for motorhomes and caravans'*. Umm . . . it was just another car park. No extra-long bays, as the signs led us to believe. So Mike reversed Bessie's overhang (sorry Bessie, that sounds rude) over the grass and left her nose jutting forward.

'Too commercial. Too many people. Not as I remember it. It's spoilt my memory. I wish I hadn't come,' I grumbled, over and over again. Before we left, though, I joined the scores of other tourists of many nationalities in snapping a few photos, including one of this seat carved from wood. We immediately thought of our friend Keith, who enjoys making furniture. So this one's for you Keith – I feel another project coming on.

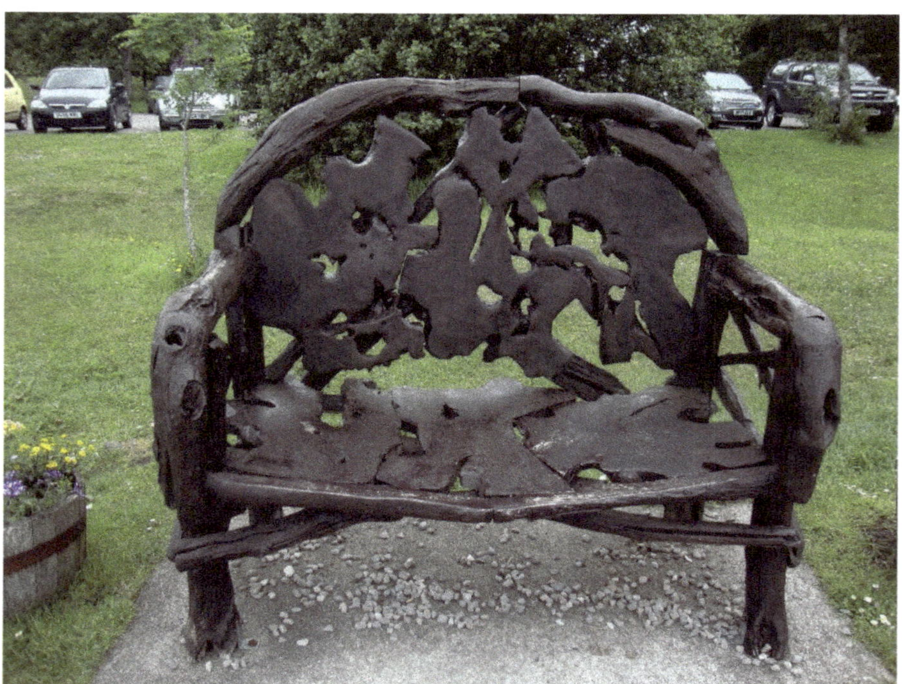

We crossed to Skye on the famous road bridge spanning Loch Alsh – no longer a toll – and our next stop was Broadford Bay in the Inner Sound. The entire island is dominated by the massive Cuillins, a range of mountains that boasts 12 Munroes – meaning they are all higher than 3,000 feet – that today were dark and mysterious in the mist.

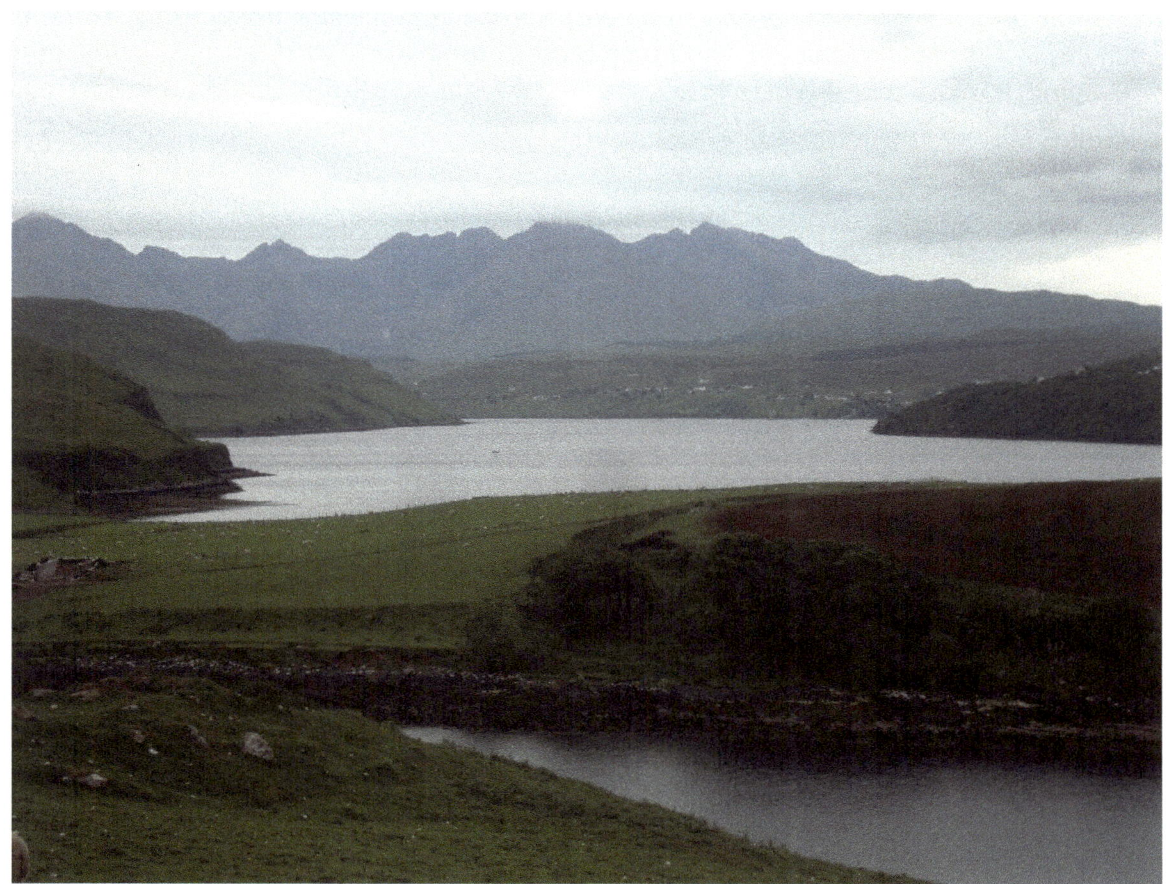

Cuillins as seen from Colliore

My favourite place during this morning's drive was Dun Beag Broch. During our tour of Scotland I'd already noticed brown tourist signs pointing to brochs but as we didn't know what they were we just passed by without visiting them. But now I know what these archaeological and architectural treasures are, and I want to see more.

Brochs are a type of roundhouse that date from the Iron Age and are an impressive testimony to the expertise of the early stonemasons who constructed them. When you consider they were built maybe 2,000 years ago and some are still standing, albeit in varying states of disrepair, you can't help but be blown away by them. Originally, they were enormously tall, circular towers, a bit like a lime kiln in shape, with just one opening and, believe it or not, cavity walls! They had no windows but, according to the information board, archaeologists believe they had several floors, with staircases to each built into the cavity. It is likely that animals were kept on the ground floor. Brochs were probably built as status symbols by tribal chiefs and served as protective, although not particularly effective, forts but eventually their popularity declined and they went out of fashion.

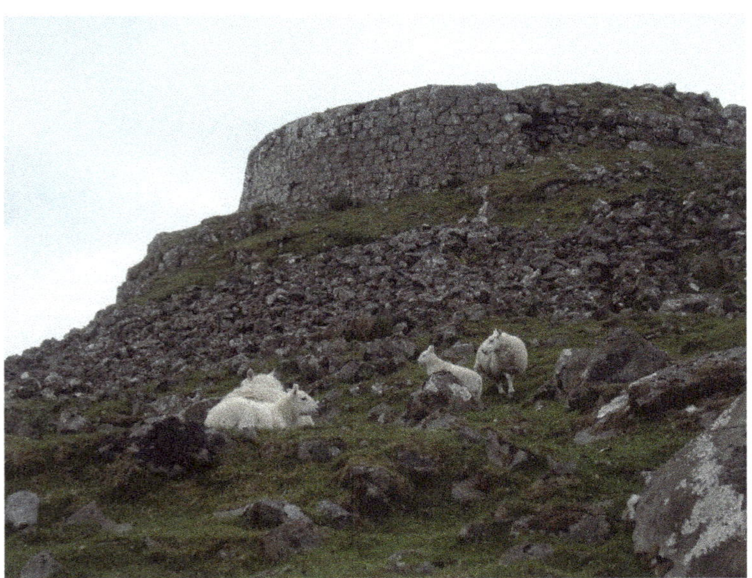

Dun Beag Broch

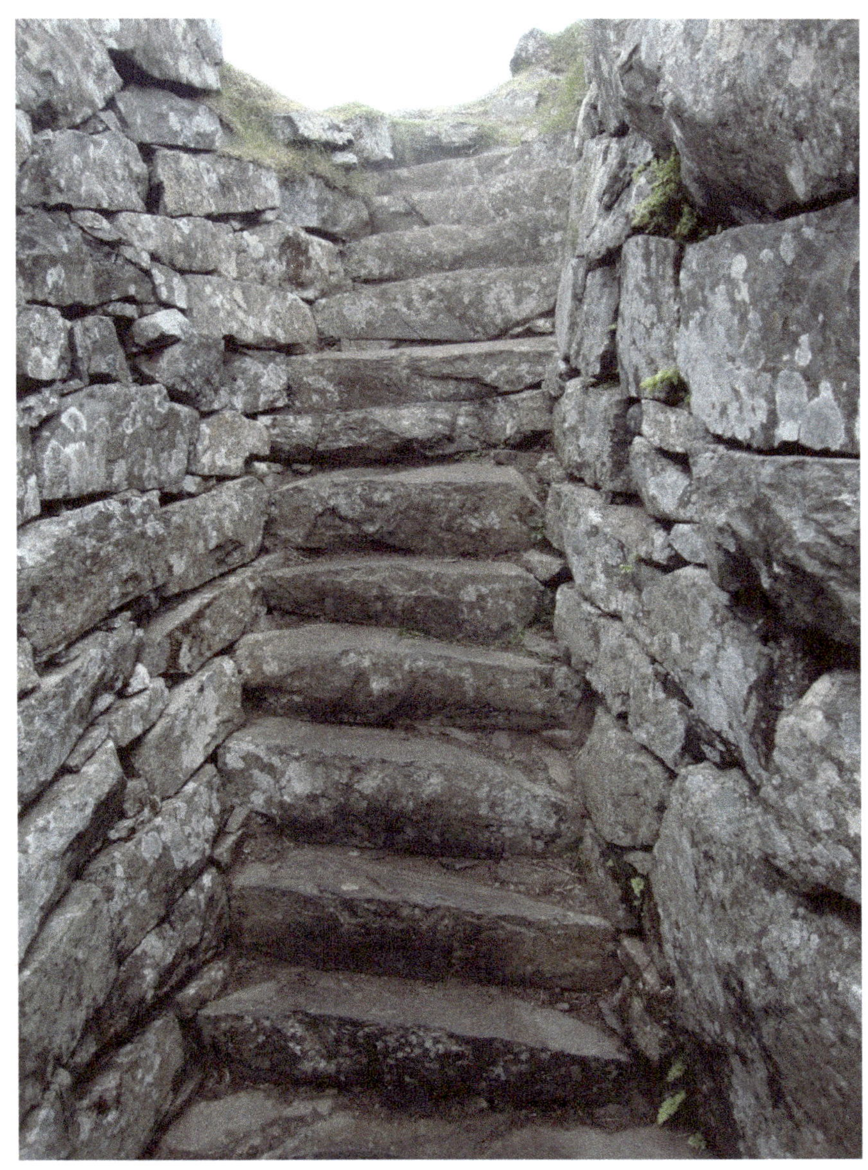

Inner staircase in the cavity wall

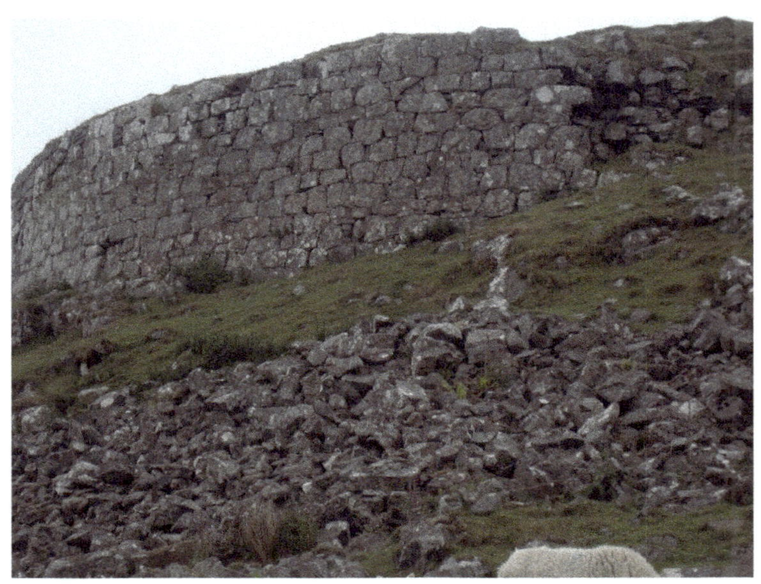

It's hard to believe this beautifully constructed stone wall was built maybe 2000 years ago

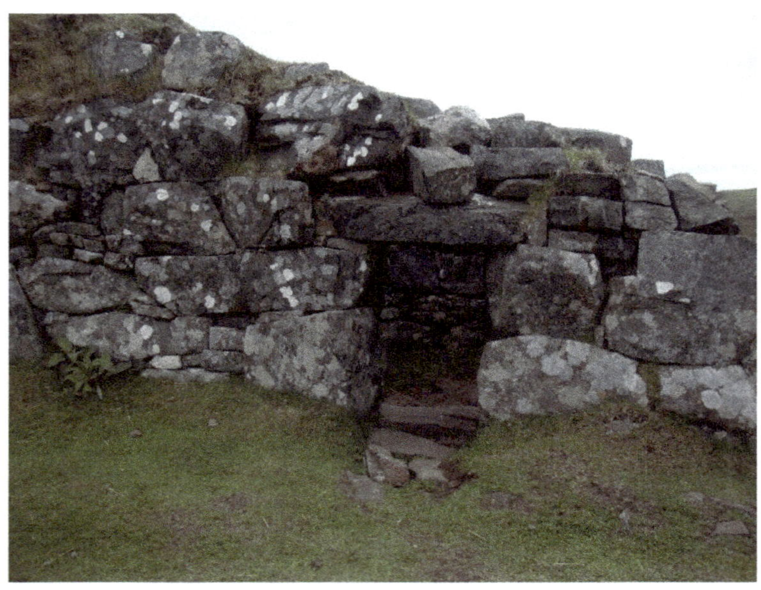

The entrance to the broch

Perched on a hill with 360º views, Dun Beag Broch has lost much of its stonework to the ravages of time and weather, and you can see where the stones have tumbled onto the grassy banks around it. Despite this, it is easy to absorb the atmosphere and imagine the once thriving community that relied on it for shelter. These days, of course, it has only sheep, wheatear, skylark and the ever-present cuckoo for company.

Not far from Dun Beag Broch, in Dunvegan, is the Giant Angus MacGaskill Museum and although we didn't stop there, I wondered who Giant Angus MacGaskill was. It turns out that at seven feet eight inches he holds the record of being the tallest Scotsman ever to have lived.

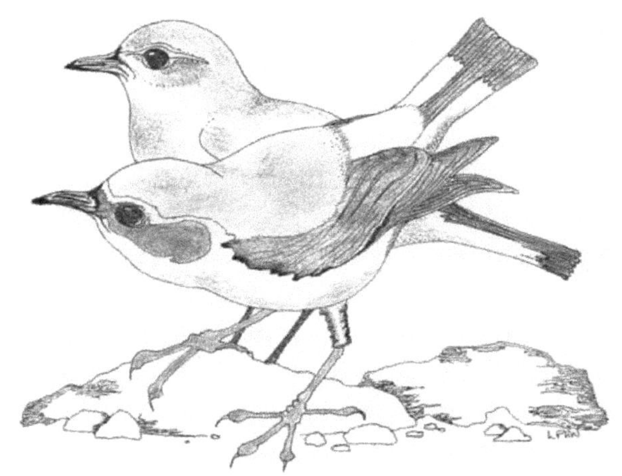

Wheatear

Although he was born on the Island of Berneray in the Outer Hebrides, he spent most of his life in Canada, after his parents were forced from their home by the Highland Clearances when he was still a child. As I mentioned earlier, this was a time of great distress and hardship for significant numbers of crofters who were dispossessed of their homes during the 18th and 19th centuries. Landlords needed to create pastureland so they could increase their incomes by introducing sheep and they did this by evicting their tenants and clearing the land. Many of the families who were dispossessed of their homes chose to emigrate to North America, especially Canada, in a bid to make new lives for their families.

Giant Angus carved out a career for himself, and no little fame, first as a strong man and later as a performer in Barnum's Circus. At the beginning of August, 1863, he became ill with what his doctor diagnosed as a 'brain fever' and he died peacefully in his sleep a week later, at his parents' home in Halifax, Nova Scotia. He was 38.

The museum is housed in a picturesque thatched cottage. Neither Angus nor his family ever lived there but it was established by a local man, Peter MacGaskill, as a lasting memorial to his fellow clansman.

Shortly after we set off on our holiday, and while we were still in Ireland, I lost the bag of potatoes that I'd brought from home. When our thorough search of all Bessie's cupboards proved fruitless – or should I say spudless – I guessed I'd either used them all up or thrown them away, and forgotten I'd done so. Today, Mike found them. They'd fallen behind a cover over the wheel arch in the wardrobe. We couldn't help wondering what would have happened if we hadn't found them. Few things smell worse than rotting spuds and we would never have been able to trace where the pong was coming from. Luckily, these were only wrinkled, soft and sprouting, but given time . . .

This evening we found a space in an empty lay-by at Armadale Bay, overlooking the Sound of Sleat, so we would be ready for tomorrow morning's ferry back to the mainland.

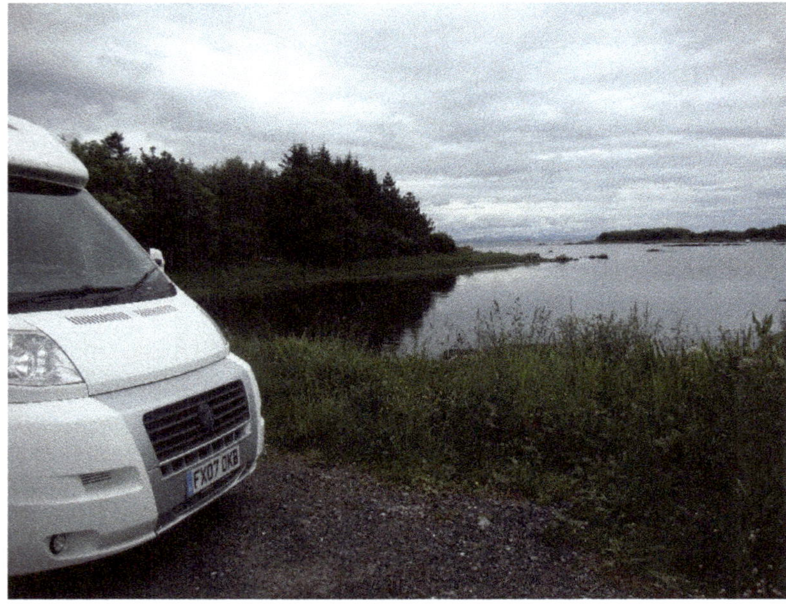

Armadale Bay

We had a walk around the port, where I rescued a little gurnard that was lying in the road. A seabed dwelling fish that uses its 'legs' to dig for food, the poor thing was way out of its watery element. I popped it back into the sea where it belongs and watched it flop around for a bit before it swam gratefully away.

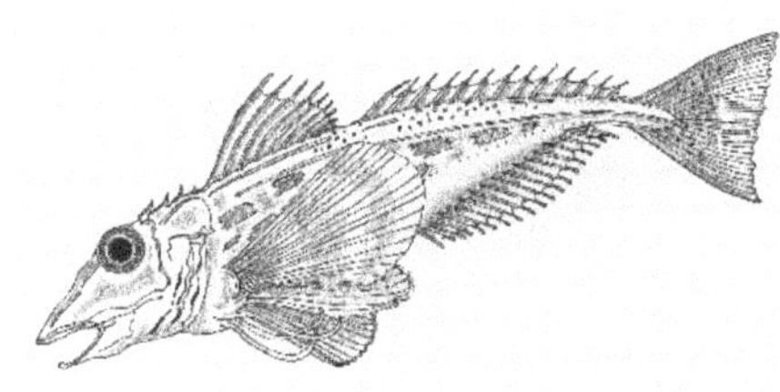

Gurnard

Mike enjoys angling and we stopped to chat to a couple dangling their rods from the seaward end of the pier. They told us that whilst they loved touring around Scotland they were constantly getting lost because their satnav hardly ever worked and they didn't know where they were. I poked Mike in the ribs to stop him telling them to get a road atlas but even I couldn't help being amazed that people would come to such a remote and mountainous region without bringing paper maps for back-up. Technology has its benefits but, as Mike said, 'you can't beat a good map!' Then we had a wander around Rubha Phoil: an enchanting wooded peninsula and eco campsite, before returning to Bessie.

We shared a bottle of wine, ate a ready-meal for dinner and spent the rest of the long light evening totally enthralled as we watched two otters frolicking in the shallow waters of the bay.

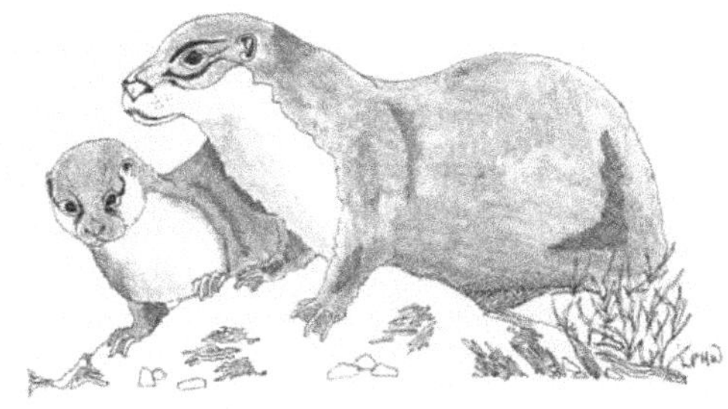

Otters

Today's mileage: 132

Armadale to Malaig and Glen Righ Forest

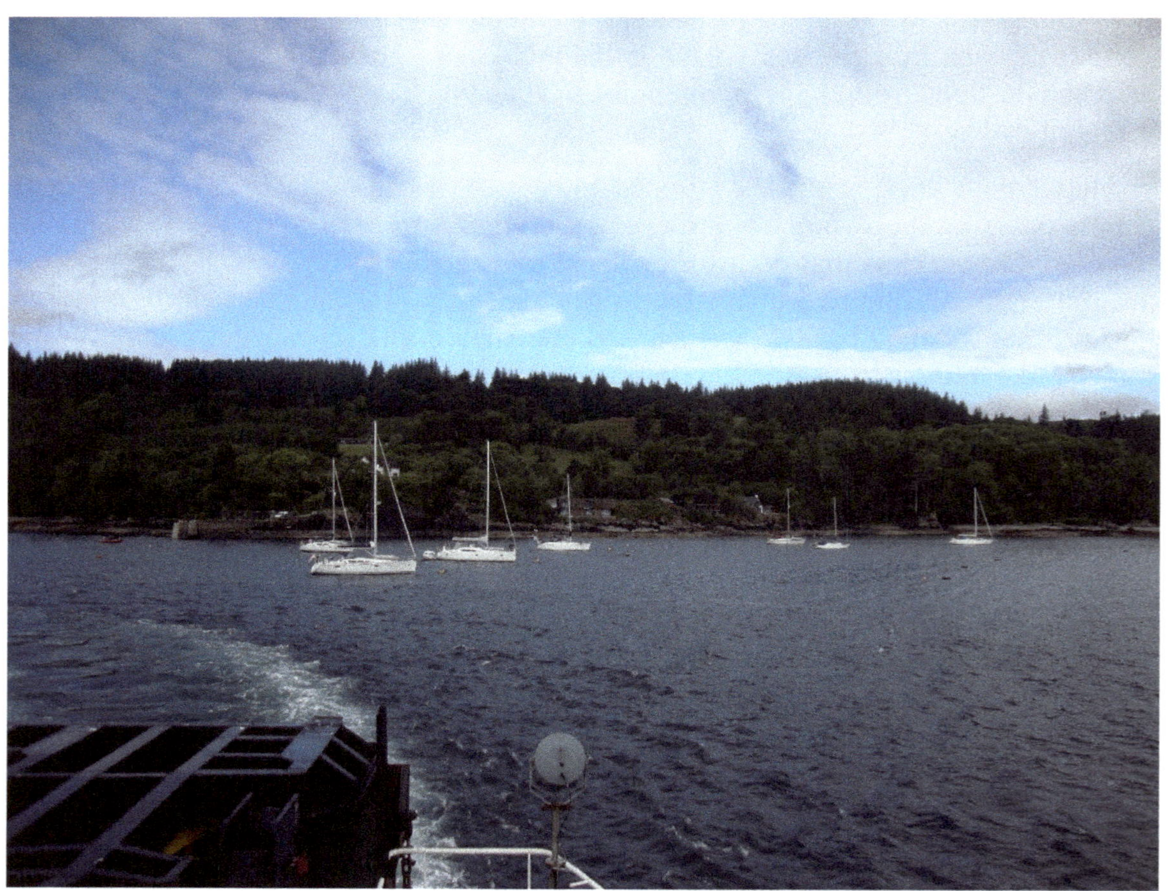

Leaving Armadale behind

Friday, 9th June

We woke up at five this morning to tune in to Radio 4 to get the results of the general election. At 5.30 we switched off the radio and went back to sleep. National politics seem a long way from us right now.

The ferry from Armadale to Mallaig left on time with three spare places on the car deck. Most of the passengers, including us, scrambled up to the top deck to make the most of the fine morning. The jagged peaks of the Island of Rum in the Small Isles, and the distinctive, flat-topped Eigg were just visible in the mist and it's a miracle the ferry didn't roll over with the weight of everyone leaning over the rails to take photographs.

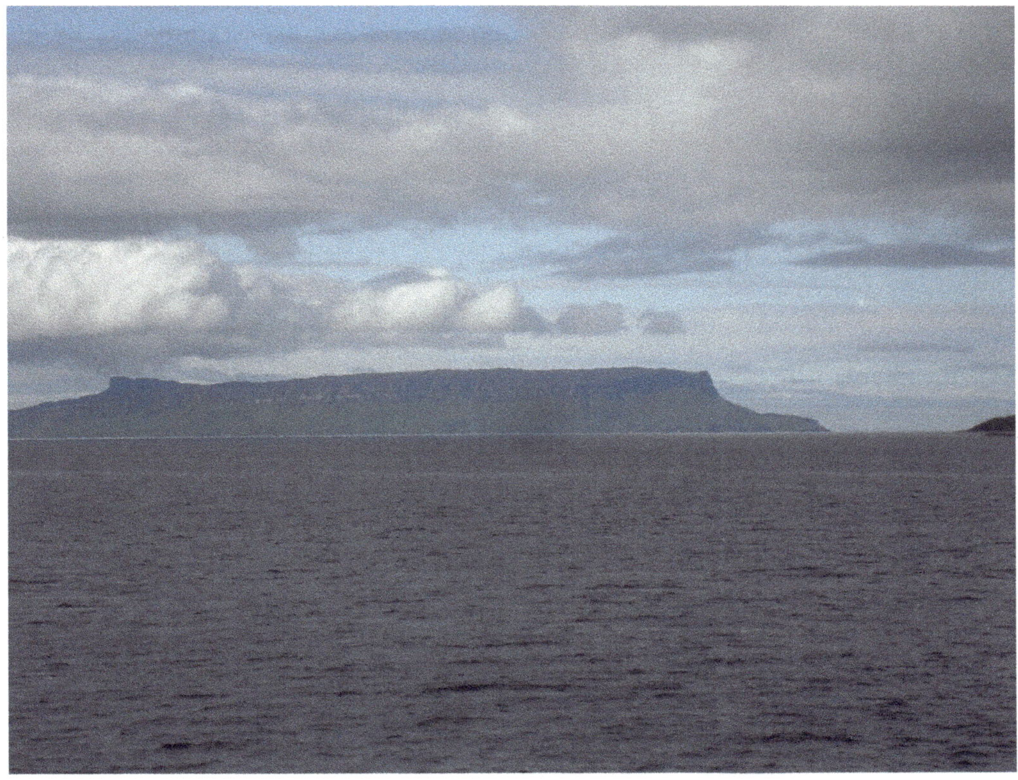

Eigg

Once we'd disembarked, and after we'd enjoyed a thirty-minute coffee stop at Mallaig, we carried on towards Corpach at the southern end of the Caledonian Canal, where we intended to spend the night. This stretch of the A830 is dominated by tall, pointy mountains, their heads in the clouds, and the Jacobite narrow gauge steam railway that runs from Mallaig to Fort William. Although we didn't hitch a ride today, we reckon this would be a train journey well worth doing and we are already planning to include it during our next visit to Scotland. The Jacobite has featured in a number of Harry Potter movies, and fans especially enjoy the train's crossing of the spectacular twenty-one span Glenfinnan Viaduct, which curves above the River Finnan a hundred feet below.

At the head of Loch Shiel is the Glenfinnan Monument, erected in 1815 as a tribute to the clansmen who died as a result of their support for Bonnie Prince Charlie during the Jacobite Risings of 1745. Unfortunately, we were unable to stop and visit as an attendant was guarding the entrance to the already full National Trust Scotland car park and all we got was a glimpse-in-passing of the kilted highlander atop the sixty-foot tower.

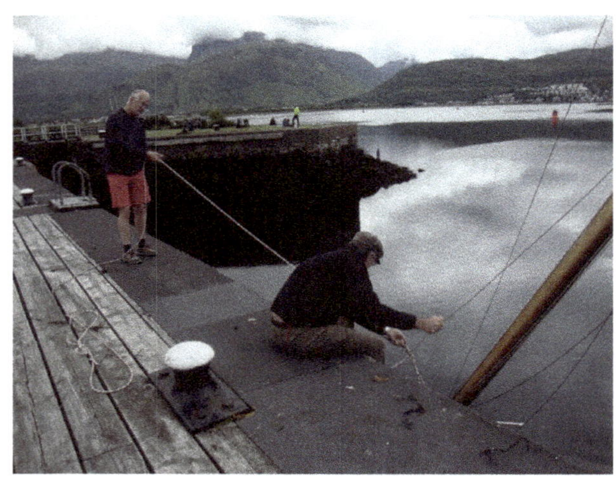

Mike helps to un-mast a visiting yacht at Corpach

We abandoned our plan to spend the night at Corpach after we were unable to find somewhere to park so we had lunch and a wander around the loch basin. We noticed two men attempting to un-mast a visiting yacht that was moored against the wall. Never one to resist anything to do with sailing boats, and in the universal tradition of sailors, Mike strolled over to help with the ropes.

From there, we drove to a lay-by overlooking Loch Linnhe, on the A82 north of the Corran Narrows. This barely navigable stretch of water reduces the width of the loch from a mile at its widest to just 200 metres at the Narrows, although small cruise liners are still able to pass through. Minutes after we arrived a police motorcyclist stopped all the southbound traffic and directed it into the lay-by. We guessed an accident ahead. But no, it was an abnormal load – three massive low loaders transporting heavy machinery. Once they'd got through, the lay-by cleared again and we were back to our usual solitude.

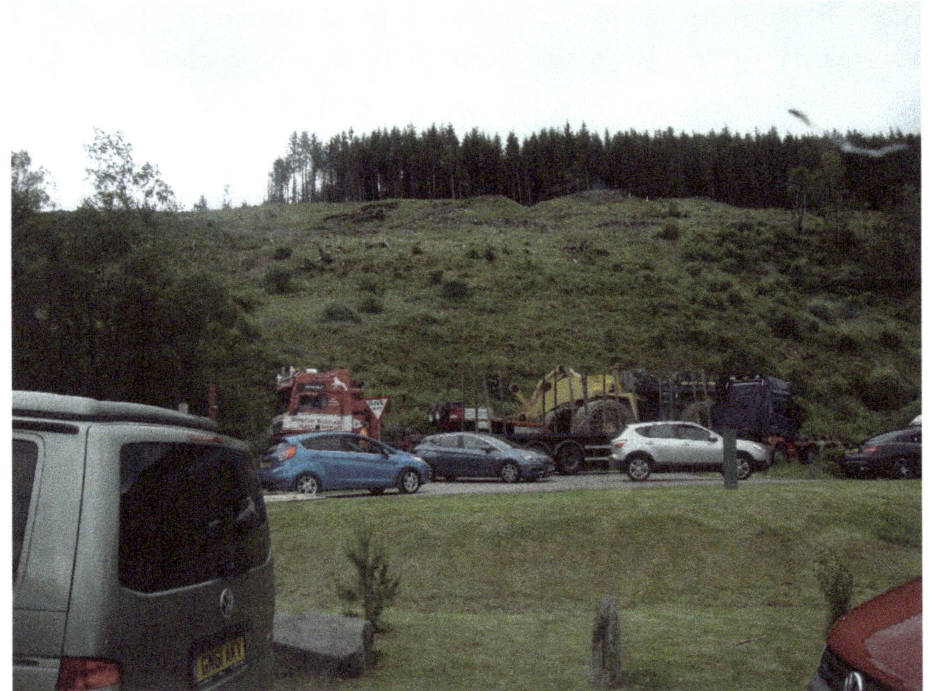

Road block

One thing I've noticed is that there is little or no ivy suffocating the trees in the parts of Scotland we've visited so far, and there has been no sign of the dreaded Japanese knotweed. Until today, that is, when we came across a big clump of it growing beside Loch Linnhe. If nothing is done it will take over and choke the indigenous plants, such as this clump of increasingly rare ragged robin that's thriving in the boggy ground around the edge of the loch.

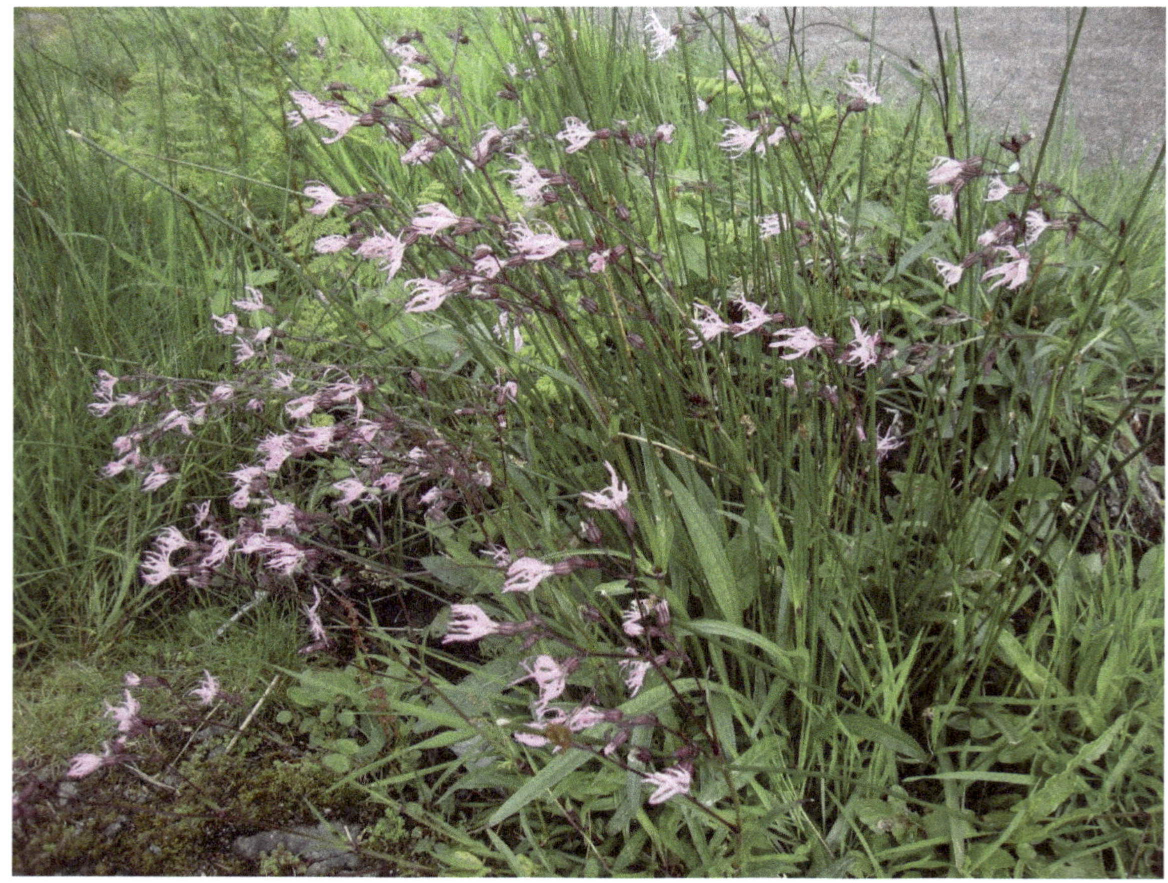

Ragged robin

After we'd been there a while, Mike spotted a not-very-obvious sign on a green post: no overnight parking. Unusual for Scotland. Should we ignore it, risk upsetting the locals, and stay? Or should we go? Who would be around to move us on in the middle of the night anyway? We debated it for five or ten minutes, but it was clear that Mike wouldn't have been comfortable or able to relax if we stayed, so we moved on.

We were very glad we did, as we arrived 15 minutes later at Glen Righ Forest, which features an excellent red squirrel feeding station. The first birdsong we heard on arrival was . . not a cuckoo on this occasion but, to our astonishment, the clear hoo-hoo-hooo of a tawny owl. In broad daylight. Then a cuckoo! We peered through the peepholes of the squirrel hide to watch them feed, but they were obviously not hungry as we didn't see any.

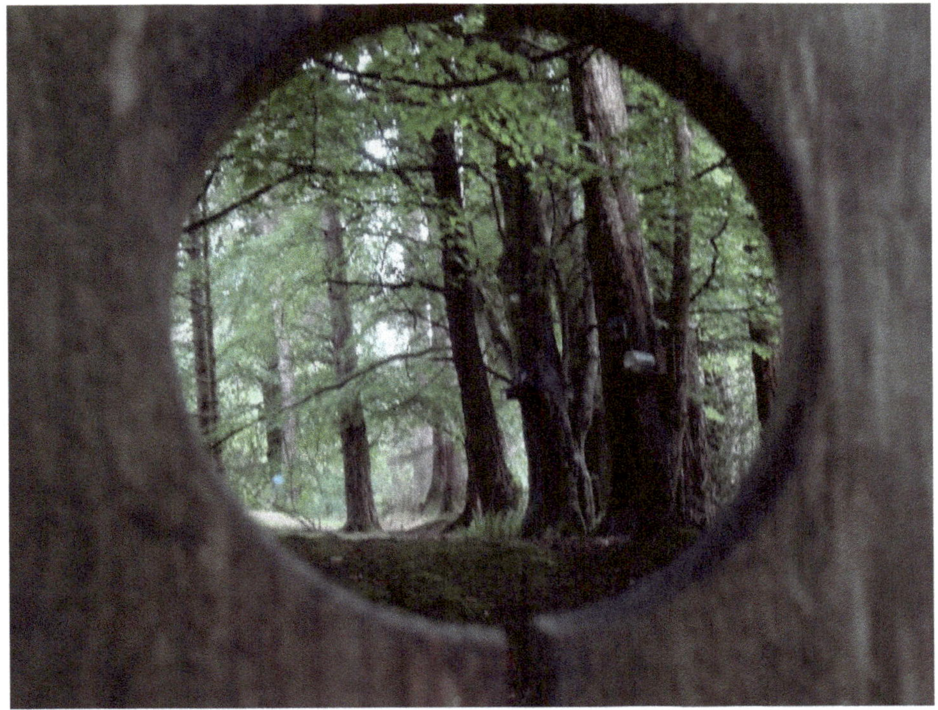

Through the round window . . ..

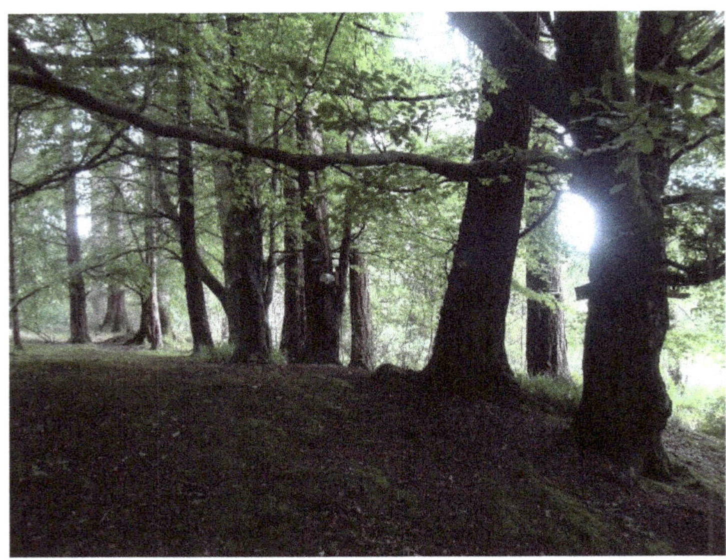

... to the squirrel feeding station.

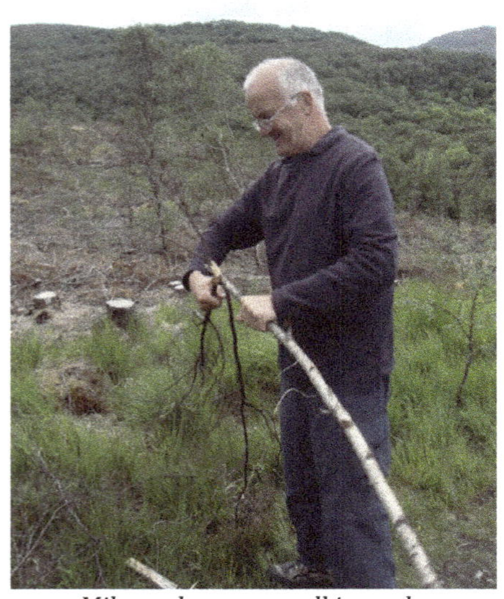

Mike makes me a walking pole.

Our walk took us on through the woods and up a steep mountain path to the Inchrigh Falls. A man making his way down told us the waterfall was 'well worth the walk up there' but what we found was a small cascade with a tiny model house tucked into the side of the bank. We were not impressed.

We carried on a bit further anyway, and as we reached the high point of the track, we spotted what we are fairly certain were two golden eagles soaring above us. They were silhouetted against the cloud and too high for us to be 100 per cent sure but they didn't look right for buzzards, with which we are very familiar. One bore off out of sight but the other continued soaring, with no wing beats. While buzzards go flap, flap, glide, this bird was just gliding with the swept back wings that are distinctive of golden eagles.

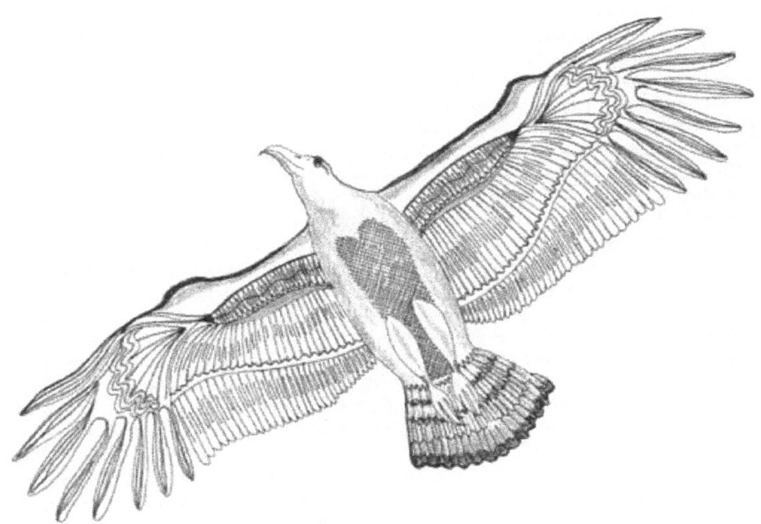

We watched until they rose so high that they disappeared from our sight and then we ambled on, following the clearly marked circular waterfall trail, rounded a bend and there in front of us were the falls. Spectacular. We'd gone up the downward path, the wrong way round the track, which was why we'd missed them. The sides of the gorge were full of rhododendrons – I know they are considered to be a pest but the hillside looked glorious. It was as though we'd been transported to the Himalayas!

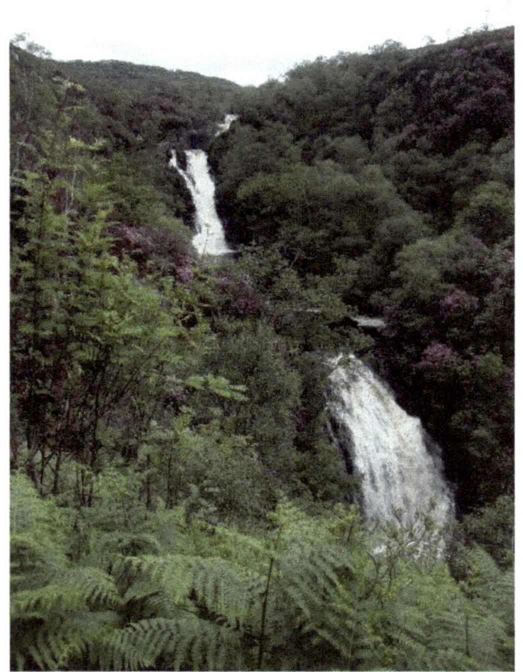

Rhododendrons adorn the banks of the Inchrigh Falls

Back in Bessie it was time for wine, crisps and, later, dinner. To begin with on this holiday I was cooking the way I do at home. That's all gone straight out of the window now though. It's ready meals and meal-deals for us these days. No preparation, no fiddly cooking, very little washing up. And jolly nice food too!

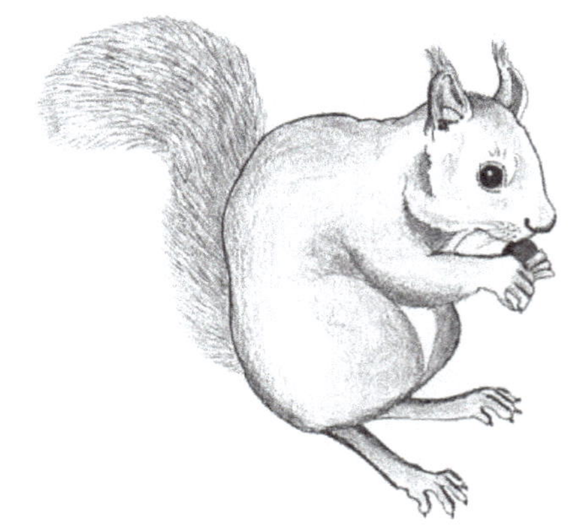

Today's mileage: 54

Argyll and Bute

Glen Righ Forest to North Ledaig

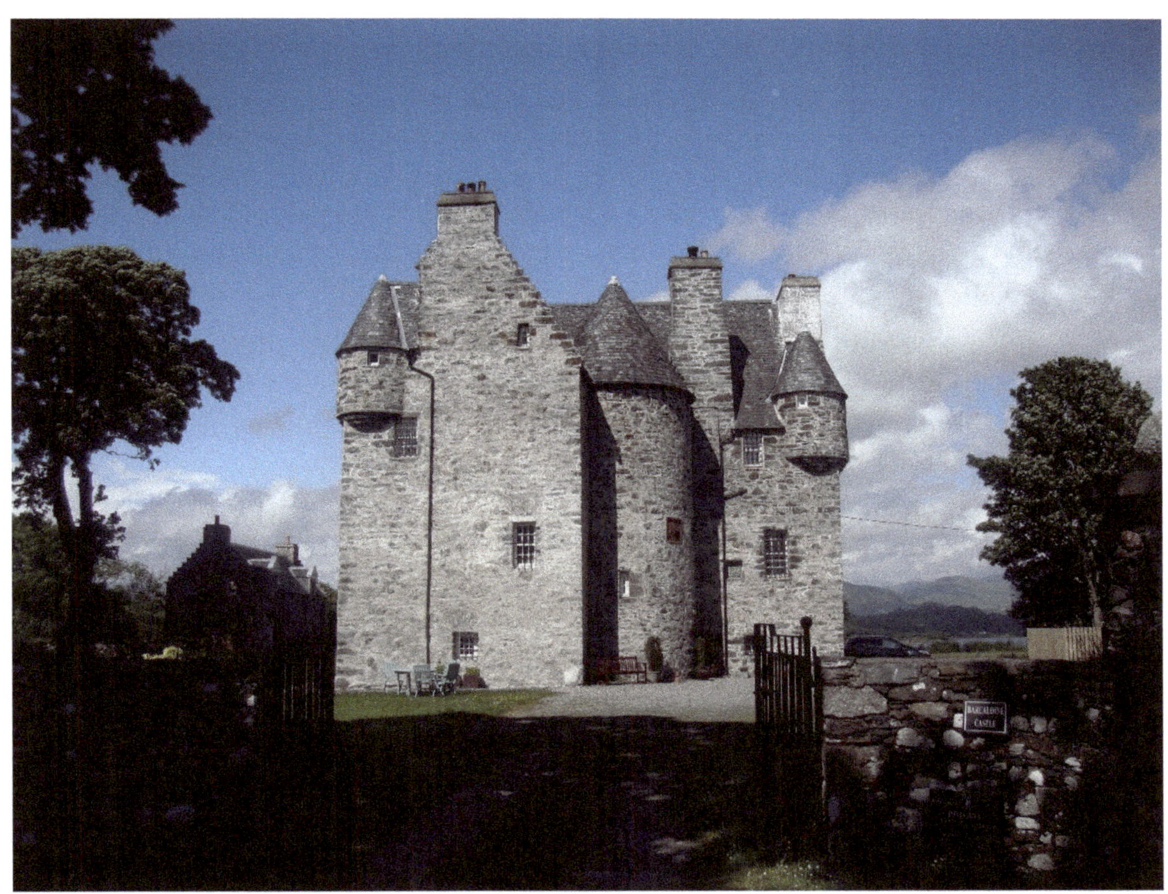

The Black Castle

Saturday, 10th June

We spent much of last night listening to rain hammering on Bessie's roof. It was still pouring as we left the forest and headed towards Oban. As we drove over the Connel Bridge, an historic cantilever bridge that spans the head of the estuary of Loch Etive, we slowed down to try and catch a glimpse of the Falls of Lora below. The bridge, originally a rail crossing, spans the narrow estuary close to the point where Etive, a sea loch, spills into the sea at the Firth of Lorn.

The Falls of Lora is a tidal race that forms white-water rapids during spring tides. These tides occur just before or just after a full or new moon, when there is the greatest difference in height between high and low water. When the level of the Firth drops lower than the level of the water in the loch at low tide, water gushes out through the narrow mouth of the loch over a rocky shelf, causing turbulent overfalls and a strong current.

In 2002, when Mike and I were members of Banbury Sub-Aqua Club, a group of us visited Scotland's west coast. The dive here is challenging – something of a bucket-list ambition for many UK divers – and was the one we all wanted to do during the trip, albeit it was the one that filled us with the most trepidation.

Diving these overfalls is, shall we say, memorable. If you can imagine the sensation of being in a tumble drier, out of control and 12 metres down in a current of fast running water, that pretty well sums it up. The dive has to be not only well-planned but accurately timed and perfectly executed if you don't want to risk being hurtled around and bashed against the underwater rocks, which was what happened to us, despite our meticulous calculations! However, we all emerged unscathed and exhilarated, and once we'd got our breath back, we were ready for another go.

My log from the second dive brings it all back: *After our decompression break, water speed had increased considerably so we decided to have another go to catch the drift. It was a high-speed roller-coaster – an exhilarating rough and tumble, crashing into boulders and rolling over and over. No control whatsoever. After a minute we had to release our buddy line and just go for it. I surfaced without knowing whether I was up or down, and then got taken back down for another whirligig along the riverbed. No time to look for or at creatures! A great dive to end on.*

I remember it seemed to last for ever, and was astonished, on finally surfacing, to see from my computer my total time underwater was a rather less than impressive three minutes. However, we'd been hurled along at a speed of around 20 knots, and covered quite a distance in that short period.

Computer? I hear you asking. Underwater? Yes. This vital piece of equipment, worn on the wrist, monitors everything you need to know to stay alive and well: depth, length of time underwater, water temperature and how much diving time you safely have remaining.

By mid-day today we were comfortably ensconced on the thirty-acre Caravan and Motorhome Club site at North Ledaig. This is an idyllic and well cared-for site with first class facilities and a great little shop with a good range of food and other essential items. Just a couple of miles from Oban, it has a two-mile stretch of beach with views to the Isle of Mull. By the time we'd had lunch, the sky was blue, the sun was shining and we unloaded the bikes.

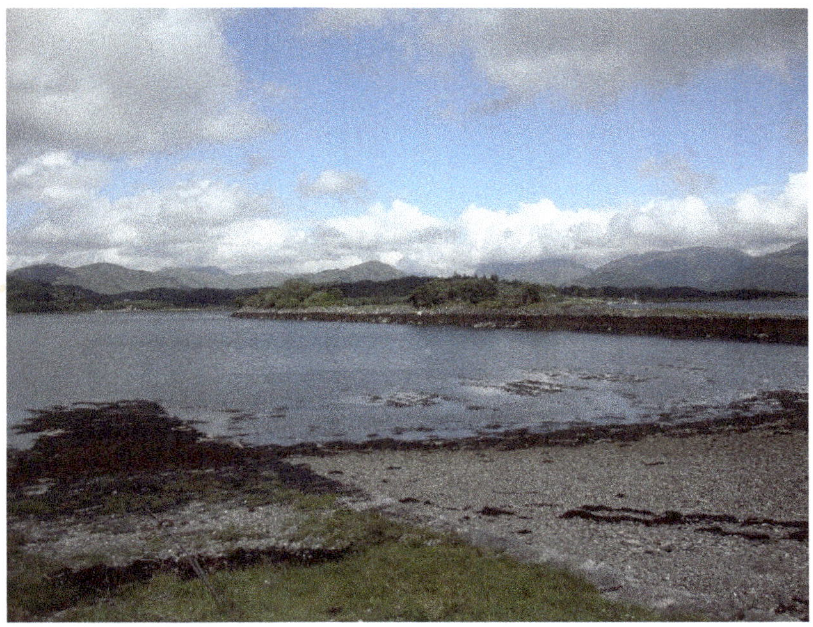

Loch Creran, Benderloch

Our cycle ride took us along a tarmacked cycleway that was originally part of the Ballachulish railway line, to the village of Benderloch, which was also one of the stations on the route and is close to the site of the former Pictish city of Beregonium, the legendary capital of ancient Scotland. The Picts were a mix of various tribes of Celtic-speaking people who lived in eastern and northern Scotland in the Iron Age. Remains of their settlements, such as the broch we saw on Skye, are still evident.

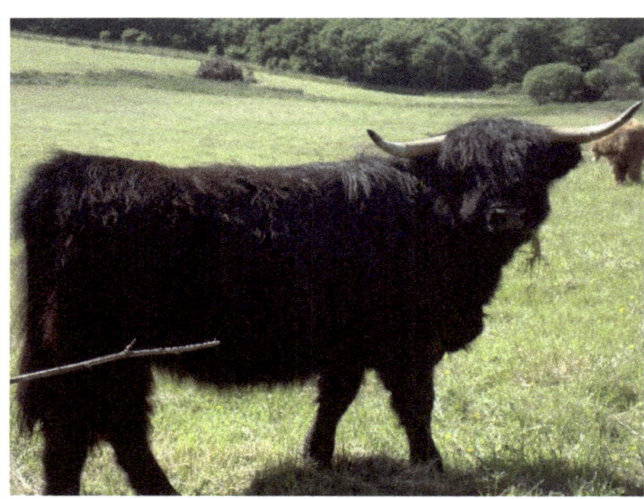

Leaving Benderloch we followed traffic-free country lanes for a few miles, passing a big salmon farm in Loch Creran, a field full of black and brown Highland cattle and Barcaldine Castle.

Also known as the Black Castle of Benderloch, because of the dark stone used in its construction, it was built between 1601 and 1609 by Duncan, 1st Lord Campbell. It is one of the few medieval castles in Scotland that is still habitable, with nine-foot-thick walls that rise to a height of thirty-two feet. These days it is used as a wedding venue and hotel, for which it enjoys its reputation for being haunted.

Because, I think, of his hair colour and his choice of headwear, Lord Campbell is remembered, and depicted in paintings, as Black Duncan of the Cowl. However, he was probably better known as Black Duncan of the Seven Castles, a reference to the string of fortifications he built across Scotland as a means of protecting his extensive estates.

We got back to Bessie just in time to get the bikes loaded back onto the rack before the skies darkened and the rain came down again.

Today's mileage: 52

Stirling

North Ledaig to Loch Lubhair

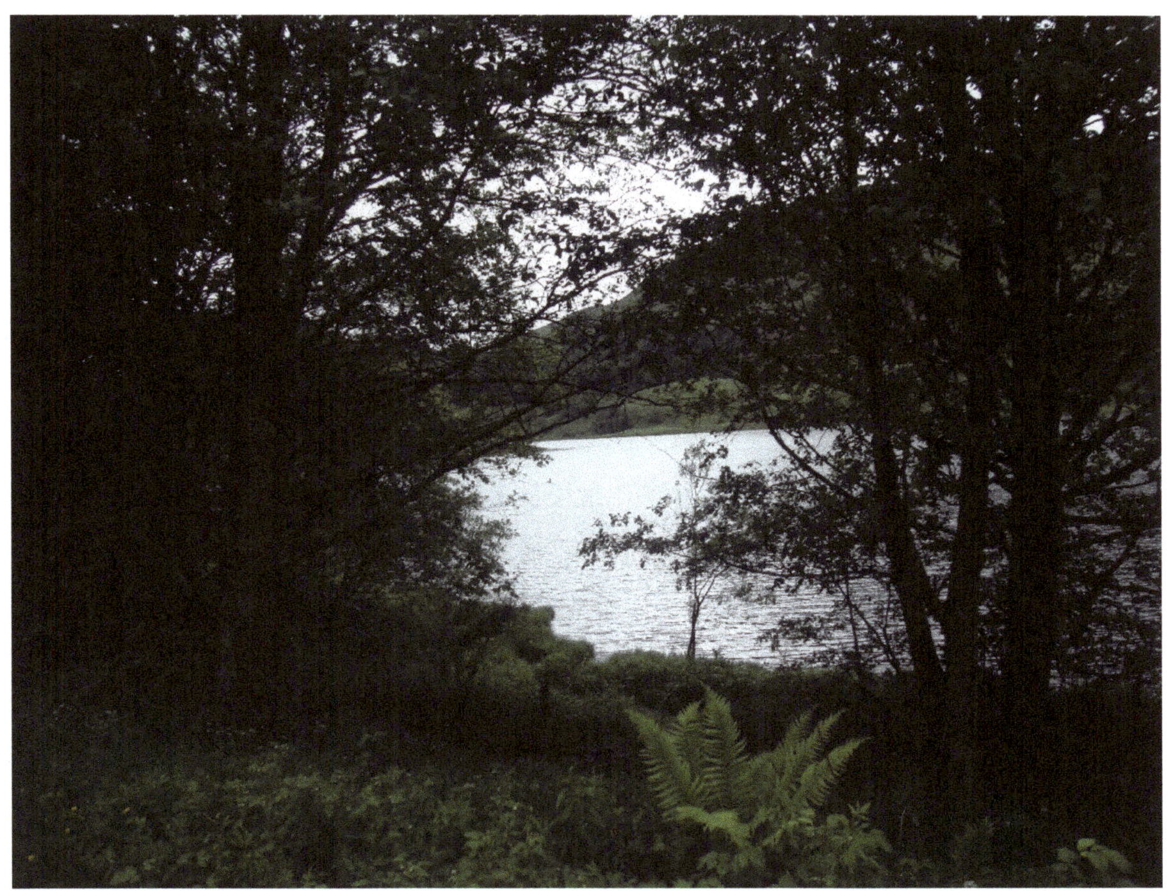

Loch Lubhair

Sunday, 11th June

Forests, mountains, rivers, glens, lochs, castles, waterfalls and the sea. We've seen all of these, every day since we arrived in Scotland and today we saw every one of them within two hours of setting off.

Loch of the day was Loch Awe, whose verdant banks are lined with trees right down to the shore. Close to the water's edge the road passes the entrance to Cruachan Power Station, the turbine for which is buried one kilometre below the ground, deep inside Ben Cruachan: the 'hollow' mountain. As we rounded the north-eastern tip of the loch, we could see the ruined 15th century Kilchurn Castle, home for 150 years to the powerful Campbells of Glenorchy, builders of the castle we saw yesterday at Benderloch. They left in the 1700s for the much grander Taymouth Castle, after which Kilchurn fell into ruins.

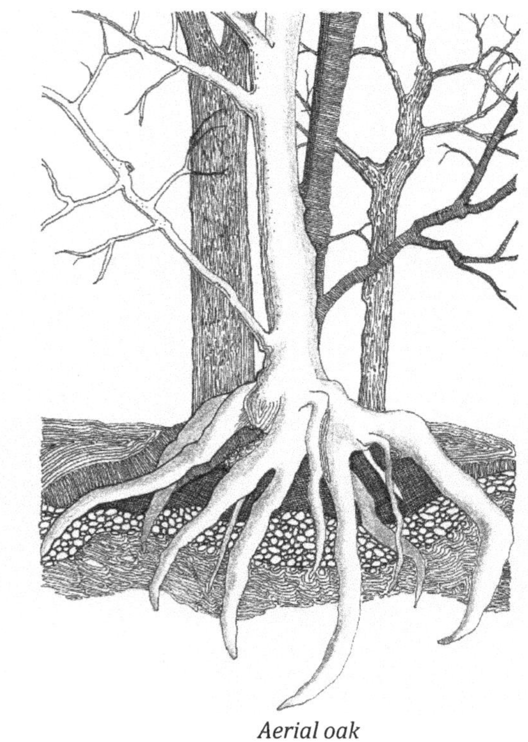

Aerial oak

This morning's first pit stop was Strone Hill, yet another welcoming area of woodland, tended and nurtured by Forestry Commission Scotland. As ever, there are neither fees nor restrictions on motorhomes entering the car park. We resisted the temptation to stay for the rest of today and overnight, instead satisfying ourselves with a gentle stroll before going on our way.

We followed two easy, circular walking trails through oak, birch and rowan, looking out for the 'aerial tree', an ancient oak. It has roots above the ground and the trunk growing above them. Foresters believe it self-seeded into a fallen trunk and as the oak grew and matured the host trunk rotted away, leaving the roots exposed.

Annoyingly, I only took one photograph and didn't realise until later that it was blurry and out of focus but, in any case, Lesley Hall-Wood's drawing gives a better idea of its appearance than I can describe.

All the trees were mature and impressive, including another ancient and massive oak that was almost as wide as it was tall.

Back on the road in Glen Lochy we were also in the land of snow poles marking the edges of the carriageway, and mile after mile of forest clearance with thousands of branches and bits of tree trunks littering the slopes. Further on we saw that the logging tracks on the mountainsides were punctuated with huge piles of tree trunks awaiting collection and transportation – double articulated lorries are a common sight on these roads. The weight of the loads they carry must be phenomenal.

By then it was late morning and we were getting peckish. But where have all the Scottish bakers gone? Have they been put out of business by the proliferation of Spar shops? Most of the villages we've driven through have a Spar, but very few, as far as we could see, have a bakery. We fancied bridies* for lunch, but you need a proper baker for them and we haven't seen one since we left Wick, ten days ago.

By lunchtime (rolls in the absence of bridies) we were approaching Crianlarich, a village just north of Loch Lomond. Famed as the Gateway to the Highlands, it is the junction of two major roads, the A82 and the A85, that link central and north west Scotland, and is a well-known overnight stop for walkers and backpackers tackling the 96-mile West Highland Way. It was pouring with rain and blowing a gale when we got there and hardly conducive to walking. But four miles further on the dreadful weather failed to detract from the beauty of our wild camp site for the night, a lay-by in Glen Dochart on the shores of Loch Lubhair. Pronounced yoo-ar, the name means yew loch but I wasn't aware of any yews there.

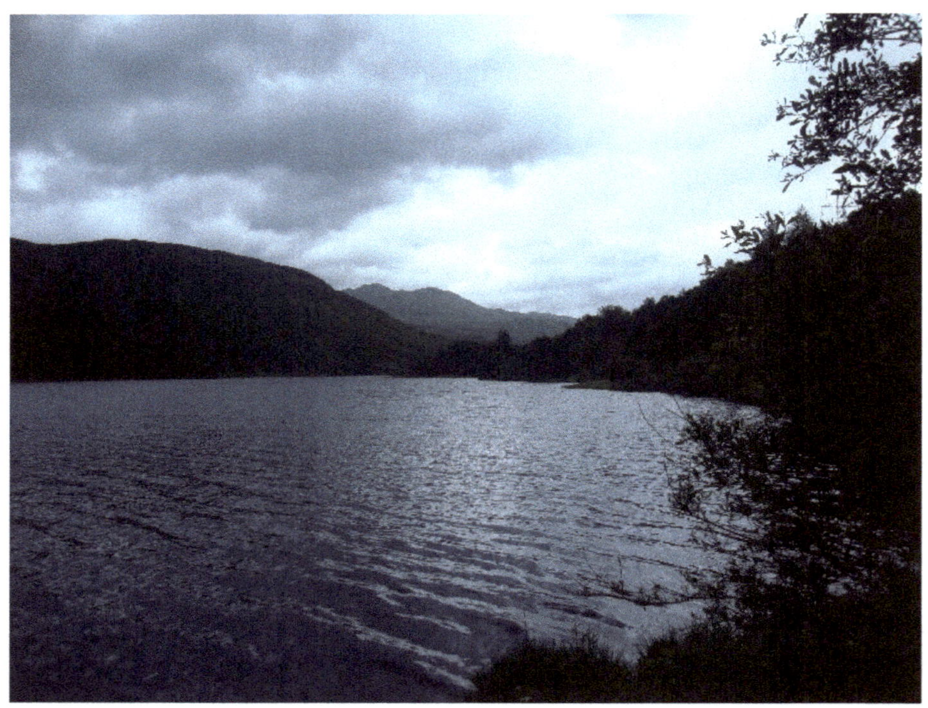

An overcast Loch Lubhair

Sometimes it's nice to have bad weather as an excuse for shutting yourself inside and spending time just reading, resting and drinking tea. So that's what we did for the rest of the day.

Today's mileage: 41

**Bridies: Scotland's answer to the Cornish pasty, they originated in Forfar and consist of minced steak seasoned with salt and pepper, and come in two varieties – with or without onion.*

Perth and Kinross

Loch Lubhair to Perth

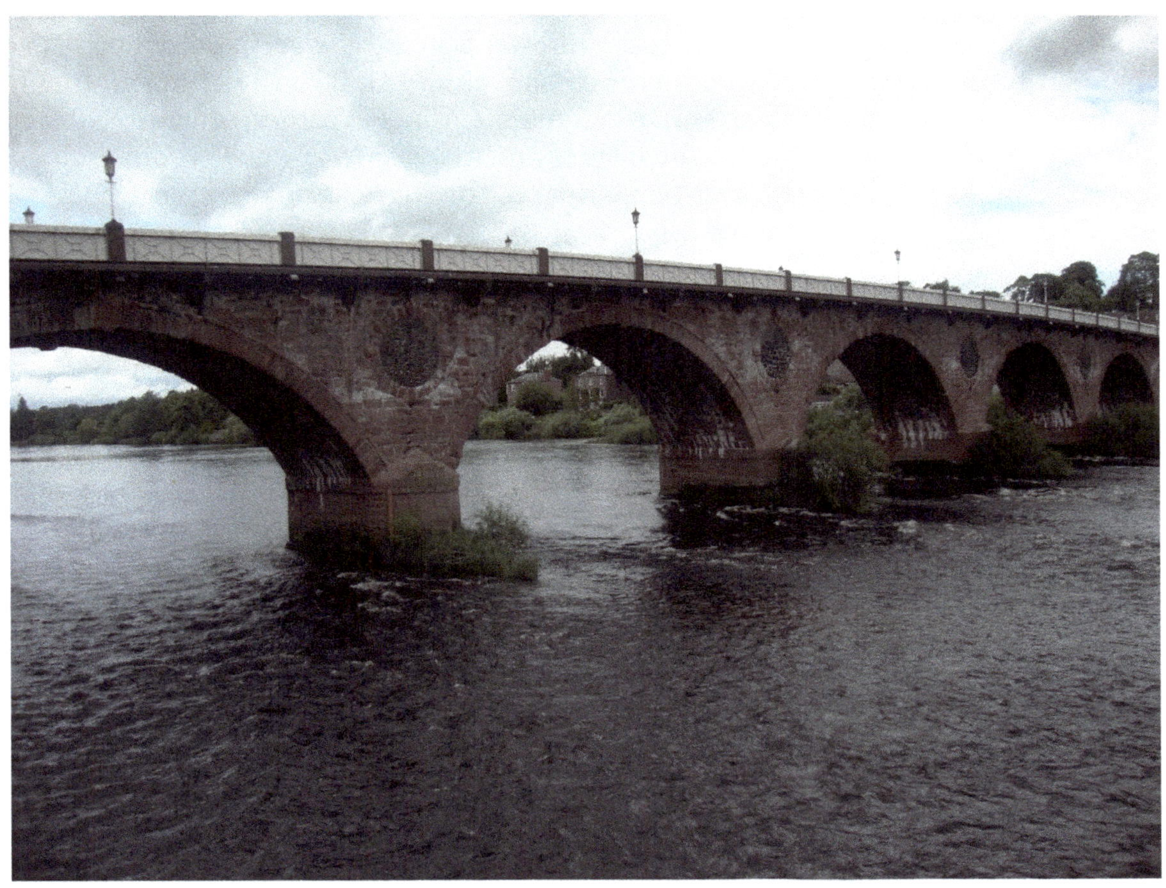

Perth Bridge straddles the River Tay in Scotland's former capital

Monday, 12th June

At last! We found a proper baker, Campbell's of Comrie, and bought two onion bridies for lunch. So delighted were we with this that we ate them for elevenses. And very good they were too, with a delicious filling and crisp flaky pastry, as opposed to the traditional shortcrust pastry used in Forfar, original home of the bridie. The smell of freshly baked bread filled our nostrils and teased our taste buds, so while we were at it, we stocked up on Scotch rolls and two of Scotland's famous strawberry tarts. They didn't last long, either! Unbelievable though it may seem, given the country's general reputation for bad weather, Angus, Fife and Perthshire are famous for their strawberries and raspberries. Dundee is the sunniest city in Scotland and the east coast regularly tops the charts for having more hours of sunshine than anywhere else in Scotland.

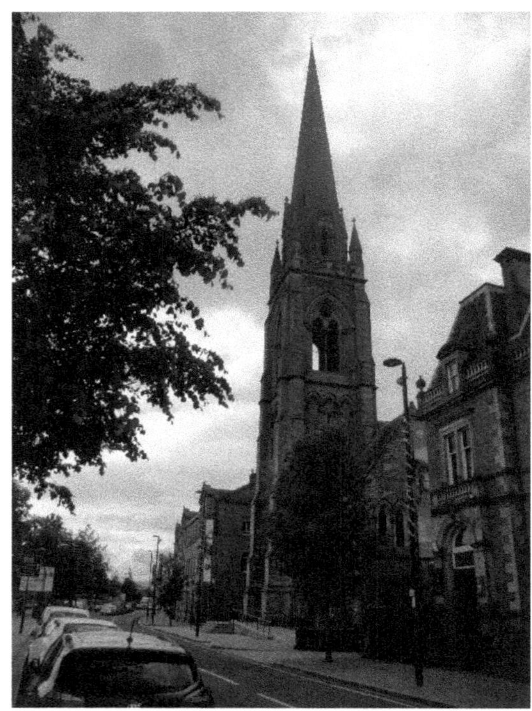

An example of Perth's gothic architecture

We'd left the rain and wind of Loch Lubhair straight after breakfast. The sky soon began to clear and we enjoyed the scenery through Glen Ogle and along Loch Earn, through Lochearnhead to Comrie, and on to Lochty, just outside Perth, for our coffee stop.

I am not a city person but I do know that in many cities you have to look up to appreciate the full splendour of old architecture, and this was certainly the case in Scotland's one-time capital, the 'fair city' of Perth.

St Ninian's Scottish Episcopal Cathedral, on the edge of the city and just across the road from the river, is more handsome inside than the impression given by the dour Victorian exterior. We were given a warm welcome by one of the cathedral's gentlemanly guides, who told us about the £750,000 restoration fund-raising appeal. He said most of the money raised so far was a result of the efforts of elderly members of the congregation holding events such as coffee mornings. I hope it will soon be possible to carry out the necessary work to prevent the ingress of water from the old internal downpipes.

Our overnight stop was a lay-by at Kinnoul Hill Woodland Park, overlooking the city. By now it was hot and sunny, and we appreciated the shade of the trees as we walked up through the woods to the top of the hill. From there a panoramic view takes in the city of Perth and the River Tay, snaking its way eastwards towards Dundee. In the far distance we could just make out Birnam Woods. Celebrated in Shakespeare's Macbeth, it is part of what remains of the remains of the ancient Caledonian Forest that once covered much of Scotland. It was the only hill we could see that had trees growing right to the very top.

Known as Scotland's rainforest, the Caledonian is now one of the country's endangered habitats. At one time it covered more than 1.5 million hectares but these days, thanks to deforestation by humans, over-grazing by deer and the introduction of sheep over the past two or three centuries, it is down to less than five per cent of that. As the human population grew, trees were burned to eradicate predators such as wolves and this resulted in an explosion in the numbers of red deer roaming the Highlands and eating the seedlings.

What remains of the forest is now being looked after largely by the charity Trees for Life, and the possibility of re-introducing wolves here, as well as to other parts of the Highlands has not yet been entirely ruled out. The UK Wolf Conservation Trust has carried out a feasibility study but says further detailed studies need to be carried out before a decision can be made. In the meantime, I am pleased to know that there is still an abundance of wildlife thriving in what is left of the native pinewoods, including red squirrels, pine martins, rare sawflies, ospreys, wood ants and black grouse.

It was only when we reached the top of Kinnoul Hill, with its sheer cliff-edge drop onto rocks 728 feet below, that we appreciated the importance of the sign we'd seen at the start of our walk.

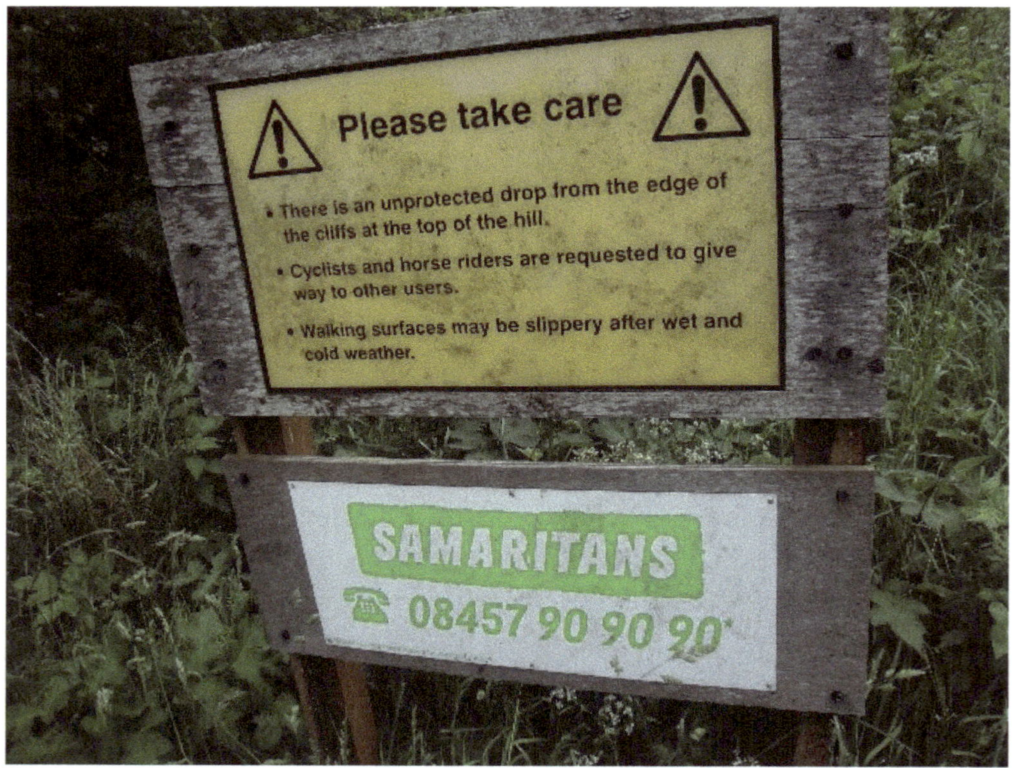

Help for desperate people

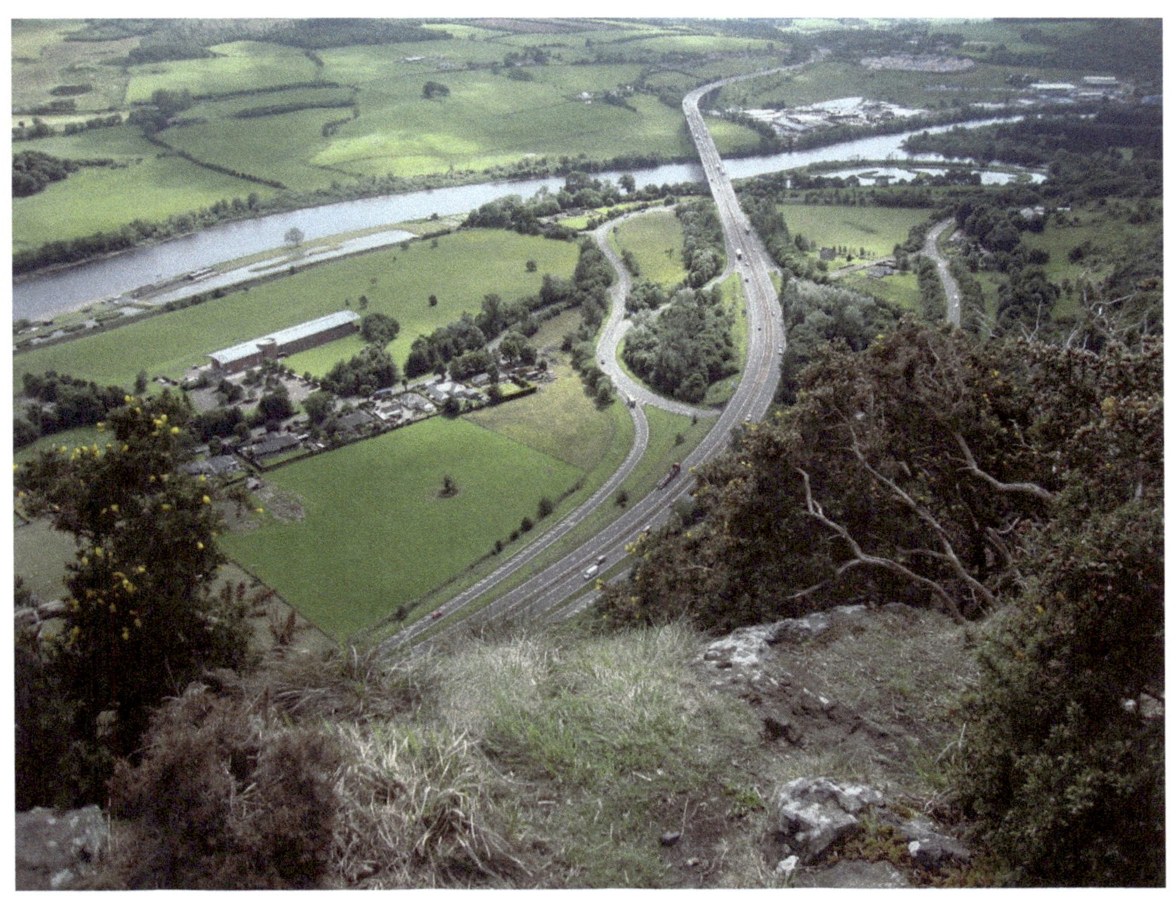

On the edge

Today's mileage: 53

Perthshire and City of Edinburgh

Perth to Edinburgh

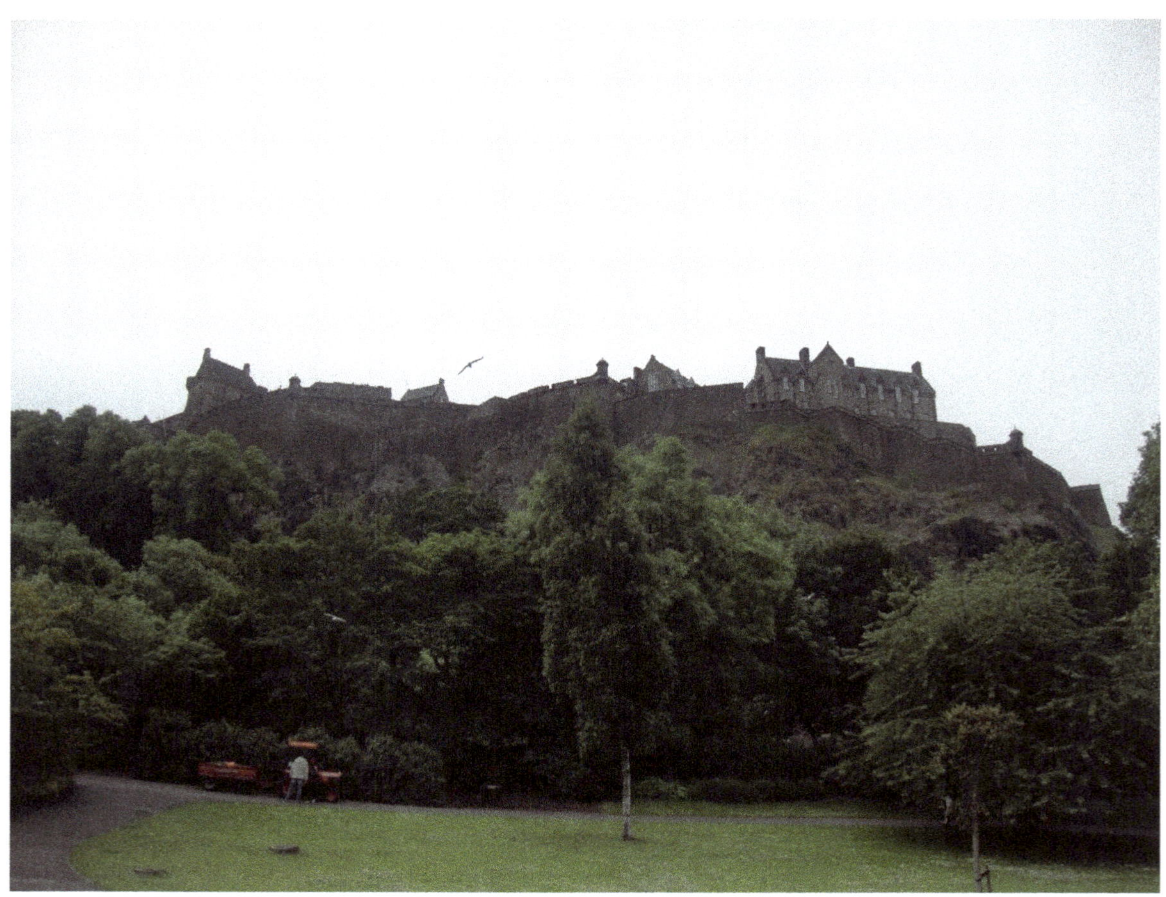

The nearest we got to Edinburgh Castle

Tuesday 13th and Wednesday 14th June

You can't really go on a touring holiday of Scotland without visiting its capital city. Two days of city life would be more than enough for us, but we felt it would also give us sufficient time to work our way through the list of things we want to see and do:

- Open-top bus tour
- The castle
- Royal Yacht Britannia
- The Old Town
- The Georgian New Town
- The Royal Mile
- Arthur's Seat and Salisbury Crags

Here's what we did:

- Royal Yacht Britannia (on Tuesday afternoon)
- Open-top bus tour
- A bit of The Royal Mile
- Went back to Bessie

Feeble or what? But the truth is, after nearly six weeks of living in wild spaces, peaceful countrywide and calm campsites we were completely unable to cope with the crowds, the noise and the bustle of Edinburgh – for example, the road up to the castle was as packed as the centre of Cardiff on the day of a big rugby international!

We caught a bus from the splendid Caravan and Motorhome Club's site on the outskirts of the city, to Ocean Terminal in Leith, the permanent berth for the Royal

Yacht Britannia, but weren't able to see much because of all the security fencing. I was too mean to let Mike pay for us to go on Britannia's tour but after we'd cheered ourselves up with lunch in the Marks and Spencer café at the adjacent Ocean Quay shopping precinct, he persuaded me.

'We're here now and you said all along you wanted to do it' and before I could protest, he joined the queue for tickets.

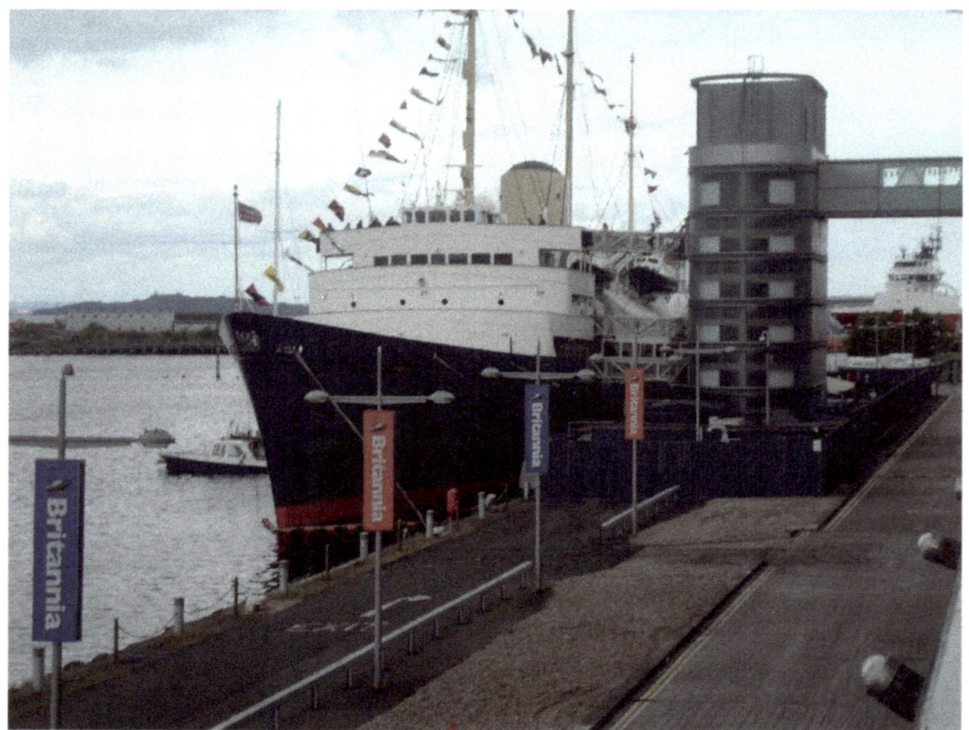

This is as near as you can get to Britannia without paying to go on board

Whether you are a royalist or not, the yacht is worth a visit. At around £15 a ticket (concessionary price for wrinklies) it isn't cheap but if you wait until after 2pm you get a 10% discount. By the time we left, even I thought it was worth it. The tour is self-guided: you are given a handset with a commentary and you can take as long as you like. There is no restriction on photography, either:

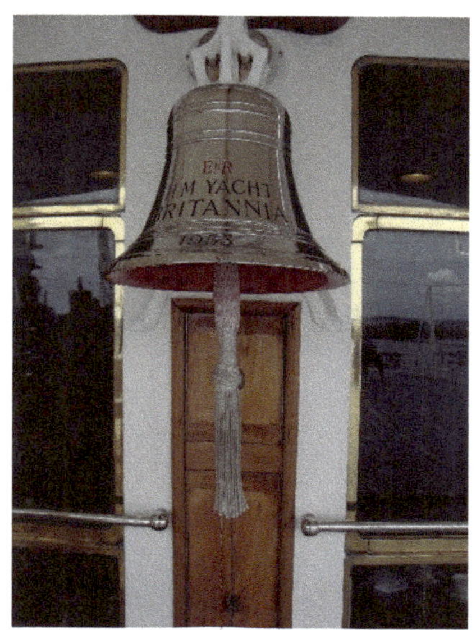

The ship's bell

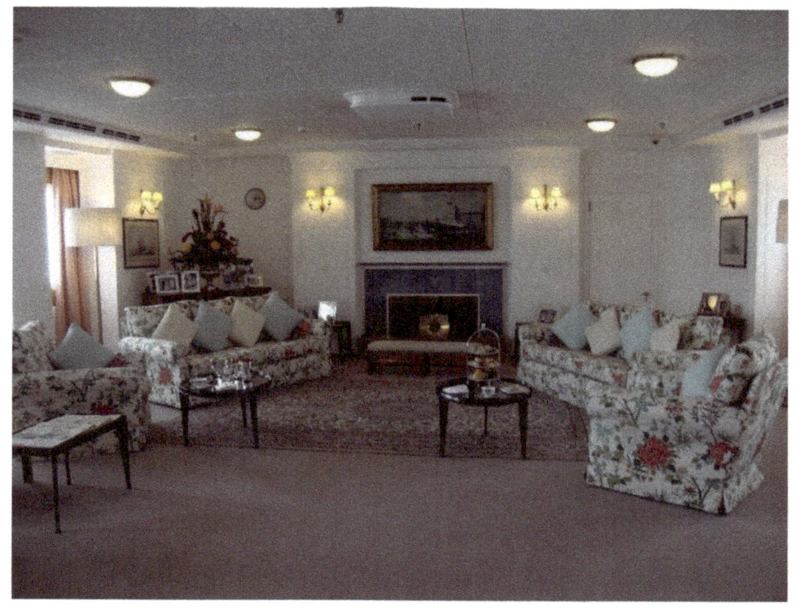

The Royal sitting room

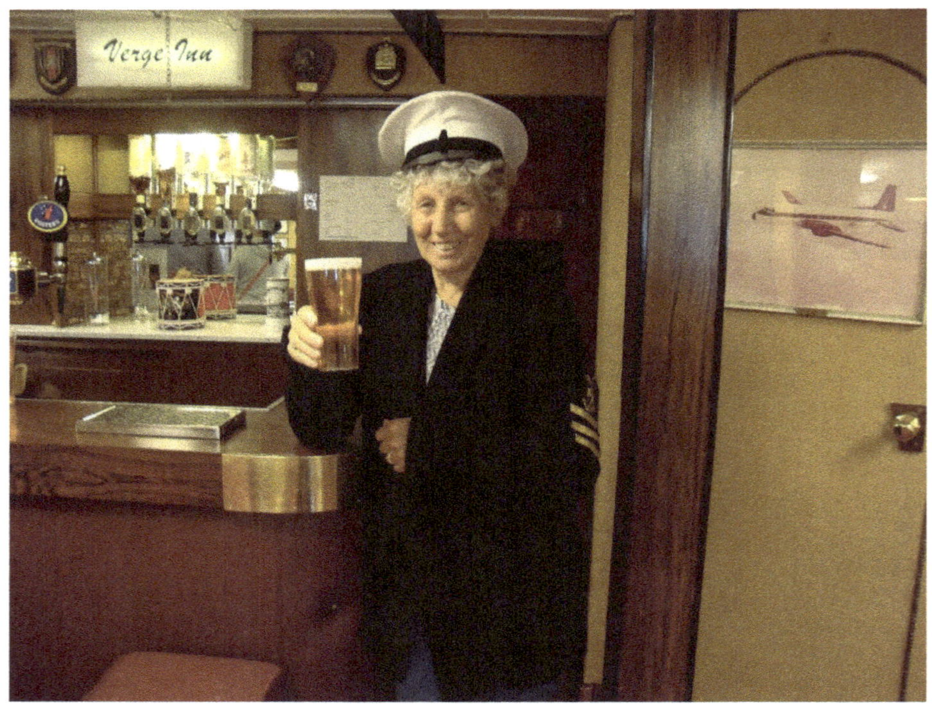

Jackie, propping up the bar in the ward room

For Wednesday's open-top bus tour we paid £14 each for about 90 minutes, and it is well worth doing especially if, as we did, you are lucky enough to get a good and knowledgeable guide. It's a hop-on-hop-off service, with three different routes from which to choose, so you can tailor your tour to please yourself. Interesting and enjoyable though it was, by the time it had ended and we'd walked a little way up The Royal Mile, we'd had enough and before long we caught the bus back to the camp site.

Sorry Edinburgh, but we probably won't be visiting again!

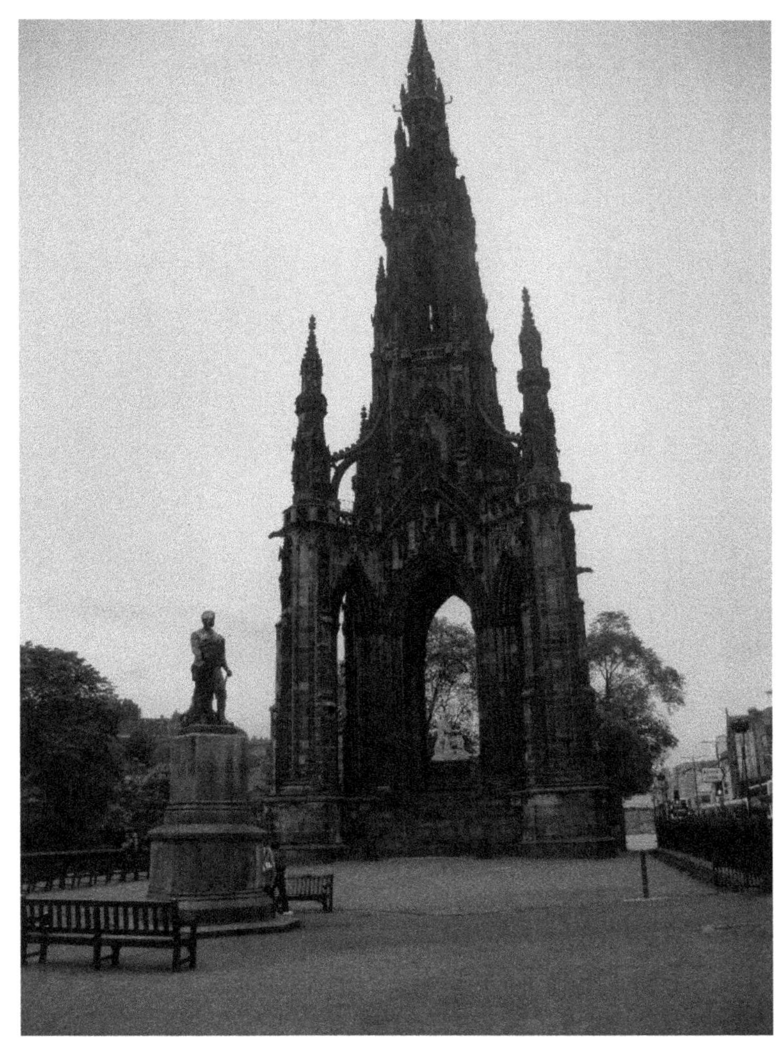

The Scott monument stands tall on Princes Street

Mileage on Tuesday: 48

Dumfries & Galloway to Cumbria

Heading for home

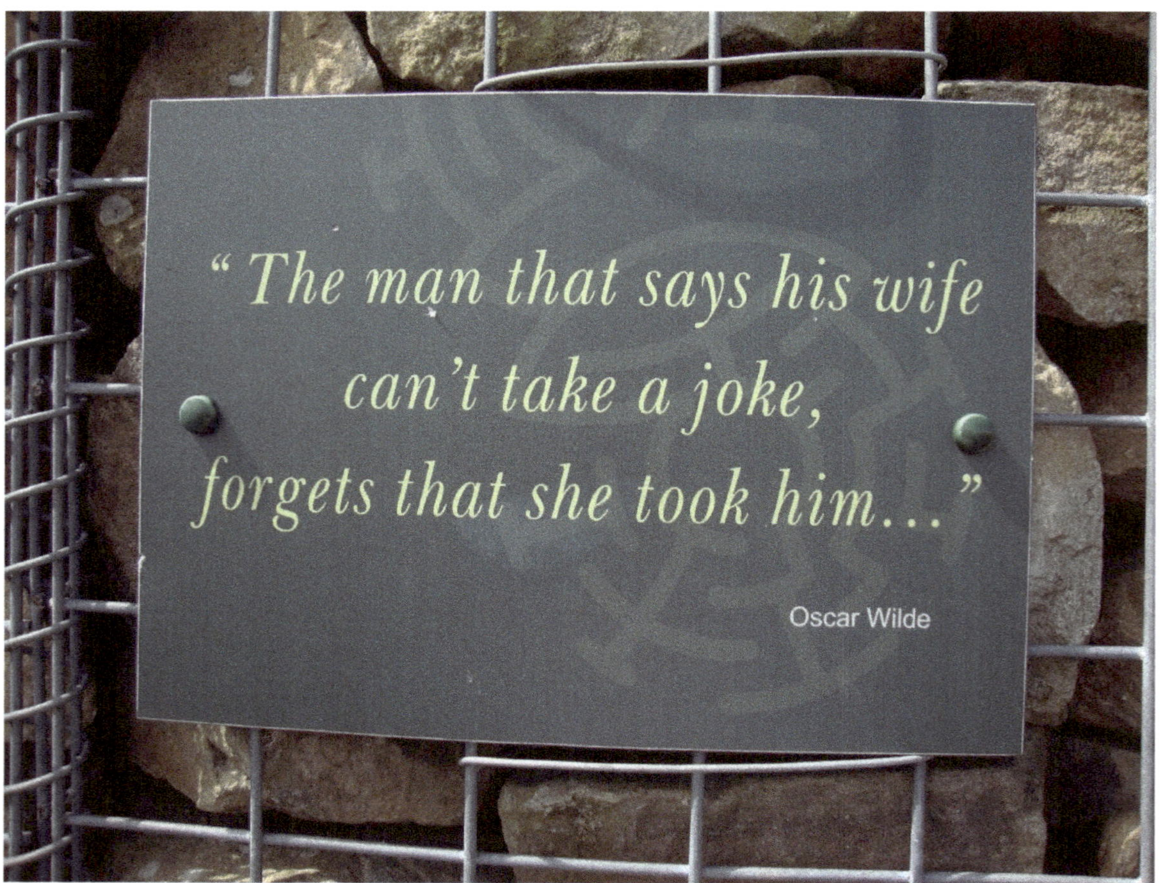

Oscar Wile quotation in Gretna's Courtship Maze – for all my married women friends!

Thursday, 15th June

This was our last morning in Scotland and we were planning a comparatively long drive today to Kirkby Lonsdale in England. But first we wanted to visit The Old Smithy at Gretna Green and, pair of old romantics that we are, to have our photograph taken at the marriage anvil.

Alas, this was not to be. As ever with these tourist hotspots, the place was heaving with visitors; the anvil was hidden away somewhere in the depths of the visitor centre and, in any case, a wedding was taking place so the area was roped off. It makes you wonder why a little three-hundred-year-old smithy on the Scottish borders should be such a great magnet for visitors and I think it's the romance and history of the place having once been the 'go-to' destination for young couples in a hurry. In 1754 a new law in England meant that couples had to wait until they were twenty-one to marry without parental consent. But Scotland was more relaxed. There, from the age of twelve for girls and fourteen for boys, anyone was allowed to wed, with or without the consent of their parents. There were no legal or religious formalities either: all they had to do was make simple declarations that they were free and of an age to marry. Another other big advantage was that anyone could officiate.

When the new law was introduced in England, love-struck young couples flocked to Scotland, crossing the border by way of a new toll road. The first place they came to was Gretna and as the blacksmith was viewed as the most senior member of the community, the forge became a favourite, if unconventional venue. The marriage was sealed by the striking of the anvil.

The forge is now licenced for weddings and for modern couples of all ages and from many different parts of the world it is still the 'go-to' destination. By the way, the legal marriageable age in Scotland is now sixteen, in line with England and Wales, but Scotland is still the only one of the three nations where parental consent is still not required prior to the age of eighteen.

All the time we've been in Scotland I've been looking for real Scottish thistles to photograph. As with the heather, I think our visit was a bit too early in the year as they aren't yet in flower. However, Gretna Green came up trumps in this respect, with this nice sculpture.

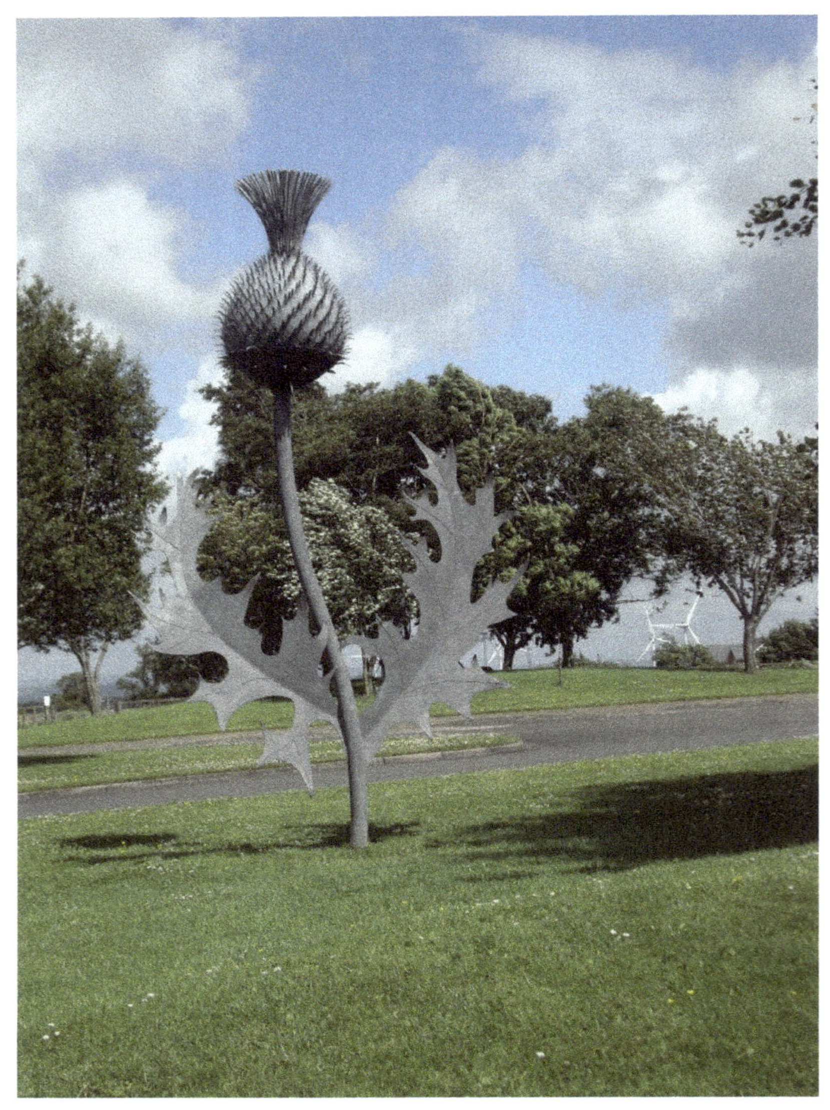

The Old Smithy is, not surprisingly, a massive attraction for people from all over the world as well as the UK and, as usual with us two, it wasn't. I couldn't even get close enough to photograph it.

Away from the hurly-burly of The Old Smithy is the Courtship Maze. In the shape of a pair of interlocking wedding rings, the maze has two entrances, with the paths meeting at the centre. The idea is that it represents the coming together of two people in love and marriage. We had a wander around there, each taking a different entrance. Of course, with his superior spatial awareness prowess, Mike got to the middle while I was still bumbling around in dead ends, reading the romantic quotes painted onto slate slabs and nailed to the stonework of the maze.

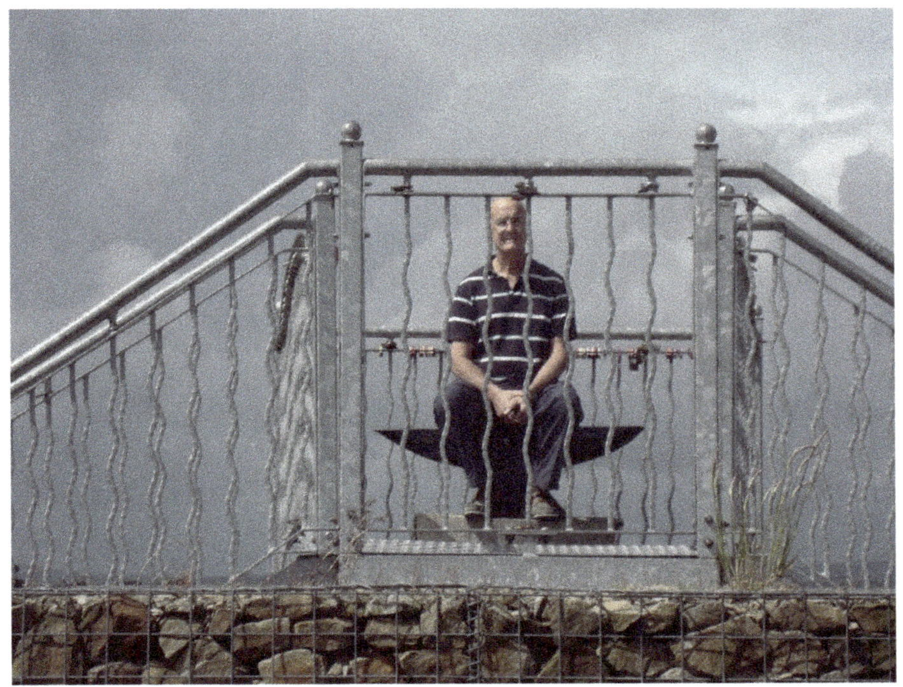

Mike reached the middle first

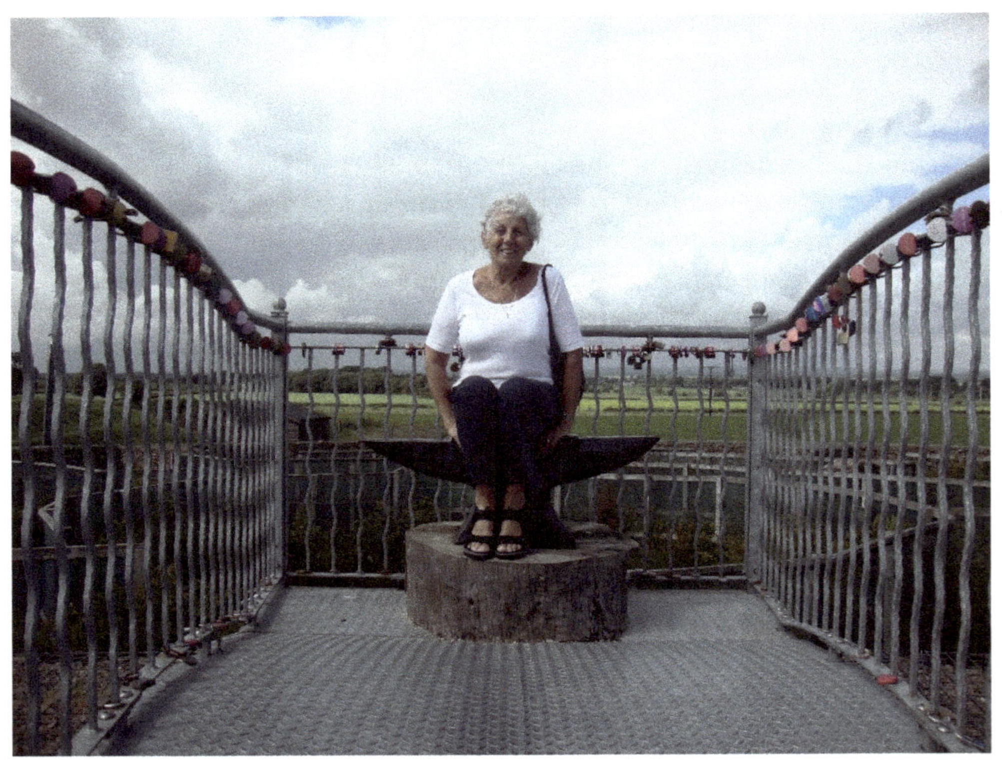

But Jackie got there in the end!

It was late afternoon when we reached Kirkby Lonsdale in Cumbria, a small market town on the edge of the Yorkshire Dales National Park. After driving around looking for somewhere to wild-camp for the night we eventually parked in a lay-by at Devil's Bridge on the River Lune. This was a happy coincidence and completely by chance, for we immediately recognised it as a place we'd visited with old Harry Beagle when we came to the Dales for our 25th wedding anniversary in 2015.

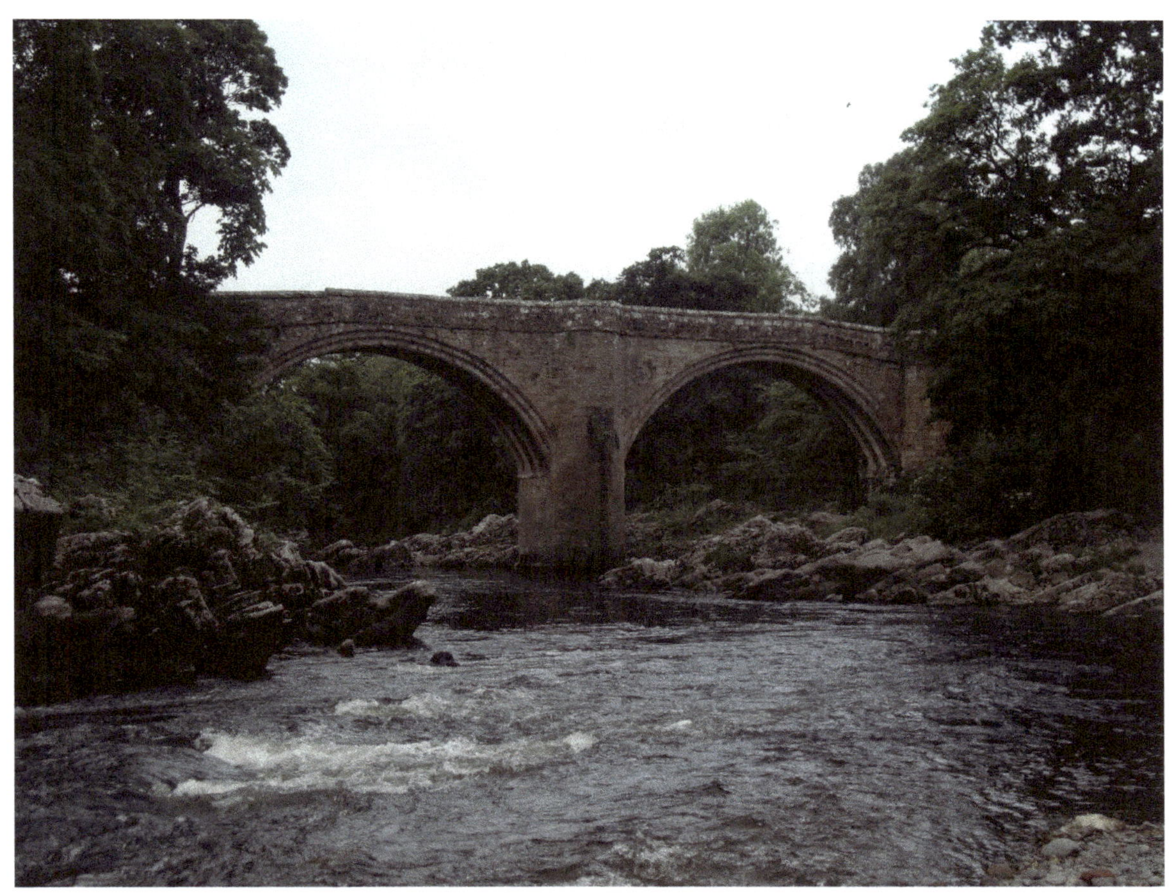

Devil's Bridge and the River Lune

Devil's Bridge is high above the river, with its clear water and boulder strewn banks. As we were leaning over the parapet looking for fish, we were joined by a council workman who told us the water in the middle of the river at that point is about 25 feet deep, and there had been several deaths there. That explained the warning notices we'd seen at each end of the pedestrianised footway: NO PERSON SHALL WITHOUT REASONABLE EXCUSE JUMP FROM DEVIL'S BRIDGE.

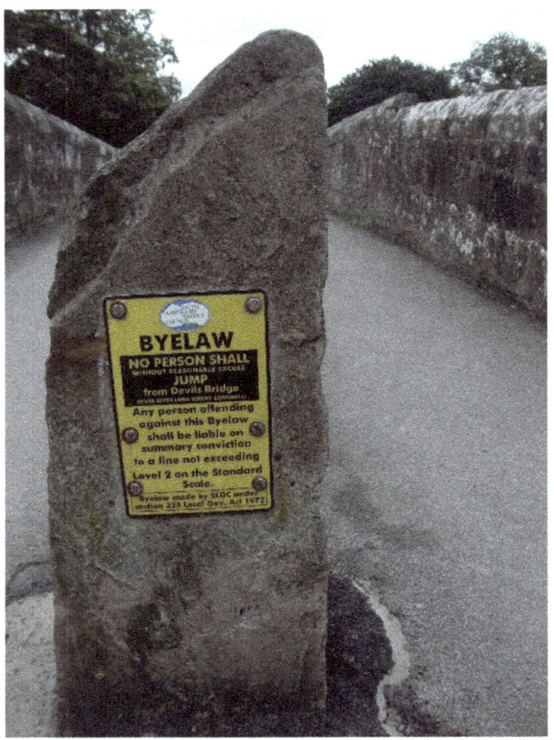

'I used to jump off here when I was a kid,' said our friendly workman. 'But I wouldn't do it now.'

He told us the bridge was built in around 1370 and criminals used to be hanged from it. Apparently, in the days before the bridge was built, the Devil appeared to an old woman and promised to build a bridge in return for the first soul to cross it. She agreed. After the bridge was built, she sent her dog across, and the Devil was outwitted. The legend isn't clear as to whether dogs have souls!

Our lay-by is a popular stopping and meeting point for motorcyclists, and several arrived during the course of the evening. Mike has never lost his love of motorbikes, although it's now more than a decade since he rode the police Pan Europeans for work, so the range of machines coming and going were a real treat for him.

We walked into the town via a path along the banks of the river and a stone staircase, the Radical Steps. At the top we enjoyed Ruskin's View, which was a favourite with the famous Victorian philanthropist and artist, John Ruskin, and has probably changed little in the years that have passed since his death in 1900.

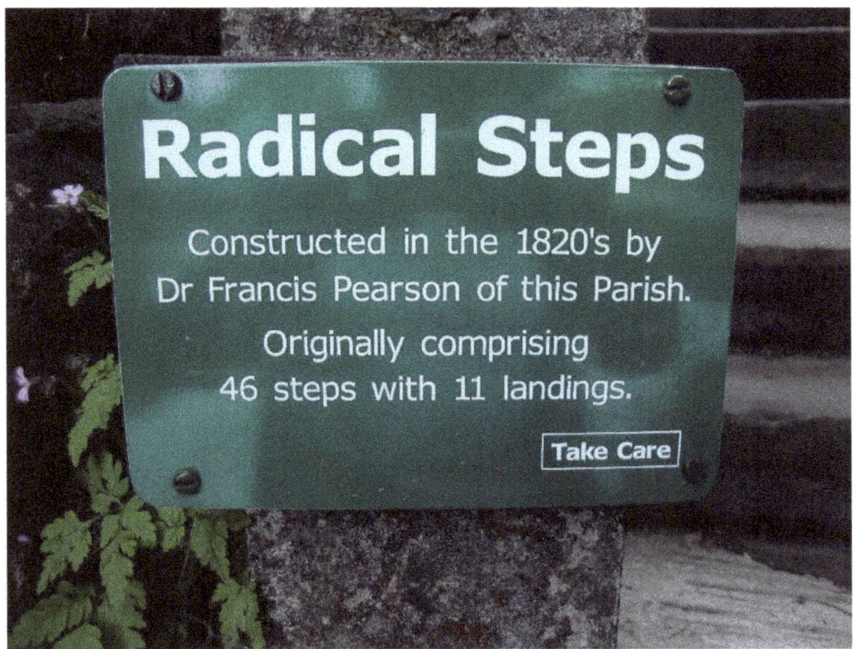

Only 46 steps? We lost count at 80!

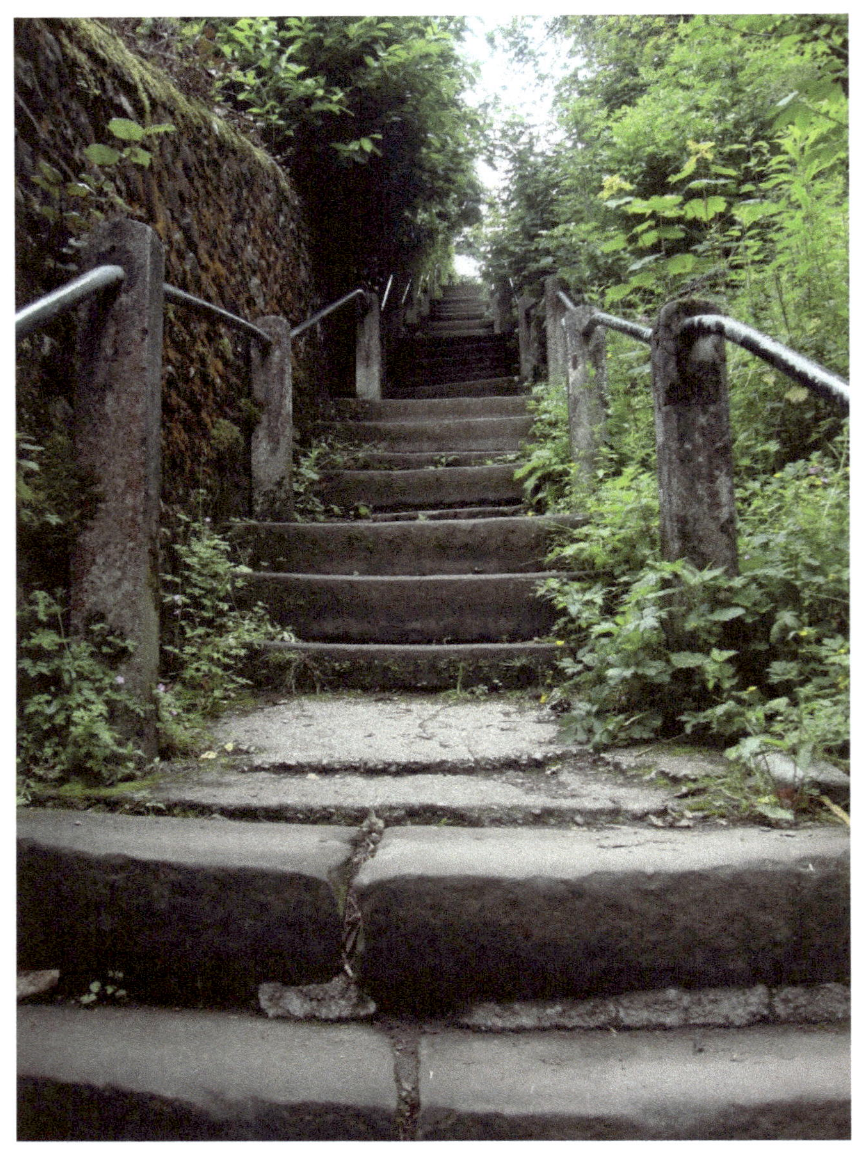

The Radical Steps today

Kirkby Lonsdale is a lovely little town with a strong sense of community. It is full of old buildings, winding alleyways and narrow closes and has a nice artisan bakery too. Despite its popularity with holidaymakers, the town has lost none of its charm and character. It's well worth a visit and we hope to go back.

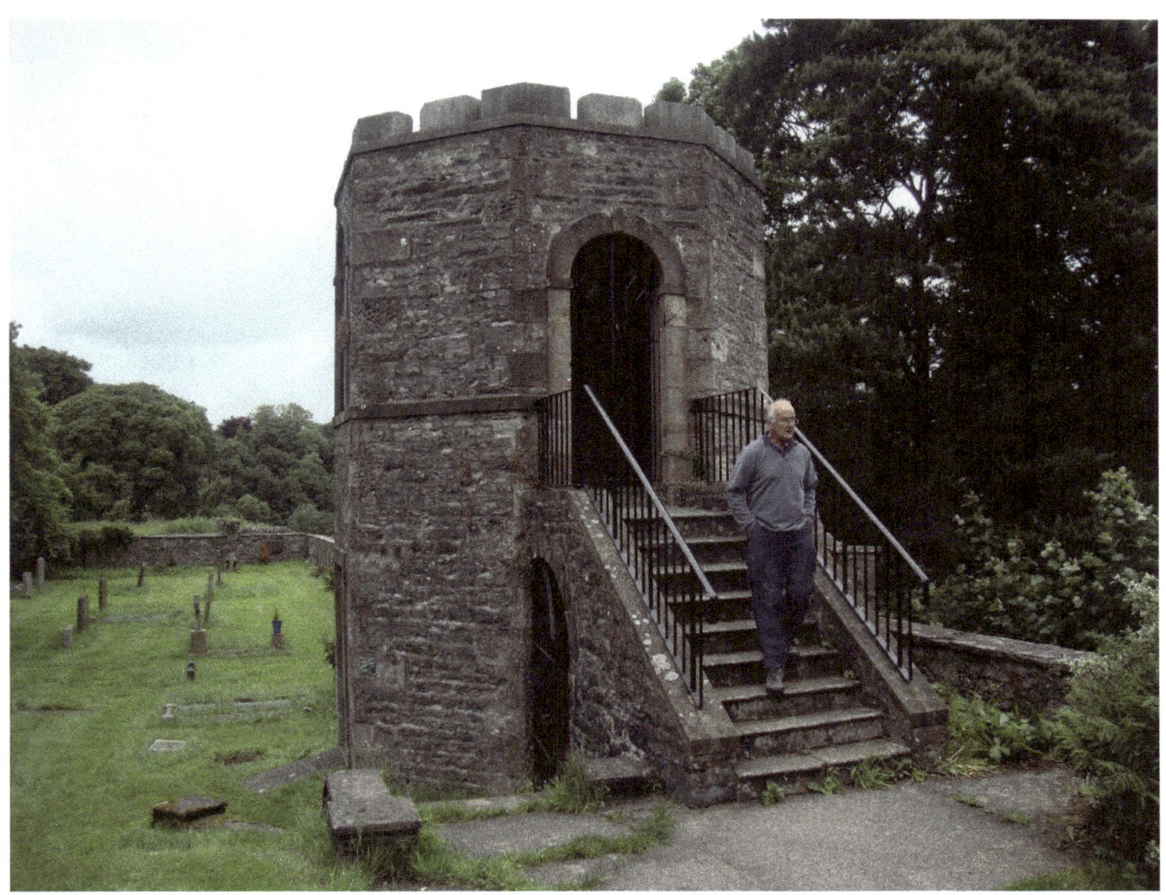

This stone gazebo is in the former vicarage garden of St Mary's Church

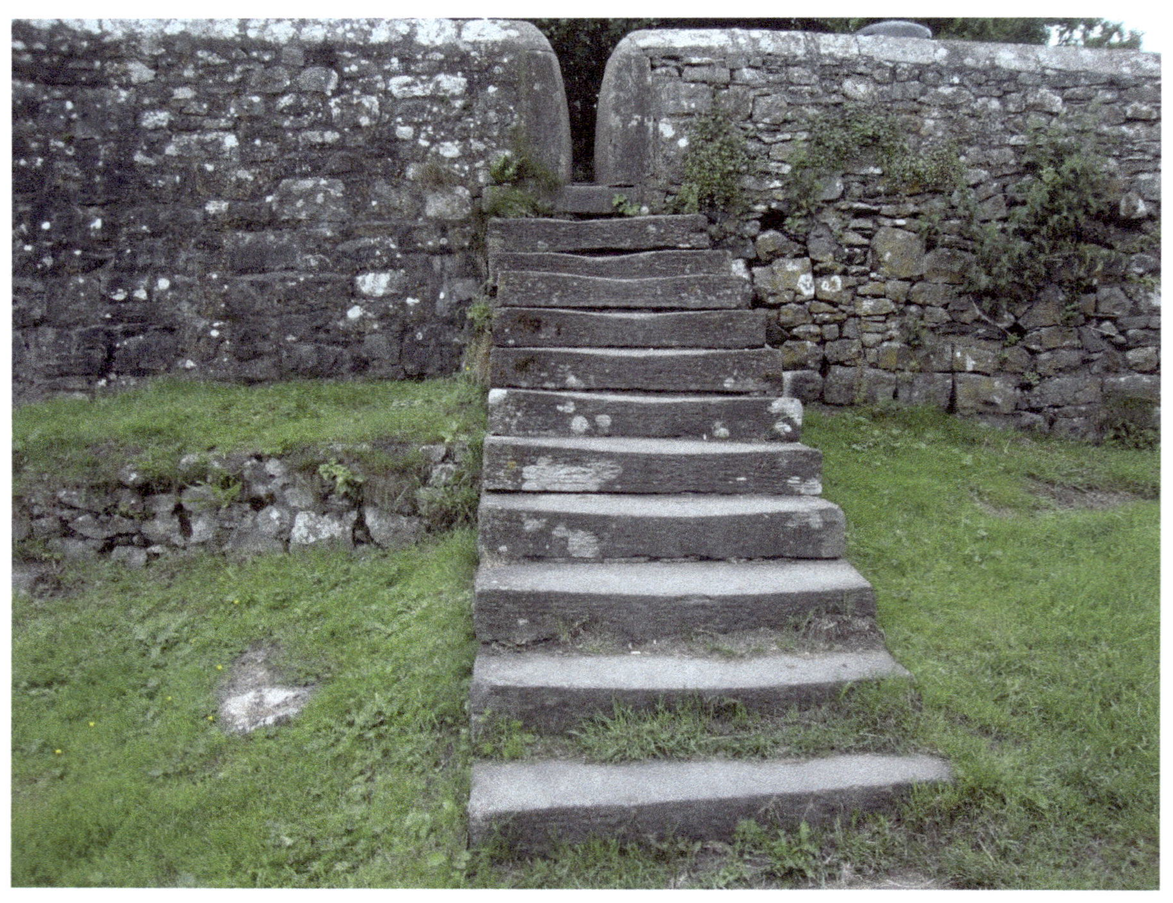

Ancient steps from the riverbank to the bridge. People were clearly much slimmer in the 14th century!

Today's mileage: 173

Bessie Goes Home

Kirkby Lonsdale to Chirk

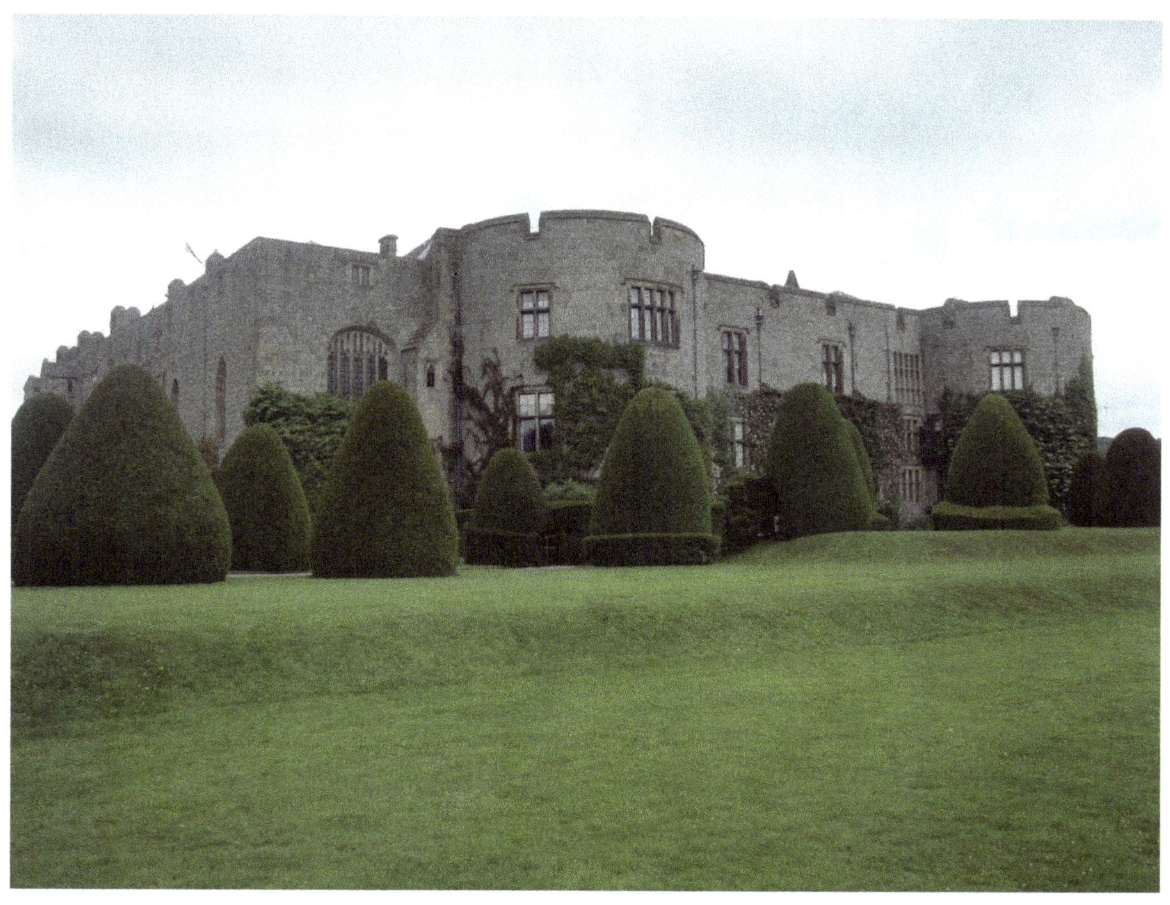

Chirk Castle. Medieval fortress of the Welsh Marches

Friday, 16th June

Chirk is another nice town, with lots of cycle routes and interesting places to visit, including the massive Chirk Castle. There is also a huge factory, smelling of chocolate and with a big sign at the entrance proclaiming it to be Mondelez. This, it turns out, is a 'cocoa bean processing factory'. That, to most of us, means chocolate. And if it's chocolate, it has to be Cadbury.

Today the weather has taken a definite turn for the hotter and by the time we reached the Caravan and Motorhome Club site shortly after eleven, the temperatures were creeping above 30 degrees Celsius and the sun was dazzling through the leaves and branches like strobe lights in a disco. Lady Margaret's Park is a charming campsite and we would both love to return one day.

Despite the heat we walked the two miles or so into Chirk and back, and then a couple of uphill miles through a tree-lined drive to the castle, now a National Trust property.

Dating from1295 Chirk Castle was built by Robert Mortimer de Chirk and was one of the chain of eight castles built by the English King Edward 1, as he completed his conquest of Wales. It holds the distinction of having been lived in continuously for almost 700 years.

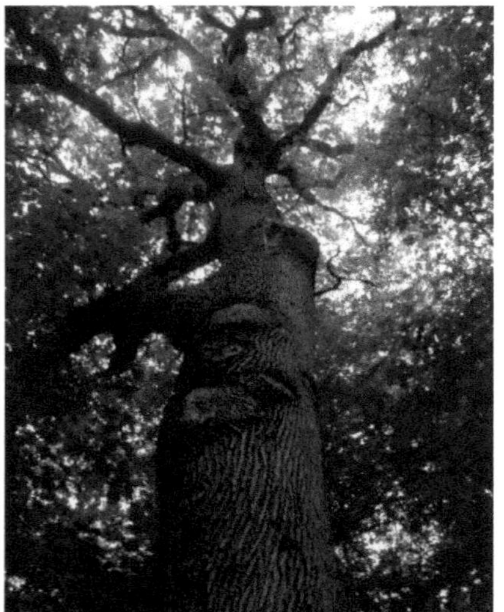

Beautiful old oak tree on the road up to the castle

I had a quick nose around the gardens, which are tended by three gardeners and a team of volunteers. We hadn't paid to get in and it was a bit cheeky of me, so we didn't stay long before picking our way back across some fields and returned to Bessie.

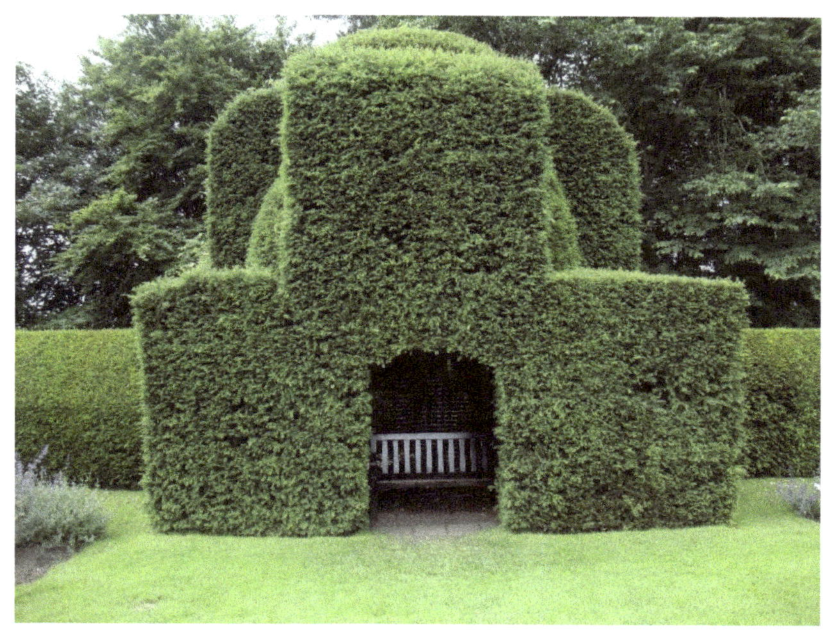

I want one of these!

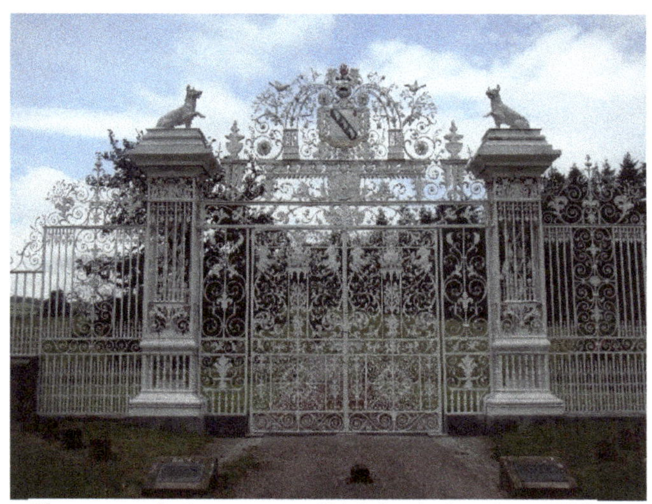

These wrought iron gates at Chirk Castle date from 1712.

The evening remained warm and we relaxed in the late sunshine over a meal of barbecued steak and a bottle of red.

Today's mileage: 121

PART THREE

Powys to Pembrokeshire

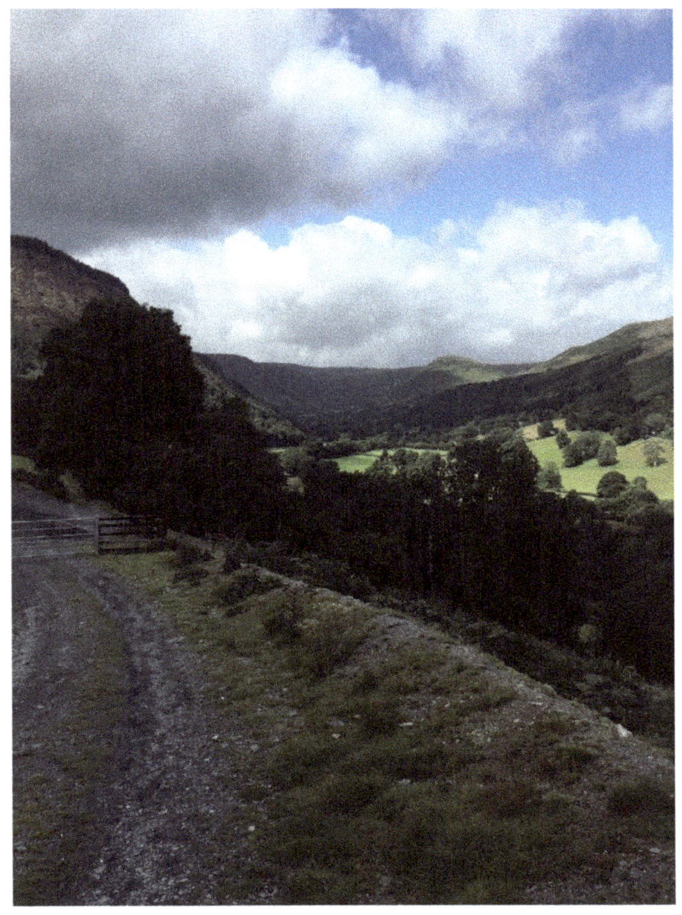

The Berwyn Mountains as seen from Llangynog. Pic by Wayne Musgrave

Saturday 16th June

Well this is the penultimate day of our six-week tour of Scotland and Ireland by motorhome, albeit it's taken in a bit of northern England and now, north Wales. Today we arrived in Llangynog, in the Tanat Valley below the Berwyn Mountains, home to Mike's younger sister Liz, her husband Wayne and their daughter Alex. It's also home to his mother, Vera, who is coming back to Pembrokeshire with us tomorrow.

It's day two of the heatwave with the temperature already soaring into the thirties as we left Chirk. It's only 24 miles from there to Llangynog but it took an inordinate amount of time as our chosen route took us through narrow country lanes and tiny hamlets.

In the evening, Liz and Wayne plied everyone with food and drink – especially drink – and it was an enjoyable, and rare, family gathering, especially as Mike's sister Chris and her husband John had driven over from their home in Shrewsbury for the occasion.

Thank you Liz and Wayne – great hospitality.

Today's mileage: 24

Sunday, 17th June

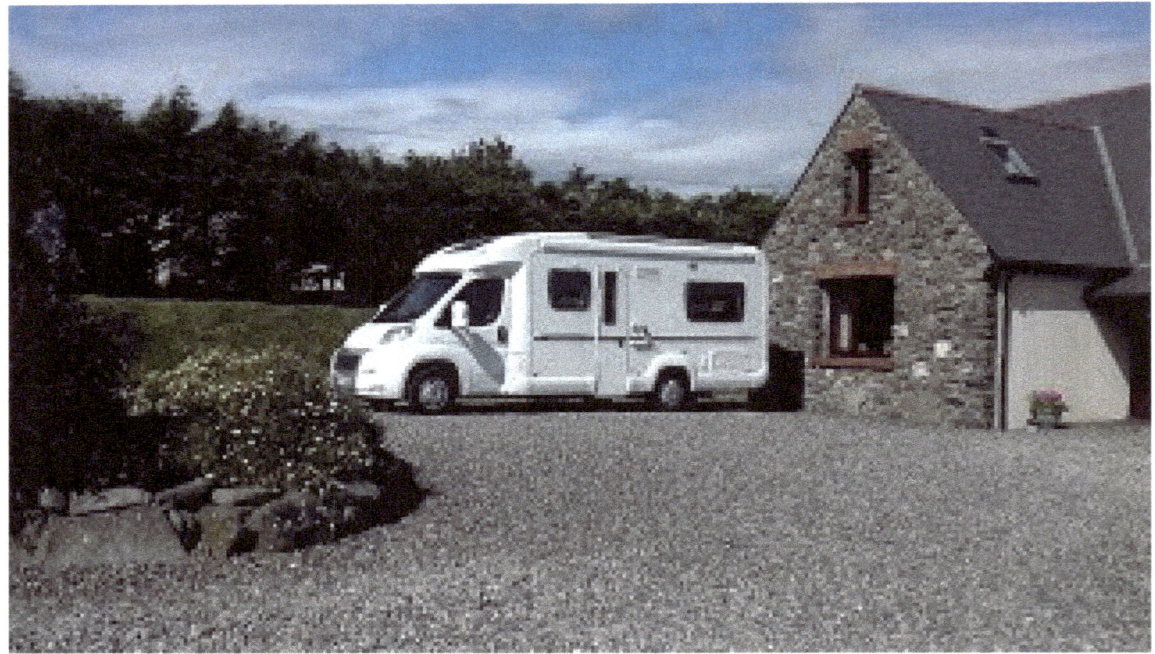

Bessie comes home!

Home at last, after what seemed like a very long drive via Welshpool, Aberystwyth, Cardigan and Fishguard. What made the journey considerably longer was that today was the day of the Tanygroes Tractor Run, in aid of Blood Bikes Wales*, and traffic diversions were in place. It is very easy to lose your sense of place in the back lanes of Ceredigion without a satnav, even with a road atlas on your lap. You have to know where you are to find out where to go, something I found impossible in these remote and unfamiliar places.

In our absence, our near neighbours Carryl Westoby and Jane Williams had done a brilliant job of keeping an eye on the house and, even more heroic, keeping our grass cut. We have around one and a third acres of lawns and paddock and at this time of year it grows at what seems to be easily an inch a day. We know how hard the two of you work at your day jobs, so huge thanks to you both.

I wish I could sum up the holiday in a few, succinct words. But I honestly don't know how to, other than to say it was truly wonderful. Bessie proved herself to be a comfortable and reliable home, and gave us no trouble throughout the six weeks. Both Ireland and Scotland are indescribably beautiful and I would do the entire trip again tomorrow.

Today's mileage: 149

*Blood Bikes Wales provides a brilliant and free service to the various hospital trusts in Wales, moving blood, plasma and documents to where they are needed. To find out more or to donate, please visit https://www.bloodbikeswales.org.uk

Bessie Goes to Ireland and Scotland: the bottom line

Length of time: 42 days / six weeks

Total mileage: 2,801

Ferry fares: Fishguard to Rosslare and Belfast to Cairnryan £288; Armadale to Mallaig £19.70

Total cost of diesel for Bessie: £525.10

Total cost of campsites: £572.28

Gas top-ups for cooking and running the fridge: £14.79

Supermarket shopping: £586.15 (equal to £97.69 per week)

Total cost of six-week holiday, for two people, excluding spending money: £2006.02

The End . . .

. . . yes, it really is. In September 2018, accompanied for the first week by our friends Dave and Faye Underhill in their Carthago motorhome, we took Bessie for a tour of Brittany and Normandy. It was not without drama. Three days before we were due to catch the ferry Bessie's fuel filter failed, causing diesel to pour onto our drive every time the engine was switched on. With the hugely appreciated help of our friend and near neighbour Tim Murray, Mike managed to obtain a replacement filter and the specialist tools to get it fixed in time and we made an uneventful Channel crossing from Plymouth to Roscoff.

As we travelled from place to place, Mike was constantly stressing. Can we smell diesel? Is the fridge working okay? Do we have enough gas? Where can we get gas? Where are we going? Where can we stay tonight? And waking up in the middle of the night, worried because he couldn't see the blue indicator light on the fridge – the reason being that I'd covered it up with a tea towel as I didn't like it glowing in the dark.

Then to cap it all, in the early hours of Saturday morning in the second week, we were woken up by the piercing shriek of the carbon monoxide alarm. We leapt out of bed to investigate. Everything seemed to be in order so we assumed it was nothing more concerning than a low battery warning. Mike removed the battery, the unearthly noise stopped and we went back to bed.

In the morning I was worried by a strange smell. 'I think we have a gas leak,' I said to Mike. He wasn't too concerned as I have an ultra-sensitive nose and am always complaining about some unsavoury whiff or another. But after a while it was getting worse and he began to worry too. We sniffed our way around the van, trying to work out the source of the gaseous pong.

It was emanating from the locker under one of the bench seats in the saloon. The locker in which the leisure battery was positioned. The leisure battery that was boiling hot, bubbling and very, very smelly.

We were on a campsite site at Beauvoir, near Le Mont St Michel, where the manager spoke good English and she was able to point us in the direction of a garage about four kilometres away, that might be able to help. Bear in mind this was a Saturday morning in rural, and to us unfamiliar, Normandy, and our French language-speaking abilities are rudimentary to say the least. With the help of my trusty Collins French *dictionnaire*, we rehearsed:

'Bonjour monsieur. Nous avons un problème. La batterie loisir est très chaude. Elle a une odeur mauvaise'.

We found the garage and Mike delivered his speech. A young mechanic clambered on board, looked in the locker, waved his arms in true Gallic style and uttered two words: *'Whoosh. Volcan!'*

I was right all along. I just knew we had a mini volcano under that seat!

One new battery and a €160 hit on the credit card later, we were on our way, comforted in the knowledge that we could now run the fridge and turn on the lights in safety. We spent the final few days of our trip discussing whether motorhoming was for us, and whether it was even a holiday – Mike couldn't relax and I was on constant meal-planning, shopping and cooking duty. We decided to give it more thought before making a decision.

A month after returning to the UK, we took Bessie for a short, end of season break. Our destination was Swansea, where there is a great cycle path from Mumbles, right round the bay to the city centre. We left home in good spirits. That was to change. We'd gone about forty miles when Mike said: 'Can you smell diesel?'

I could. We pulled into a garage forecourt near Carmarthen and the old problem was back – diesel was pouring out again. Now what? We could go home, but the sole Fiat dealership that could deal with the problem was in Swansea. This time, Mike decided, he would replace the entire unit. He already knew, from some on-line research, that this was a common failing in these vehicles and didn't want to risk it happening over and over again. All credit to Day's of Swansea – a quick phone call was all it took for them to confirm they could get the necessary parts and fit them that afternoon. So we kept going, leaving a ribbon of expensive diesel all the way from Carmarthen to Llansamlet. This time the hit on the credit card was higher – around £300. Plus, of course, the cost of replacing three quarters of a tank of diesel.

So that was it. We made the decision to sell Bessie and if we want a motorhome holiday in future, we will hire a van and let someone else do all the worrying. A week later she'd gone.

We have no regrets about selling her and we have some enduring memories of the many trips we had in her: Norfolk, Wales, Cornwall and the West Country, Yorkshire, the Cotswolds and our number one favourite: Ireland and Scotland. But now, after three decades of holidays-on-the-move, whether on land or at sea, we are looking forward to relaxing breaks in sunny climes where someone else does all the hard work.

Au revoir Bessie. And thanks for the memories.

www.ingramcontent.com/pod-product-compliance
Lightning Source LLC
LaVergne TN
LVHW060637110826
845147LV00018B/998

* 9 7 8 1 8 3 8 0 7 5 2 6 2 *